SEX, LIES &TRUTH
A VERY SHORT HISTORY

**Creating a Better World Starts
With Seeing it for What it Really Is:
Uncut & Censor Free**

BY

Gerard Fournier

ZOLAR ENTERTAINMENT

For the truths of my life:

Lili, Lisa, and David

CONTENTS

Introduction

WHISPERS ALONG THE PATH

I must understand in order that I may believe.
By doubting we come to questioning,
and by questioning we perceive the truth.

— Abelard (c.1122)

CANTERBURY KNIGHTS

Truth is our most precious commodity. Everything we stand for, all our beliefs and values are based on a foundation of truth. It's what we freely exchange with others every time we open our mouths, write an e-mail, or pen a history of the world. Or not. We should never take it lightly.

When we allow spin and half-truths to go unchallenged, we step into a slippery slide that spirals downwards-ever widening, devaluing and debasing our words as surely as Photoshop's digitally enhanced images and computer-generated film images have emasculated the hard evidence of the truth of any still or moving picture. We need truth because wisdom sprouts from its seeds. Wisdom can grow in no other medium.

Truth comes in many forms and depths, as do the countless untruths that surround us like a garland of hypnotic deception. "Everybody lies," Mark Twain assures, "every day, every hour, awake, asleep, in his dreams, in his joy, in his mourning." We are consumed by the lying arts, and the greatest deception of all is that we're barely aware of it. I know from experience, having been a liar since before I could even spell the word.

Deception is the through-line of human history. All of literature and movies, TV and opera, pop music and political intrigue stand in stark testimony to our insatiable appetite to witness the endless battle between a thousand lies and one heroic truth. Where would we be without the cutting humor of Twain and the wit of Oscar Wilde to help us through the mess?

It's a total waste of effort to try and point out all the lies and untruths that are happening around us all the time, even if we limited these to just truth-challenged celebrities. There's already a long stream of bestsellers about specific hubs of misspoken spin, be they about Presidents and straying politicians, movie stars and rock divas, or CEOs and TV talking heads. In the end, what good do these revelations ever do, aside from providing us with a smug chuckle and a fleeting sense of superiority?

To tackle the real problems of the world, the ones that directly affect you and me in the strongest ways – millions of starving children, global warming, AIDS, escalating poverty, depleting water supplies, the widening gap between haves and have-nots, terrorism, rampant greed – we need to open up our belief systems and see what really makes them tick, and how they could have created the shocking world we find ourselves in at the dawn of a new millennium. When was the last time we, as a culture, dared to question our enshrined beliefs, both sacred and profane? We live in a world of 'us and them' where everyone on the 'them' side is to be feared, no matter where we draw the line. These are our beliefs in action. What if the beliefs are wrong?

It's been noted that the main thing Albert Einstein and Groucho Marx had in common was their relentless ability to punch holes in the sacred cows of our beliefs, to let some light shine in. Maybe it's time we all joined in in punching holes, starting with our own nearest and dearest beliefs.

So this book is not so much about unveiling 'the truth' as it is about challenging the shaky foundations on which the truths of our beliefs are based – and what tools we will need to separate fantasy from spin, and spin from something approaching the real world.

As to the little liar I was back in early grade school, I eventually learned the wisdom of Twain's advice that if you tell the truth you don't have to remember anything. Also eventually, I learned that the biggest whoppers weren't invented by little tikes with no respect for the truth, but were the credos daily drubbed into our trusting minds by our school systems, religion of ancestral tradition, extended family, and the cultural reinforcements of TV, magazines, newspapers, books, films, and pop music.

In short, the powers that decide which beliefs we are to hold as 'lifelong beliefs' – inserted as these are from earliest memories into every layer of our life — in essence control and limit our possibilities. Until we learn to challenge the truth of these beliefs, we only kid ourselves in believing that we are free to change our world, and ourselves.

So it comes as a shock to most of us that gullibility has become the benchmark of our times. As a culture we unquestioningly believe the moronic nonsense that is served up before us simply because we have been informed since early childhood that it is unnecessary to think for ourselves. How ironic, the one quality that separates us so starkly from all other creatures on this planet is the one we forfeit so readily. I mean, how many others are aghast that an excellent work of fiction like the *Da Vinci Code* can be mistaken by so many as a history lesson?

At times I feel like I've fallen into some bizarre version of the Canterbury Tales, a reality TV version where each pilgrim tells his tale, but in the end none is any wiser. There is no end of the road in sight, but then there are oh so many voices to be heard; exotic voices, quaint esoteric systems, strange sounding lexicons; a babble of conflicting and competing beliefs. The pilgrims amble on, spellbound in a sea of credulity.

A searcher for truth today is like the knight in shining armor who left on his quest for the Holy Grail...only the modern knight more often than not has left without his shining armor. Not only that, but he has somehow failed to take along his trusty page/assistant. Not to mention his steed. In fact he doesn't have a sword or lance or shield, or practically any clothing at all. He has pretty much been ripped off, ill-clothed by those responsible for outfitting him, like that near naked emperor of long ago.

Alone he tramps not knowing which way to go. He is confronted and accosted at seemingly every turn, at every crossroads, by suspicious looking characters of every sort. They point left, right, here, there, back, forth. Well meaning, or so they seem. But are they truly knowledgeable, or just as lost as he is? And what of those who are only too happy to lighten his pockets in exchange for a map to his cherished grail?

The world is freely bequeathed to us, a gift wrapped in thousands upon thousands of years of accumulated knowledge, much of it written down in just the last few millennia and lovingly preserved for our benefit. The findings and understandings of cultures from every part of the globe are available to us all, virtually at our fingertips. Without leaving the comfort of our homes we experience the horror and triumph of war, the ecstasy of sublime love, the building of a pyramid, and the utter abandonment of being shipwrecked on a desert island. We climb inside the stupendous mind of Aristotle, sit on Michelangelo's shoulder, walk at the side of Jesus of Nazareth, sit quietly under a tree with Buddha, and learn that it is unwise to pet certain types of poisonous snakes.

Our heritage is rich, vibrant with the experiences of countless lives. Yet, like an ever-shifting landscape, truth morphs, in constant need of editing.

Wisdom is our lifelong quest, truth, our day-to-day discoveries.

* * *

In *The Dragons of Eden*, Carl Sagan wrote about the emergence of a new form of thinking, a multidisciplinary thinking that would produce a remarkable new range of possibilities not only for our individual selves, but for all human cultures. It's to this consilience type of thinking that I turn in this book to help us awaken from our stupor, to construct a world vastly superior to the bottom-feeding zeitgeist we see all about us.

To think clearly we need to identify which of our thoughts are really our own, and which are the remnants of ideas woven a thousand times over, since earliest childhood, through the synapses of our brain.

Also, assaulted as we are by a matrix of cultural imprints from TV and film, Internet and blogs, chatrooms and DVDs, we must halt our precipitous descent into an Orwellian world of Big Brother mind spin where the tenor of our times is fear, and that hesitant smile on my face is called anxiety. This brave new world is conspicuously bereft of happiness and abundance for all, the twin pillars upon which we gambled our future.

We all long to be happy, but somewhere along the way so many of us seem to have forgotten just how to go about it. Part bright-eyed child, part enthralled artist, part inspired genius; we are a many-layered palimpsest of imagination and invention beneath the conventions of our socially sanctioned façades.

What we need is a powerful stimulant, a shot of ocular Viagra to awaken us to what we really are, a way of opening our eyes to the real world beyond the illusions that are paraded before us on a daily basis. If we're ever to turn the tables on the insanities and outrages that regularly assault us, and create a *user-friendly world*, we'll have to create it with our eyes wide open.

This is a book about the power of our personal wisdom. It's about how it was marginalized over centuries of cultural development, then anesthetized for each of us individually as we marched toward adulthood. Keeping in mind that 'power is never relinquished willingly', we will focus our stealth at what lies beneath the apparent.

To do so with the keenest eye possible, and in keeping with the genius in questioning everything, I have divided the book into three parts, covering roughly the past, present and future of who we are.

In **Part 1, Harvesting Our Roots**, I start by checking out our cultural foundations; how do the beliefs and worldviews of our ancestors hold up when brought face to face with what we know today? Are we continuing to build on increasingly shaky assumptions? Scientific discoveries, archeological digs, and cognitive reasoning point in one direction while we, as a culture, steadfastly continue moving in quite another, simply because it's tradition — what we've always done, what our forefathers believed in. Is this wise?

In **Part 2, A Masterwork In Progress**, I take a close look at the incredibly gifted creatures known as 'we'. Our mental powers are expanding by leaps and bounds. Each of us has learned more since childhood than our ancestors did in thousands of years — the more we learn the more we're capable of learning. It's time to reassess this extremely complex conscious being, dump all our preconceived notions about his limitations, and put into use the full slate of mind tools at our disposal.

In **Part 3, Reinventing Our Future**, I envision a vastly different world we could step into, one created by daring to use the innate powers we have at our disposal. As a people, as a culture, as a species, we are at a critical crossroads. Either we take the high road and revive some sense of truth and reality behind the decisions we make on a daily basis, or we continue on down this delusionary back road which has served up the Machiavellian world we now call our daily lives.

The choice is a simple one of intent: do we choose to question and enlighten, or like the near-naked emperor, continue to deceive – ourselves.

PART 1

HARVESTING OUR ROOTS

The baggage each of us carries:

- *A history of deception, how it has become the standard of social exchange, and why we are so adept at lying to ourselves;*
- *How humans only recently became conscious, were banished from 'Eden', in turn setting in motion our never-ending quest for truth;*
- *How modern-day myths are every bit as effective in controlling our perceptions of reality as ancient myths were at dictating the beliefs of our ancestors;*
- *How cultures far and wide were persuaded to denigrate the feminine in favor of the masculine, placing man in sole position as lord and master, and relegating woman to the role of victim.*

Without coming face to face with these underlying strands of cultural DNA we cannot hope to uncover any truth at all.

I
THE WHOLE TRUTH
&
LOTS OF LIES

The power in knowing at least some truth, the weakness in clinging to lies.

A 'short history of wisdom.' Although wisdom may seem to be everywhere about us, true wisdom isn't exactly easy to nail down.

What the media, elected leaders, and expert commentators solemnly inform us is the real world, oftentimes is anything but. Hocus-pocus and snake oil, both ancient and modern, are ubiquitous magic bullets. Spin doctoring and clever advertising haven't made things any easier.

Wise advice on what to look for and what to avoid from:

- Socrates
- Joseph Campbell
- Edward O. Wilson
- Sam Keen
- Epicurus
- John O'Donohue

1

THE POWER OF KNOWING

*Today, everywhere we turn we see corruption
dishonesty, deception and Humbug.*
— Diogenes, (during the reign of Alexander the Great)

Truth, we are assured by distant memories, is always the first casualty of war, which given the life-or-death nature of the situation, doesn't seem such a bad idea. But if it's the first casualty of war, then surely truth must be the norm in peacetime. Our natural state, as it were, is a state of truth; truth is beauty, peace is beautiful, and as long as we keep war at bay, our lives will be bathed in truth and beauty. "So then," the credulous child asks innocently, "when exactly was the last time we were at peace?"

When did our culture declare war on itself, this civil war if you will, where we lie to ourselves as a daily practice? We lie to each other compulsively, yet in no way consider ourselves to be liars. We've become so complacent about its everyday reality; we barely notice that deception has become the standard of social exchange. "Misspeak" is the new truth.

Not too long ago, bending the truth and concocting streams of misinformation was the prerogative of the proverbial used car salesman. Today this very unsettling mindset is the status quo in business, in politics, in virtually every walk of life. More so, we expect it. We expect our politicians not to keep their campaign promises because they just said them to get elected. We expect businessmen to tell us fairy tales about the quality of our investments because their only interest is in getting their hands on our hard-earned money. And we expect our friends to lie about how they really made out on last night's date, or how superlatively well their careers are soaring.

Tom Harpur, noted deflator of cultural delusions (*Would You Believe?),* put in unvarnished terms our penchant for falsifying the truth. "We live in a culture that is prone to lying. Thrives on it, in fact. Of course, nobody wants to admit this. In fact, it's only possible on a massive scale because of a more or less tacit conspiracy to ignore the phenomenon unless it becomes so blatant as to cause an overt scandal whether in business, in government, or in the church."

In fact, when it comes to believing in matters spiritual, people are at their most trusting. Railing, rightfully, against the dubious fabrications emanating from the White House or TV networks or corporate halls of infamy is somehow easier than doubting those laughably deluded who claim, with head piously bent, to have been in personal conversation with God, or to have been chosen by Jesus to deliver messages of importance for all mankind, or to be channeling the syrupy ramblings of ethereal entities from far-off galaxies. Tragically and invariably, this naiveté grows in direct proportion to our cultural level of fear.

It's not just a matter of being outright lied to. The milieu of our times can fairly be described as an unpleasant concoction of hogwash, baloney and flim-flam. From the moment we're welcomed to the new day by some artificially animated newscaster until we hit the pillow to embrace the merciful reality of our dream world, we are forced to wade through it, and indeed to make our own noteworthy contributions.

Before reflexively laughing at the spread of this potent fertilizer we should perhaps pause to see where it's all leading. What does it say about our treasured freedoms, about our quality of life? In *On Bullshit*, Princeton professor of philosophy Harry Frankfurt wrote in 1985 that "Bullshit is more insidious than lying, because lying arouses people's anger while bullshit is simply accepted as a fact of life." He blames its phenomenal rise on our delusional postmodern take on reality — that reality is whatever you make of it. With this kind of laissez-faire thinking, everyone is free to decide for themselves what is real and what isn't. Or as Francis Wheen wrote in *How Mumbo-Jumbo Conquered the World*, "If all notions of truth and falsity cease to have any validity, how can one combat bogus ideas — or indeed outright lies?"

Of course, humbug and its kin have likely been with us since humans first discovered that they could lie and get away with it, but never has it engulfed an era as extensively as this one. But then never before has our species been exposed to such a flood of voices that may not exactly have our best interests at heart.

Change is overtaking us at an astounding rate from all directions. As physicist Michio Kaku (*Hyperspace*) puts it, "we have amassed more knowledge since World War II than all the knowledge amassed in our two million year evolution on this planet." It's a result of the way our brains, senses and inventions (including language), cooperate in acquiring knowledge, a mushrooming expansion wherein the more we learn the more we are capable of learning.

Or to put it another way, whatever knowledge we had amassed by the time we graduated from formal education (presuming we haven't just got out of school), is already but the introductory chapter to whatever field we labored in. Twenty plus years or so of intensive development is all we need to prepare us to face the world. My pet dog learned everything she needed to know in just a handful of months. The extra time, it would seem, is well spent learning the finer points in the ancient and revered art of inventive storytelling.

What is truly astounding in this scenario, though, is not that humankind has learned more in our lifetime than our ancestors did in millions of years, but that so many of us actually rely on such dubious arbiters of reality as TV, popular magazines, and carefully crafted press releases. I mean what's the point of uncovering this incredible mass of knowledge only to pull the shades over our eyes? Living with our 'eyes wide shut' as Stanley Kubrick's final masterwork described it.

No, this is not about television bashing. The medium has incredible potential to inform and enlighten, as well as entertain. But like the spamming and scamming that now proliferates on the Internet, it's becoming progressively more difficult to distinguish what is real from all that is not. Many different sorts of quasi-truths besiege us from program to program, channel to channel, sound bite to video clip.

News As Truth

Even network daily news, which used to impart a certain modicum of the important events of the day, is now either a dumbed-down News-Lite or a propaganda service for a particular political party or corporate interest. (Or in Leonard Cohen's poetic phrase, "Of this you can be sure, the rich have set their channels in the bedrooms of the poor.") Naturally enough people tend to dial up those news stations that support their own biases and political/economic outlook, thus polarizing neighbors and communities even further in their understanding on what is going on in the real world- as it does to citizens of different countries.

During the recent war on Iraq, I watched in amazement, programs from BBC World (England), TV5 (France), Telelatino & RAIuno (Latin America & Italy), CBC Newsworld (Canada), snippets from Al-Jazeera (Arabic Network), as well as flipping from NBC to FOX to CNN. The same events, different angles, different interpretations, all with one thing in common – depending on their audience's mindset, very precise descriptions of tusks or ears or feet or an outsized sexual member, but not a single portrait of the seven ton elephant.

Or worse still, in desperation to maintain their viewership numbers, the media drops its newsgathering standards so severely that we're left with little other than celebrity-driven sound bites of inconsequential value. Ever try to find the news value in the media circus surrounding the latest Blacksburg or Columbine?

Sam Keen, scholar and author (*Hymns to an Unknown God*), describes our situation as being locked in a room with this horde of very secular evangelists who inundate us with 'images' of the good life, and nothing much else. "Year by year, we grow more cynical because we know that our opinions are manipulated by sound bites and attractive images." Who can we believe, and on what basis can we decide what to believe?

Cynical becomes our collective perspective, and through this perception, we filter our view of the world. It's easy to justify holding back the truth, or simply being apathetic about it altogether, when cynicism is our guiding light – "The Ten Commandments and the Golden Rule are fine as far as they go, but this is the real world! We're talking business here! Besides, everyone else is doing it."

In the long run we are simply lulled into a false sense of security, that there is no need to question. The powers that be, no matter whom or of what variation through the ages, have largely retained the right to create the truth and insist that the masses believe in it. Socrates took his measure of poison hemlock not because Athenians objected to his theories or propositions, but because he dared to doubt their absolute truths, and taught others to do the same.

The Age of Enlightenment, which was catalyst to both the American and French revolutions, taught that people could only free themselves by learning to question. That is, we don't set people free; each person must 'free himself' by learning to think for himself, by reasoning things through, by questioning and doubting. By seeking the truth, he sets himself free. Freedom and ignorance do not go hand-in-hand.

Open debate is the price we pay for this freedom. Questioning is what makes it work. So why is it acceptable today that disagreement is met with name-calling and denigrating remarks, or what is becoming more common, labeling the other as unpatriotic or anti this or anti that, when in fact the one doing the name calling is the one stifling our freedoms? Increasingly, this sort of ad hominem attack is heard coming from politicians and from the airwaves of powerful national media. Radio talk shows are a growing Mecca for this totalitarian mindset. Or maybe, while we were distracted by trifles like 9/11 and the invasion of Iraq, Mini-Me's in brown shirts assumed the role of media watchdog.

What's unique about our times today is that never before has the world known mass communication that literally blankets the entire globe, as it blankets each of our lives. Moreover, in recent years its control has fallen into surprisingly fewer and fewer hands. In a nutshell, is that new Hollywood release gracing the front cover of Time magazine because the movie is of such cultural significance, or because the conglomerate that owns Time also owns the studio that made this overpriced turkey?

The same applies to the reporting on foreign wars and political double-dealings. Vested interests are rarely in the interests of the public. Just ask the followers of Socrates as they watched him succumb to the poison.

Further to the point, how did we devolve from being citizens to mere consumers? How did we allow the global village, as envisioned by Marshal McLuhan in the 60s, to be hijacked by globalization? How did "We've only got this one fragile planet, so let's help each other do our best with it", become "So let's all dine at the Golden Arches and shop for all our needs at Wal-Mart"? Wow, the thrill of flying all the way to New Delhi to feast on a Big Mac! What a brave new world.

Noble Peace Prize winner Aung San Suu Kyi said we begin a revolution in our spirit "by first learning how to liberate our own minds from fear, apathy, and ignorance."

Well I'm all for getting rid of our incessant fear, debilitating apathy and manufactured ignorance, but what we really need is not so much a revolution, as a new Enlightenment, one that emerges from our inner *Network* exclamation that "I'm mad as hell and I'm not going to take it anymore." How else are we to reclaim our sanity amidst the mind-altering narcotic emanating from the brilliant minds who bring us The Evening News and 'Reality' TV?

2

THE COST OF ENLIGHTENMENT

Like lambs being lead to the slaughter, so the unwary line up and sign up, and buy up everything on the market. After all, they have no choice. The experts have convinced them of how truly miserable they are. It seems their happy quotient just doesn't make the grade. Their relationships are the antithesis of true romance. Their lives are mundane and boring, and those were the good years. And their careers...well, Bill Gates they are not.

Then, once thoroughly distressed and depressed at being such miserable failures, they get hit with the punch line, the remedy of all remedies, the 'cure' that will put happy faces back where they belong. Just follow the 7 laws, 12 steps, 5 principles or 10 secrets of the cosmos, available for $39.95 for the book, or $550 for the weekend seminar, or $195 in six hour-long cassettes, or $12,000 for the week in Fiji, and we are assured of a healthy long life, of wealth and prosperity, of doing nothing but good deeds, and loving all of mankind.

Hey, sign me up right away. It's amazing what $40 will buy these days!

It's so easy to be cynical, isn't it? And cynicism, as Oscar Wilde succinctly described it in *De Profundis*, "is the perfect philosophy for a man who has no soul." He also pointed out that to the cynic, nothing is ever revealed. And so, properly chastised, that will be the end of that.

Steps and programs are not exactly new to our age. We tend to idealize images of the past, where great thinkers and prophets taught on the 'steps' of sacred places like the Acropolis and the Agora in Athens, or the Temple in Jerusalem. All that passersby of the time had to do was to stop and listen, and their lives would be filled with wisdom. How lucky could they get? Why are we not so privileged today?

A nice thought, naïve as it is. Then as now, those same steps were crowded with scores of others hawking their goods, their produce, their esoteric ideas and schemes for changing the world.

The great teachers had to compete with all manner of potions and quick-fix solutions, and a myriad of 'spiritual steps' to eternal happiness. And we can well bet that the quick-fix solutions, for a handful of shekels or denarii, won out hands down over all others.

Today, as in all times of great change and uncertainty, people are questing, searching, for a meaning to it all, for a point or purpose to their life, for a "What's it all about, Alfie?", for something other than just consuming more and enjoying it less. And what do they get for the most part? Come-ons from spin doctors and geniuses of the advertising universe.

The essence of advertising is not, as one innocent tried to inform me way back when, the business of placing spot ads in public places in order to inform the citizenry of the latest products on the market. Far from anything so benign, real advertising is about creating a lack, a lack that is so profoundly serious that people will not rest until that void has been filled. And lo and behold, the advertiser just happens to have at hand the product to fill that very need. From creation of lack, to grateful fulfillment, all in the span of 60 seconds. Or 30, or less.

It's a very simple yet powerfully effective formula. Our consciousness is lulled into a sense of invulnerability (see any Advertising 101 course), then a rapid succession of video cuts and mood altering music insinuates itself into our inner being and lays claim to our longings. "Consumerism is the worship of the god of quantity," John O'Donohue (*Eternal Echoes*) observes keenly; "advertising is its liturgy."

I first tweaked to the nature of this insidious skullduggery when I was a kid in the late 50s. Back there when *Leave it to Beaver* land and the *Ed Sullivan Show* were gently interrupted by a series of ads that ran on the only TV station we could get at the time, housewives were informed, in a rather commanding male voice, that it was time to get rid of their old-fashioned electric carving knife and replace it with a new type, one with a curving blade, or whatever it claimed to have (I can't actually remember what it looked like, but the message remains indelible). Any woman worth her salt surely had to do better than to cut her family roast with one of those ordinary electric knives.

Of course we didn't own an electric knife back then, nor as I discovered did any of my friends have such a gadget in their homes. So how to upgrade to an even better one? Still the commercial played over and over again for months on end. Eventually, a shiny new electric carving knife — not the advertised one — found its way into our kitchen, as one did into the homes of most of my young acquaintances.

How many people today, searching for real answers to serious questions, or for some semblance of truth in a sea of misspokeness, have in fact ended up with a shiny new carving knife?

3

THE WISDOM HUMBUG

If the electric carving knife didn't work when it was plugged in, few of us would hesitate in sending it back for a full refund. As we wouldn't hesitate returning that new state-of-the-art television, if we didn't get a clear picture to see those carving knife commercials. And if after completing his driver-training course, my son still didn't know how to drive a car, I would certainly demand an explanation. The same if he couldn't compose a coherent essay upon completing high school. There are certain standards to be met, and there's no fudging on this.

So why do the same people come back again and again to the same media-driven gurus, or to very similar 'masters', whether they base their miracle make-overs on pop-psychology or spiritual revelations, real estate acumen or dietary supplements? I know they are the same people because, in connection with our PBS *Quest* series, my wife Lili and I have been to a number of these weekend conferences, usually in big hotels in major cities — New York, San Francisco, Chicago — and I see many of the same faces. When talking with them, I find that this is their umpteenth trip to the well; yes, they have all the books, and the CDs they play constantly in their car, and they are lined up to buy even more, and they just don't know how they are going to get to see all these experts in the short time allotted. Choices, choices. But something is wrong here.

Are these experts' solutions so shallow as to be uplifting solely for the duration of an afternoon seminar? What about the claims they so boldly make — to effectively alter our lives for the better, to make us overnight millionaires, to reinvigorate us with a youthful vitality for decades to come. I realize that television and its sound-bite style of presentation has drastically shortened our attention span, but I doubt that most people have spent all this time and money for a few feel-good hours.

Then why this uncontested tolerance for all these seminars and books and tapes and trendy mentors? Why don't people rush to the next set of seminars and demand their money back from the last set that didn't work (including airfare, hotels, meals, etc.)? Why don't they sue the publishers of books claiming "Seven Steps to Happiness", which though they followed them faithfully, certainly did not make them happy (though the result of the lawsuit just might ease the pain)?

If it's just entertainment they're looking for, there are dozens of amusements that cost far less than the hundreds of dollars demanded by most of these gatherings. At least when we spend the money on a thought-provoking play or a great Broadway musical there are no further demands put upon us, and no consequent feelings of guilt that we weren't able to sustain this euphoria over a period of days or weeks.

Perhaps it's this very guilt that keeps drawing people back for more and more sessions, that it's somehow their fault that their life didn't change for the better, so they must give it another go. And pay better attention this time! Heaven forbid, it simply couldn't be the system itself that is void and vacuous. It certainly couldn't be humbug; after all, the inspirational spokesperson is so warm and charming and charismatic

4

THE MAGIC BULLET

In the end, the irony is that we ourselves are responsible. This eats to the very core of existence. And all these bestsellers proclaim this at some point or other in their wordy pages — or at least that's what I assume is indelibly written between the lines. The subtlety however is magnificently lost on our advertising-addled minds. The implication is clearly and simply that by following the steps outlined inside the book (tapes, whatever), all our floundering will be pushed aside, and our life will take a decided turn for the better.

What should be emblazoned across the jackets of these books (instead of the glowing raves from fellow experts) is that none of this is of any use unless we take full responsibility for *every step of our lives*. *There is no magic bullet.* There is no such thing as any number of steps to nirvana.

Absolute truth is viewable only in the theater of a closed mind.

And so we come to the essence of what is being offered in these many books and tapes. Most of the authors and speakers in the business, at least the ones I've met, seem to be pretty decent people, though what some of them have to offer may not exactly pass muster. However, not all are as talented or well informed as the next, though we wouldn't know it by their success as best-selling authors.

On the one side there are the genuine experts with their hard-earned doctorates under their arms who seem to have read about everything there is to read on a subject, from ancient times right up to the moment, and who possess an amazing ability to synthesize all of this and apply it to our modern conundrums in an easy to understand and entertaining fashion. What rare gems they are.

On the other side are those vociferous know-it-alls who seem to have lifted their central theme from a trite saying on the back of some matchbook. This they have turned into a catchy title, which became an article, which was expanded into a book, which became a bestseller. The bestseller lead to a stream of bestsellers, all saying essentially the same thing (but hell, that title *is* catchy), and the person in question is hailed as an unparalleled expert. Need I say this type of author far outsells the former?

The majority of writers questing for truth tend to have some kind of background in psychology/psychiatry, medicine/biology, philosophy/spirituality, or physics/cosmology.

It's in this group that most seekers get lost. That is, how is the average person to go about distinguishing between those with merely a touch of 'hands-on' experience, and those with impeccable credentials, be they academic or experiential; let alone ferreting out those whose Ph.D. is of questionable origin. What guidelines do we use? The number of copies sold worldwide? The cleverness of the title? The praise on the back cover?

One commentator uses a very simple acid test. He looks at the jacket of the book: the larger the Ph.D. plastered across the cover, the less likely he is to find genuine words of wisdom inside. A true scholar does not hide behind his degrees. Wisdom has its own voice.

In the course of filming for our *Quest* series of documentaries on PBS, Lili has interviewed dozens of the top selling authors, not all of whom have ended up in the series. One of these, a very well known personage whom all would recognize, insisted that he didn't need to sign the standard release form for his appearance in the show, as he didn't believe in contracts. His word (and permission) was his bond, and that he had already given. When I pointed out that the release was required by the network, he waved his hand dismissively, saying his agent would take care of it. He then sat down for three hours of taping in which he informed us that he was 'enlightened', and in response to a follow-up question of what he would do if he came face to face with God, calmly replied that he would shake His hand and say, "Hi, me. How am I doing?"

I guess this bit of buffoonery — I mean we (and the crew) did have a difficult time suppressing our smirks, despite his straight face — should have tipped us off to what lay ahead. Weeks later we received a letter demanding thousands of dollars up front for the privilege of having him in our documentary. We replied that no one gets paid to be interviewed, that we were in debt financing (house mortgages to pay for the shows), and that PBS was *given* the shows for free for its fund raising pledge drives.

The great man himself responded that "you should be ashamed of yourselves", that we were "using" other people to make our fortune, and that no signature would appear on the release until we came up with the required funds. This all from an 'enlightened' man ('God' if you will) whose word is his bond. A stand-up comic could not have come up with a more outrageous caricature. Need I say he didn't make the cut to the *Quest* series?

Then there was the woman who, also after the fact, requested a few thousand dollars to "make things interesting for me", given as how her star had risen since the actual filming, and now she was "number one in the world!" The fact that very few have ever heard of her is, I'm sure, of little consequence.

Wise observers through the ages have told us never to lose our sense of humor, especially when looking at ourselves, for it is in humor that the serious issues are truly tested.

Humbug Wizardry

Motivational speakers, I used to think, were a pretty innocent breed, requiring no professional credentials other than their contagious enthusiasm and inspirational take on "I can do anything I set my mind to." Alas, having seen over the years the true damage they do to people's lives, I no longer believe them to be harmless.

Many of the most popular are itinerate modern day snake-oil salesmen/women who cavalierly toss around concepts of self-help, pop psychology, and devious unscientific takes on quantum physics, all designed to confuse and amaze the credulous, while convincing them that everything they have been doing up to this point in their lives is wrong. The expert at hand (fill in the blank) is there to rectify this by starting them on a nice long course of his teachings.

Dale Carnegie wrote *How to Win Friends & Influence People* back in 1936. Read it and amazingly we find that virtually everything the above authors have to say is straight out of this book — except for the modern addition of guilt and feelings of inadequacy for not yet being a thorough success. Carnegie's book after all was a manual for good salesmanship.

The bait dangled by these modern-day wizards as they pass through our local Learning Annex or similar umbrella speakers group, is that they are somehow privy to "The Secret" which has been passed on to them by the great minds of antiquity, a secret which they will share, for an escalating fee, with those who can no longer stand being outside the wrought iron gates of success and wealth and power.

Unrealistic dreams of boundless money and social prestige are kindled and sold to millions on the promise that they will all reach to the top of the mountain — bounty enough for all who subscribe – though in reality less than one percent will ever come close, secret or no secret. This is the big lie, the lie that does so much harm to so many desperate lives.

The Real Secret, if it must be put in such prosaic terms, is that only a few percent of the world's population possesses real wealth and power. They do not give it up easily, a severe attitude that trickles right on down through the ranks, thus further restricting anyone's efforts to join them. A positive attitude will indeed succeed in getting one pointed in the right direction, but the catalytic ingredients in the recipe are work, discipline, and the consistent application of sound success principles, ingredients mysteriously absent from many tomes on personal empowerment.

"Much of it is humbug. But it sells as well as pornography," Jostein Gaarder (*Sophie's World*) wrote of the pervasive spread of this pap. "But the difference between real philosophy and these books is more or less the same as the difference between real love and pornography. Many of these books do not contain so much as one iota of genuine experience."

Or as Scott Adams, the creator of the cartoon character *Dilbert* sarcastically suggested to those who seek out self-help books for inspiration, save your money and instead "Go read any book in the History, Philosophy, or Religion section and think about what it says."

So where do we go from here? Whom do we trust? Where does all this stuff they're saying come from anyway?

5

A NEW ENLIGHTENMENT

Enlightenment is a term used in two quite different ways. The first refers to the philosophic movement of the 18th century which placed an emphasis on rational thinking, as in Thomas Jefferson's advice to "Fix reason firmly in her seat, and call on her tribunal for every fact, every opinion." The second comes from Buddhism where it is seen as a blessed state marked by the absence of all desire. When someone says they are seeking Enlightenment they are obviously referring to the latter. In the 18th century sense, one does not 'become enlightened'.

To further add confusion, in recent years several new-age types have claimed that Enlightenment is attainable by consciously pursuing spiritual self-improvement, a proposition which flies right in the face of the Buddha's assertion that "only when we let go of our striving" is this deeper truth visible.

Certainty freezes the mind. No one has a stranglehold on objective truth. Each of our stories must be filtered through our personal experiences, hidden agendas, perceptions and belief systems. But through it all something resembling the truth does begin to emerge, and in paying close attention to it we inevitably unfold our first glimpse of wisdom.

Wisdom cannot be based on illusion. Surface truth changes with every passing second; life is forever changing, we are forever changing. But wisdom resides in a much deeper reality. Like Vincent van Gogh arresting the eternal moment in his painting of a simple wheat field, we must peer past the surface details to illuminate those deeper reaches.

There are different ways of knowing, and different depths. Reason is brilliant in uncovering the reality of our day-to-day world, what science and medicine and academic matters thrive on. But there is more to reality than what meets the eye. If we are to embark on a 21st century Age of Enlightenment we would be wise not to rely solely on reason and the workings of the material world (what can be measured by a ruler or weighed on a scale), but to open our questioning to include the mysterious workings of intuition, the cause and effect intrigues of inspiration, and the almost hypnotic affect a great work of art can have on the one beholding it — to name but a few.

Sex, Lies & Truth — A Very Short History is a modest proposal for the immodest task of discovering these truths in all their depths, and then to convincing ourselves to be brave enough to live by them. That is, to set ourselves free — if we dare.

We're not alone. As experts in mythology are fond of reminding us, the heroes of every age have blazed paths through the maze of possibilities, long before us. The labyrinth is well known, though it rapidly grows over and is in need of new paths. As Joseph Campbell (*The Hero with a Thousand Faces*) so tantalizingly put it, we have only to follow the thread of the hero's path.

The 'thread', of course, is the thread woven through these chapters. It's the thread of knowledge that's been passed down to us since long before the word was written. It's the thread which Ariadne gave to Theseus before he descended into that famous labyrinth on the island of Crete to battle the Minotaur. It is the thread of our longing that binds us to our ancestors, and to our children's children yet to come.

To paraphrase Isaac Newton (1642-1727), we are but midgets in all that we know; if we appear to see farther than others, it's because we stand on the shoulders of giants. This too is the thread, the thread upon which the human race has grown to be a global society of over six and a half billion. The last million years have seen no real increase in the amount of land available, nor in the amount of solar energy reaching us, nor in the amount of breathable oxygen. Yet in that time span our species has exploded out of Africa, conquered and reshaped every viable habitat (not always wisely), and is currently venturing into space in search of new lands to settle our ever-expanding numbers. None of which would have been possible without this thread, or river of knowledge.

Of Giants and Threads

One of the giants with the broadest shoulders was Socrates (470-399 BC). Not surprisingly, it troubled him that he knew so little; "One thing only I know, and that is that I know nothing." That is, the more we know the greater the possibilities that open up before us; but also the more we learn the more our eyes are opened to just how little we actually know. He believed there was no point in telling people what to think, nor in arguing that his conclusions were superior to theirs. As Norwegian philosophy instructor Jostein Gaarder wrote in *Sophie's World*, he "saw his task as helping people to 'give birth' to the correct insight, since real understanding must come from within. It cannot be imparted by someone else...only the understanding that comes from within can lead to true insight."

This essentially is the nature of the thread. But it's not one single strand that dangles before our eyes. That would be far too simple, and totally without challenge. What kind of a quest for truth would that be? Think instead of that scene near the end of *Indiana Jones and the Last Crusade* where the eponymous hero must choose wisely from a whole slew of wine goblets and chalices to find the one true Holy Grail. There are a lot of threads out there, pretenders and fakes and impostors. Very good fakes. Choosing wisely is not as easy as it at first sounds.

Our modern world is as much a trickster and dispenser of dim-witted gibberish as it is a repository of wisdom. Like the sphinx of old with its riddles, we must learn to ask the right questions, before listening to the answers. As Harvard zoologist Edward Wilson notes in *Consilience*, "the right answer to a trivial question is also trivial, but the right question, even when insoluble in exact form, is a guide to major discovery."

The right questions are what we're here to discover. And we'll know we've asked the right questions when we start, quite surreptitiously, making major discoveries. Illuminating discoveries. Little light bulbs flashing in our mind's eye.

We'll even venture into the land beyond the mirror — a land quite ignored by the original Age of Reason — spying on Alice's looking glass world, prying open the doors of perception. We'll explore the mysteries that lay within our unconscious, inevitably altering our conscious perceptions about the way the world works, and our unique capabilities within it.

The magic is that we'll do it all by ourselves, forming the right questions, simply by attending to the whispers from the ages, whispers old and new.

As Sam Keen has noted, individuals in all cultures eventually rise up to demolish the accepted answers and in their place leave painful questions. This questioning quest, then, is not aimed at those who are genuinely comfortable with their current perception of reality. It's my experience, though, that the ranks of those who are unhappy with the humbug zeitgeist of our times are growing exponentially. Humbug quite simply means 'designed to deceive.' So it is to those who are tired of being deceived that I extend this invitation to a different sort of amusement park ride – a ride tentatively fashioned from amidst the veiled shadows of forgotten truths.

6

THE THREAD OF WISDOM

"He who does not know history," Cicero (106-43 BC) observed a few thousand years ago, "is destined to remain a child."

The trail of human wisdom is as long as that of human existence. Plato learned from Socrates, as Aristotle learned from Plato. Yet each of these was far from the only influence on the other. Their abilities were very much a synthesis of all they'd been exposed to. And these include an untraceable long line of wisdom passed on long before Socrates, as indeed his influence is large on us today. But in the past at least the movement from one set of ideas, or world outlook, or paradigm, to another was snail-like slow, taking generations or more to take hold. This was a welcome pace, one which all could easily adapt to, very much a result of the limited number of influences from both outside and in.

Much has changed in the past century. Here we are in the new millennium with instant communication to all parts of the world, to all cultures, to all heritages, to all sources of wisdom. Yet we are anything but wise. "We are drowning in information," Edward Wilson explains in *Consilience*, "while starving for wisdom."

Wisdom is not a commodity that comes nicely bundled up, but is a result of what we do with knowledge. A huge pile of information does not necessarily contain any more wisdom than a small pile. In fact, they both contain the same amount: none. Wisdom is found in the sifting. In essence we have made things more difficult for ourselves by making the pile of info so great: what a lot of sifting to be done!

The answer (we bravely hope) is to sift through piles of what has already been sifted several times. That is, where we are faced with only the 'good stuff' left over from these formerly indiscriminate meanderings. This in fact is what we do with any so-called modern work of wisdom (healthcare, philosophy, spirituality, cosmology). We assume that the author has weeded out all that is unimportant and presented us with the essential kernels of truth.

Unfortunately, today there is a penchant for doublespeak and phrase inversion that can, upon first glance, make nonsense sound like profound wisdom. In psychology it's called psychobabble. In publishing it's to be found quite regularly under best sellers, and in Hollywood it's affectionately known as High Concept.

So anyone can toss around a quote from a famous person, but does that mean that whatever lies between the quotation marks is valid? Put another way, is everything a famous person said or wrote necessarily true? What if he changed his mind later in his thinking? Or if he was proven decidedly wrong by some other great thinker?

More to the point, it's so easy to take a saying out of context and have it support something that the author never had supported in his life. We have only to look at the Bible to see how easily and how frequently this can be accomplished. People on opposing sides in heated debates have often quoted the same passage from this Holy Book to support their diametrically opposed conclusions.

So it is important not to be swayed by an argument just because a quote from Aristotle is attached to it. How well does the author's reasoning stand on its own, without the fancy window dressing?

Finally, beware of those who spew out a stream of wisdom, never giving credit for where it came from, implying that these are their own original ideas. I saw one of these thought-thieves on the Oprah Winfrey show not long ago. His talk was essentially 'borrowed' from Plato, with a smattering of 17th and 18th century British philosophy. The audience applauded and cheered his bons mots. He smiled and bowed his appreciation, with not a hint of where his brilliance came from. In writing this is called plagiarism. In whole, it is simply intellectual dishonesty.

And what truth is there to be found in dishonesty?

A THIRST AND A HUNGER

That there is a spiritual hunger today is not in question – and searching for truth after all is a spiritual, not a material, pursuit. The real question is what is meant by 'spiritual'?

I know people whose eyes roll in dismay at the very mention of the word. They figure I'm either trying to interest them in some religion they've long ago abandoned, or I myself have just been inculcated by some charmingly charismatic guru whose divine essence I just have to share with them. Thanks, but no thanks.

What was that cogent saying about throwing out the baby with the bath water? Religion, to set the record straight, is *not* the essence of what is spiritual within us. Quite to the contrary, the religions of the world were created as aids to help us address our spiritual longings, and hopefully to satisfy them.

Most of these religions were created a long, long time ago and for many people today have lost relevance and meaning. But the spiritual needs they were developed to nourish – and laughter is a serious spiritual craving that's rapidly slipping from our cultural grasp — are nonetheless still within us, and are as much in need of sustenance as are our physical cravings. Yet our modern world acts as though there is no such need. As Keen notes, the spiritual dimension is most obvious by its absence.

Spiritual longing, quite simply, is the ongoing pursuit of truths – a preoccupation as sacred to science, as it is to the arts, as it is to religion.

Creativity and the various forms of the arts are the way most people come in contact with that momentary transcendence that the spiritual craves. Some matrix in our interior landscape is stopped in its tracks by seeing a great painting, or is arrested by a hypnotic dance, or by the spine-tingling chords of entrancing music. Our physical eyes just see colored oils on canvas, but our spiritual dimension is captivated by a time-altering and deeply moving experience. It's called soul food.

Yet another way of envisioning the spiritual is as the essential truth concealed in a myth — the core at the center of the story, as it is at the core of who we are. As Tom Harpur refers to it, a spiritual myth is a truth so vast and so important to our human condition that it can only be told in the most profound language of all, the language of symbolism, allegory, and metaphor.

TV documentarian Bill Moyers, after crisscrossing the continent and other parts of the world for decades in search of deeper meaning, wrote, "any journalist worth his or her salt knows the real story today is to define what it means to be spiritual. This is the biggest story — not only of the decade but of the century."

It's time to set the record straight. The spiritual is not something to discard lightly, or to be ignored as though it doesn't exist. It's an integral feature of the human condition, not to mention an essential guiding force in every civilization.

Traveling in the Wilderness

For most of us, the quest for truth begins when we step back from the same old answers and turn instead toward fresh questions. "Nothing shapes our lives so much as the questions we ask — *or refuse to ask*," Keen reminds us. Indeed we are all questioners, but the types of questions that make us spring to life can be of a profoundly different nature.

Yet, in our eager pursuit, we find ourselves stumbling and careening off in every which direction. We demand straight answers. What we often get, as one commentator described it, is akin to a large cotton candy which we greedily devour, only to discover that it has vanished on our tongue, leaving us with little other than a sweet sticky craving for more of the same.

Somehow, we must be going about this in the wrong way. Straight answers to straight questions do not point the way through the labyrinth. The numinous or mysterious responds in a more circuitous fashion.

John O'Donohue finds that one of the damaging aspects of this hunger is the way we tend to see everything in a severe and insistent light. That our modern consciousness has lost a certain reverence and gentility, lacking "graciousness in the presence of mystery," as it strives to un-riddle and control what is unknown.

Somewhere along the line we have forgotten our reverence for what is eternal and mysterious.

And being obsessed with spiritual programs is not necessarily a good thing. O'Donohue writes that the 13th century mystic Meister Eckhart radically revised the whole notion of spiritual programs, that there is in fact no such thing as a spiritual journey. "If there were a spiritual journey, it would be only a quarter inch long, though many miles deep." No need to master complex steps, or leave home on pilgrimage and travel vast distances. The eternal resides within.

The poet Yeats said that man needs reckless courage to descend into the abyss of himself. So we seek help in our quest. The first step, that all-important first step (back to the steps are we?), is to choose wisely from amidst the hawkers and barkers, philosophers and teachers.

Sam Keen is a scholar and author who has done it all and written thoughtfully about it all, right from the 60's experimenting with free love and Eastern religions, to unmasking dangerous mind-warping schemes and pointing the way through the minefields.

To journey through this lawless wilderness, the former editor of Psychology Today suggests, we need to take along a compass and some special gear, and most importantly "we will need to construct a spiritual bullshit detector."

To follow meekly in the steps of others is rarely a wise choice. Poet David Whyte (*The Heart Aroused*) has a severe view of those who would thus abandon their own beliefs. "This is where I feel a lot of the spiritual paths of both East and West have been quite erroneous and misleading around 'desire' because the hope is that you can get to a place where there is no desire whatsoever, and I don't believe it's possible."

Instead we simply end up following the desires of those who were clever enough to keep theirs alive. And that's when real evil starts to happen, as witness the Third Reich and Jonestown and Heaven's Gate cults.

In short, beware the fuzzy-headed and their fuzzy-headed mysticism, their mind-numbing fundamentalism, and their wild-eyed conspiracies. Muddled minds make for outrageous claims, and fake 'mystery' cults will be only too happy to replace our will with their own. The trick is to never relinquish our will, our inner desires, to anyone.

The Wisdom of Becoming a Butterfly

I read recently, although I don't remember where or by whom, a wonderful encapsulation of what it takes to move into action. "How does one become a butterfly...by wanting so badly to fly that one is willing to give up being a caterpillar." Simple, yes. But sometimes a simple image is far more powerful than reams of lengthy philosophical dissertation.

Or as astronaut John Glenn exhorts one and all, "live and die for some aim nobler and better...ideals are the very stuff of survival."

8

THE HEROIC JOURNEY

In the final analysis our search for truth does not begin somewhere out there, but with the one we are most adept at deceiving — our self. In fact, according to recent studies on mind development, our survival down through the ages has frequently been dependent upon our skill at self-deception, or at lying to our self. Those who did it best, survived the most.

Evolutionary wise, our ability to conceal our true intentions from hostile others, or from those whom we simply desired to manipulate for social gain, has often meant the difference between acceptance and banishment, or even death. The problem is, when we knowingly lie, we tend to give ourselves away through subtle body postures and facial quirks – fidgeting, averting eyes, blushing, etc. – telltale signs that act as built-in lie detectors. As Mark Twain noted, "When a person cannot deceive himself, the chances are against his being able to deceive other people."

So in a survival-of-the-fittest frame of mind, our brains cleverly devised a way around the problem by confining our duplicitous intentions to an unconscious decision-making sector of the brain, while hiding the truth from our conscious self. This way, because we do not know that we are lying, we can tell what we believe to be the truth, with an honest-looking face. (More about the split brain in the next chapter.)

Which leads to another problem. If we don't even know when we are deceiving ourselves, how are we to get to the truth of who we really are, let alone to the truth of anyone else? More to the point, is what we think really what we think, or are we the unsuspecting recipients of an Orwellian mindscape courtesy of family preferences and cultural demands? Are mom and apple pie really the values we believe in? Have we ever given it serious thought, aside from laughing along at some *South Park* episode?

The first step in any quest for truth, it seems, is to break free from this fashioned mindset, no matter how well intentioned the motives. It takes a conscious effort, and a courageous will to ask the right questions.

Who then were the first to break free, to ask the first meaningful questions? What kind of a world created the necessity for such a quest? What were its beginnings, and in answer to what?

II

FROM
THE GARDEN OF EDEN
TO
REALITY BITES

Is consciousness a recent evolutionary invention?

There was a time when Mother Nature created everything as if by magic. Quite suddenly this world-view came crashing down. Now we learn that this time of innocence may well have been a time of totally unconscious living. That what has come to be called the beginning of patriarchy — the mass slaughters, massive migrations, and beginnings of all major religions — was in fact the birth pangs of human consciousness.

Amazingly, humans may not have been conscious all that long. True consciousness in fact is a lot rarer than generally presumed; infants aren't conscious at all. Our ancient ancestors may never have even experienced it. This is important to know when choosing to follow in their footsteps, believing in their sacred myths.

How the human race moved from the Garden of Eden to the conscious world:

- Julian Jaynes
- Reay Tannahill
- Amaury de Riencourt
- Carl Jung
- Carl Sagan
- Michael Gazzaniga
- Malcolm Gladwell.

1

THE POWER OF CONSCIOUSNESS

Once upon a time ...

... our ancestors stood in awe of the world in which they lived. Thunder and lightning weren't seen as electromagnetic discharges caused by the friction between rapidly colliding hot and cold air masses. They were magic events, a mysterious and powerful show put on by nature for no apparent reason. Or they were evidence of the gods in heaven, throwing bolts of lightning, perhaps angry at us and in need of being placated.

Everywhere around was mystery and wonder: the dangerous dark of night was lit by an intriguing pattern of lights in the sky, imagined into amusing scenarios of animals and gods; the ever changing face of the wandering moon set the pulse of the seasons; the invigorating warmth of the sun, so powerful that no man could stare upon its face without being blinded; the magic of fire — warming the night, lighting the way in darkened caves, scaring off terrifying beasts, making food more digestible and tasty, molding metals into useful tools and weapons and jewelry.

And most magical of all was Mother Earth, as nature came to be known. Her creativity was prolific, budding and blossoming, sprouting all over. Trees and bushes, vegetables and fruits, roots and shoots. A cornucopia of wonder and delight, of filling tastes and joy, all as if by magic appearing before our eyes. Mother Earth the creator gave birth to so much.

Some of this magic she passed on to her creations, at least to the female side. For no apparent reason, ewes and mares and hens of every type of animal created carbon copies of their species. And the greatest of these was woman. From the midst of her belly grew the human race itself.

Man, the male of the human species, was in awe of her mysterious magic. Of all the spirit gods humans created to account for the happenings in nature, the greatest were the goddesses. They alone possessed the magic of creating something out of nothing.

Sex in History

Sex in this time — from the very beginning of our species — was something people indulged in for the sheer pleasure of it. (Not that we have any nobler motivation today, just that, except when in the throes of passionate new conquest, we tend to be aware of life-altering consequences to unprotected sex.) Hard as it is for us to comprehend, our ancient ancestors as a whole hadn't a clue that there was any connection between sex and having a baby. Even in this past century, "anthropologists have been consistently taken aback," Reay Tannahill writes in *Sex in History*, "to discover primitive tribes still ignorant of the relationship between coitus and conception." Who could fathom that making whoopee would have such a magical effect on creation?

It wasn't until the first Neolithic humans started settling down some ten thousand years ago, to raise crops and herd animals that we began to notice how sex played a significant role in the development of the flocks. It took thousands of years more to sink into our collective minds that, if sex was a necessary part of the equation, then men must be more than just innocent bystanders, that without them there could be no creation at all, that woman wasn't magical at all, and that if there was power in anything at all it was in man's seed.

Swiss historian Amaury de Riencourt, in his eye-opening exploration of the sexes, *Sex and Power in History*, explains that between the 5th and 2nd millennia BC, depending on the culture and in which part of the world, the human race crossed over a "*mental threshold* from magico-symbolic thought processes to rational thinking." In the matter of sexual intercourse and pregnancy, what had long been observed as a feat of inexplicable magic, slowly came to be understood in terms of cause and effect.

Gradually, once these late Bronze Age ancestors got the idea of magic out of their heads, it dawned on them that this connection was not only essential, "but was the only one that created new life."

The World Turned Right on its Head

Then all hell broke loose. Well, not exactly. Major change tends to be very slow, more like the pony express than e-mail, especially when it is as earth shattering as this. The entire worldview of our ancestors, after all, was being turned right on its head.

After 150,000 years of standing in awe of feminine magic and worshipping the goddess, the male of the species now proudly stood in her place, and assumed the mantle of creator, lord and master. Woman went from being magic creator to mere container, charged with caring for man's precious seed. Fields were no longer seen as the magic womb of Mother Nature, but simply as the recipient of seeds of grains, and vegetables and fruit trees. The goddesses were demoted to being icons of beauty and seduction, or as consorts to all-powerful male gods, who now reigned supreme on high.

In many ancient cultures, in both East and West, once they discovered the creative power of the male, it was taught that the bones and the brain of a fetus came from the father's semen, and the flesh and the blood from the mother's vaginal secretions. The mother's contribution of an egg (and its genetic traits) simply did not exist in this understanding. She was but a vessel, a baker's oven.

Reay Tannahill, in her exhaustive study of gender differences, *Sex in History*, states, "At the beginning of the Christian era, the Alexandrians had discovered the ovaries, but took them to be an unimportant feminine version of the testes." It wasn't until the dawn of the microscope in the 16th century that debate arose as to what significant contribution, if any, babies inherited from their mothers. "Gradually it came to be accepted that a child derived its characteristics as much from its mother as its father, but *it was not until 1854* (italics added) that anyone succeeded in observing the fusion of sperm and egg that proved the truth of the matter."

Masculine Growing Pains

The tremendous plummet of the Great Mother some three to four thousand years ago, Amaury writes, was a psychological event of the first magnitude that "took place in the collective unconscious of these early cultures and shaped the relationship of the sexes ... in such a way as to assure the complete predominance, not always or necessarily of men, but of the *masculine principle*."

It isn't that the women of this time were madly cheering for the supremacy of their familiar goddesses, while men brutally forced their newly designed gods to the top of the mountain. The old maternal view of life, one that had been accepted unquestioningly for perhaps hundreds of thousands of years, was simply at an end. It was not something that happened just to men. Men and women alike shared the same culture, so when these momentous changes in perception took place, everyone's outlook was affected accordingly. (More about the power of perception in chapter 7.)

The stories and myths told around the fire and passed on to the younger generations were the same for all. This was not a battle of the sexes, but a 'discovery' of a totally new reality, a dawning of a new rational consciousness to replace our previously automatic, unconscious acceptance of a magical world.

2

THE CONSCIOUSNESS EXPLOSION

What caused this great breakdown of the matriarchal world, the suppression of the unconscious and all the wonders it has to offer? What prompted consciousness to burst upon the scene, birthed as it were by the great mother Unconscious?

As Julian Jaynes writes, the mighty themes of the religions of the world are here sounded for the first time. "Why have the gods left us? Like friends who depart from us, they must be offended. Our misfortunes are our punishments for our offenses. We go down on our knees, begging to be forgiven."

These words from Princeton psychologist Julian Jaynes mark the pivotal time when our ancestors shifted from unconscious to conscious living. They describe the anguish of abandonment as these people struggled with their newfound freedom of choice — and its companion of personal responsibility for each and every thing they did, and said, and thought.

In *Shadows of Forgotten Ancestors,* Carl Sagan and Ann Druyan describe our predicament then as akin to that of infants abandoned on a doorstep, with no note to indicate who their parents were, or where they came from.

"Repeatedly, in many cultures, we invented reassuring fantasies about our parents — about how much they loved us, about how heroic and larger than life they were. As orphans do, we sometimes blamed ourselves for having been abandoned. It must have been our fault. We were too sinful, perhaps, or morally incorrigible." These are the stories we told ourselves, to be found still in the early chapters of our holy books, first brave attempts to explain the world around us.

Just as a child starts out seeing itself as the center of its own little universe, so too we as a species started off certain in our belief that we and our home base, the Earth, were at the center of the Universe, convinced even that the planets and stars and sun were created precisely for our benefit. As Sagan and Druyan put it, this comfortable conceit has been crumbling for five hundred years now, slowly substituting our reliance on a God or gods to lend a hand, with our own ability to discover our place in the real world, and to deal with challenges using the wits we have at hand. "The cost of coming of age is giving up the security blanket."

The Birth of Consciousness

There are those who say what's the difference, who cares when our ancestors became conscious, what's it got to do with us today? But there is wisdom yet to be woven from these threads. If truth is so difficult to nail down in our daily lives perhaps it's because these lives are based on an antiquated foundation. What if we rebuilt our lives on a foundation more in tune with the way the world actually is? Would we not then have more control of where we are heading? Our inbred fear of change, alas, has locked us in a belief system that was created back when chariots were all the rage, and pollution was what a horse left behind for us to avoid stepping in. Time to move on.

Between three and five thousand years ago something truly profound and ultimately awesome occurred which more and more researchers are beginning to see as the birth of consciousness. We are still a far way from knowing the hows and whys and wherefores, and much of what follows can only in all honesty be described as highly speculative, yet the interwoven accounts of the following researchers and historians is a most compelling explanation of why the world suddenly changed so drastically. And why our myths and legends and holy books look back so nostalgically at this simpler and purer time of our collective human innocence.

The Origin of Consciousness in the Breakdown of the Bicameral Mind is Jaynes' controversial theory. It isn't as obtuse or frightening as the title at first sounds. Simply put, Jaynes proposes that during that part of the unconscious era when our ancestors finally settled down to tend crops and raise livestock, and consequently formed larger and larger towns and cities, there was a great deal of stress created for all concerned.

After all, these were people who just a few generations before were a part of some small wandering tribe, where everyone knew everyone else. All of a sudden they are living bang next door to someone who for all intents and purposes is a foreigner; they meet at market someone whose name they can barely pronounce; and they work on a community project — building a wall around their town for protection — alongside a Babel of total strangers.

This degree of stress and tension should be recognizable to any citizen of the 21st century, where ethnic and national and religious boundaries have been so erased by the global village that we can hardly tell a joke any more for fear of offending someone somewhere — perhaps the very one to whom we are telling the joke. Stress is our constant companion.

According to Jaynes, the level of stress got so high for these post-tribal folks that something had to give. Instead of mentally breaking down, the mind itself cleverly went into schizophrenic drive. Schizophrenic in that one side of the brain assumed the role of master, telling us what to do in any stressful situation; the other side, or obedient half, the one we have control over, carried out these wishes as best as possible, totally without responsibility, for it was just doing what it was told. Thus reducing the stress.

All of this is easy to comprehend when we accept that the brain, modern and ancient alike, is essentially divided into two parts, only one of which is under our command at a time.

The master side of the brain 'spoke' to the obedient side through hallucinated voices, voices which could be heard only within the individual's head, but as real as any external voice. More so even. Just listen to schizophrenics — there are many wandering the streets these days of virtually every community, thanks to powerful new drugs — and see how furtive are their arguments, how real, how dominated they are by this voice which we, of course, cannot hear. At least with an outside voice we can turn away, block up our ears, run away. But hallucinated voices are loud, they are as close as close can be, and they demand our full attention. So we obey.

The Birth of Our First Personal Gods

Thus it was, according to the theory, that our ancestors learned to cope with the stress of their brave new world. In the small, tribal world, the leader or chieftain was obeyed because he or she was close at hand. No tension. Now in the new, larger world which was ever growing before them, stress took hold, and to deal with that stress people began to hear the faraway leader's voice in their heads, close at hand where it could be easily obeyed. When the leader died, the body was buried in the centre of town, on ever higher mounds, while the dead leader's voice continued to ring in the people's heads. Thus were born our first personal gods, and their altars.

It's not essential that we accept this description of our pre-history in all its details. Certainly there are aspects of it that many critics question. But as we will see next, the theory nonetheless jives very nicely with the historical breakdown of the unconscious goddess-dominated world, and the takeover of consciousness and patriarchy.

All through this voices-in the-head period — during which human beings became aware of the power of the male seed and the non-magical status of woman — the great female goddesses were gradually replaced by new gods — the voices of revered dead leaders. As more and more of these were male, the gods soon outnumbered the goddesses, and eventually accorded a much greater respect.

But this new male worldview could not take precedence until the old mytho-poetic view was replaced by a rational and logical one. As de Riencourt put it, "All through the metamorphosis of the early myths, one perceives the discursive power of the mind attempting to awaken, and break through the primeval dreamlike forms of mythological understanding."

The conscious mind was as yet only partially awakened.

HELL ON EARTH

All hell did brake loose, finally. In the most painful and barbaric ways imaginable. Right in the midst of this gradual redevelopment of our understanding of who and what we are in the overall scheme of things, the worst nightmares struck the civilized world in the form of crazed invaders.

The Dorian invasions, as they were known in ancient Greece. Elsewhere, the Philistines, or boat people who attacked Egypt, then settled in the Promised Land. The mad Assyrians who swarmed over people after people, their wild-eyed horses whipping their war chariots through defenseless settlements, trampling all who stood in their way. These were the killers, the 'uncivilized' hordes from what is now Eastern Europe and the Eurasian steppes, who descended upon the refined cultures everywhere from the Middle East to North Africa, to India and China.

Jaynes describes how the Assyrians fell like butchers upon countless innocent villages, enslaving what survivors they could, and slaughtering the rest by the thousands. It was a nightmare the likes of which had never before been seen in history. All that was left behind were boastful bas-reliefs showing whole cities of people who had been stuck alive on stakes running up through the groin and out the shoulders. Wanton cruelty. A world gone mad. Clear evidence that all social control had broken down.

These invaders were highly mobile, always on the move. As Tannahill points out, it was in these groups that "man was dominant, and woman as much his chattel as the beasts he herded."

Abandoned by God

These invaders had shaken free from voices, from gods telling them what to do, and without a moral code to replace them, they simply ran amok. As Jaynes suggests, the very practice of using cruelty to rule by fear is at the brink of subjective consciousness.

Historian de Riencourt concludes that the period that stretched from the 17th to the 14th century BC is one of the sharpest separations in history, brought about by successive invasions from "iron-bearing, horse-drawn, chariot-riding barbarians of obviously terrifying mien and disposition." This relentless wave of callous patriarchal warriors against all settled peoples destroyed every state and empire that stood in its path.

He further describes this vicious and masculine subjugation of these peaceful peoples in rape-like terminology, wherein the invaders violently penetrated, and inseminated the female-oriented cultures from Europe to Asia and back.

Thus began the patriarchal supremacy. Thus began the preeminence of conscious human beings.

4

FROM WRITING TO ATLANTIS

The invasions of course are only part of the story. For so great a revolution as the birth of consciousness, there had to be a weakening of the unconscious from several different angles.

One of these was the development of writing. When we can read something over and over again, be it a story or instructions or laws to live by, we no longer have to rely on voices to advise us; in fact they tend to get in the way. Another was the opening up of trade routes to places quite far afield. Strange foreigners not only looked different and spoke differently, but they obviously marched to a different drummer — the voices they heard were not at all like ours. So the unconscious slipped yet another notch.

But the greatest attack on the power of the unconscious was the ultimate failure of the gods themselves. The voices may have been fine for handling the stress of day-to-day living, but for helping out during times of major chaos, they were useless. And as luck would have it, there was major chaos afoot, at least in those parts of the world where we have numerous records.

Around the time of the barbaric invasions, there were a couple of major earthquakes in particular that literally destroyed the world as it was once known. The tale of the lost continent of Atlantis was how Plato described the destruction of an advanced Mediterranean civilization in the neighborhood of Crete. A volcano blew its stack on the island of Thera (Santorini), collapsing a vast area of land to the bottom of the sea.

The shock waves that blasted through the air are estimated to have been hundreds of times more powerful than a hydrogen bomb. "A *tsunami* or huge tidal wave followed," in Jaynes' rendering of the disaster, one towering some 700 feet high and smashing into the coasts of these fragile states of the Aegean at up to 350 miles per hour. The islands and mainland settlements were destroyed for two miles inland. "A civilization and its gods had ended."

Chaos reigned supreme. Refugees scrambled in panic in any which direction. Murderous invaders on the one hand, the wrath of Mother Nature on the other, and now the civilized peoples themselves were at each other's throats, desperate for land, for food, for shelter. It was a do-or-die situation. They either ceased to blindly accept the old view of the world and became conscious and learned to fend for themselves, or they were slaughtered. The old ways of peaceful isolation were gone forever.

Of promised Lands and Oracles

Eventually resettlement occurred. Those who were late to find suitable land continued to wander around the edges of these new civilizations. Scholars agree that they were collectively known as 'Khabiru,' the likely source name of the wandering Hebrew tribes in search of a promised land.

As for those who continued to hear voices? For several centuries after the new era began, while moral codes and laws were being worked out to define acceptable 'civilized' behavior, those who still heard voices were pretty much revered. After all, the gods still spoke to them. They must be favored. So they were consulted on everything from how to defeat the enemy, to how to pray to the deities. To the Israelites they were known as the Prophets; to the ancient Greeks they were the Oracles.

In the end, however, when cultures became more confident in their human capabilities, they tired of these bothersome types, and slaughtered most of them. The world from here on was to be home to conscious people only. In today's world, schizophrenics are fully conscious, their voices but a remnant of our common past. But it is interesting to note that there is not a society on this entire earth, no matter what its history or technological development, that does not have a small portion of its members — about 1% according to psychiatrist Tim Crow of Oxford, England — who are schizophrenic. All humankind from the same cloth.

5

UNCONSCIOUS OVER BUT NOT OUT

The overthrow of the Great Mother Goddess's supremacy, as de Riencourt says, meant the submerging of all those qualities associated with the unconscious, and the female spirit — instinct, emotion, intuition, empathy, and sensitivity to the needs and concerns of others. The Wise Old Man archetype, well known to Western religious tradition, assumed supremacy in the name of consciousness, and the male spirit — creative intellect, seminal thought (logos spermatikos), analyzing and categorizing. Creation no longer sprouted from the matriarchal womb, but from the mind (word) of God. *In the beginning was the word.*

Mythology, which had so well guided and informed us in the days of the Great Mother, was now pushed aside by increasingly unmythical thought processes, a form of thinking rooted in rationalism and logic. The royal battle between myth and logic, between the abstract thinking male and the concrete feeling female. As old religions were replaced by systems of ethics, "myths were reshaped into parables; and uncertainty, spiritual questing, took the place of the quiet passive acceptance of nature and destiny."

And so began philosophy. Such was the beginning of history, as a progression of events that lead to some goal or purpose. It was a giant step for our ancestors. The good old certainties of repetitive rhythms and cycles were replaced by unknown tomorrows, by worries over whether we made the right choices, by the burden of personal responsibility for every step of the way. A new quest began in earnest, a search for old assurances in a world which shouted clearly, "there are no guarantees!"

The Price the Human Race Paid for Freedom

The new world order, as we see from the story of Eden, is one of original sin, of death and violence, of heaven and hell — of ultimate responsibility. But of far more significance than all of this, Eden is a story about the price the human race had to pay for its freedom. The cost of leaving childhood and innocence. What it takes to develop into a fully rounded and capable adult. To go forth on one's own in search of real truths.

Most importantly, we bear witness here to the birth of a new human, endowed with a Promethean drive to become lord and master of nature and to dominate the earth. Conscious at long last, able to reflect and to ask questions about destiny and the meaning of life, and life after life. Cut loose from the earthbound embraces of Mother Nature, the metaphorical apron strings of motherly care, Homo sapiens sets out bravely on its journey of exploration.

Past, present and future, before this blurred by endless cyclical repetitions, are now sharply perceived. Instead of the old 'once upon a time,' people begin to see history as a linear development of unique and unrepeatable events, all endowed with moral significance.

We were happy once to be a part of nature, to see our lives as not much different from that of grizzly bears or jungle cats or bull frogs in the pond. But this 'I-thou' relationship soon deteriorated into a 'subject-object,' or master-slave view of our place in this brave new world. This was no minor change, our placing ourselves outside of nature — its effects are still glaringly seen in our present day rape of the environment and extinction of countless species.

And don't be fooled into believing that the names we give things (animal, human) and actions (genocide, ethnic cleansing) are *just* word changes. As Jaynes warns, the words we choose affect our perceptions, and our perceptions precede our actions. "Word changes are concept changes and concept changes are behavioral changes." All of history, of politics, of religion, and of science cries out in witness to its devastating power.

6

A SUDDEN PERCEPTUAL CHANGE

The reign of the unconscious, like the reign of the goddess, is over. As Joseph Campbell described it, just like a butterfly opens up from its cocoon, so the human mind opened to full waking consciousness. Modern mankind emerged from its ancient ignorance as the dream-web of myth fell away. No longer was there a hiding place for the gods in this brave new world; indeed there no longer exists on this entire planet a society like the ones once supported by the gods.

We are as a species grown to maturity. We take responsibility (in theory at any rate) for our actions, for our thoughts, for our intentions. We have free will and freedom of choice. There is no going back.

The reign of consciousness, however, has proved thus far to be considerably less than ideal. So we look back with fondness at this time before our supposed Great Fall, when we reportedly lost our paradise on earth by performing some dastardly deed in defiance of the ineffable will.

We know now that our ouster from Eden was a significant myth, not a history lesson. That there was no original sin beneath an apple tree. That the only fall was the one out of our infant crib, where we then learned to stand on our own two feet, and make our way in the world.

Awareness, Consciousness and Something in Between

The main problem most of us have with all of the above is the idea that somehow the ancients created so much – Egyptian and Sumerian cultures to name just two — while stumbling around in some unconscious state. It just doesn't seem to make sense. Or maybe it's just our definition of consciousness that is in need of fine-tuning.

Recently Lili interviewed Jane Goodall, who lived for many years in the wild with chimpanzees, performing astonishing breakthrough research which has greatly altered our perceptions of mankind's closest relative. Goodall opened our eyes in many ways to the reality of these magnificently complex creatures, our cousins, who before had been seen in rather simplistic terms. When Lili asked her — totally off topic and thus unwittingly putting her on the spot — if she considered these primates to be conscious as we are, Goodall's response was both direct and equivocating.

"There's no doubt in my mind that chimpanzees *are* ... we know they're rational. We know they have emotions and they are conscious of self. They understand the difference between me and you. And the extent to which other animals have the same degree of consciousness is something which is still being discussed. ...certainly the other great apes are conscious."

She continued, shedding light on the slipperiness of the problem. "Elephants, dogs, I would go way down the animal scale...probably varying degrees of consciousness. The thing is that only *we* know that we're conscious. Only *we* question the meaning of our lives. Only we wonder what it's all about. Is there a plan? So we have a different level of consciousness."

A different level of consciousness, or more correctly, a different definition of what consciousness is? Too often, as in this instance, consciousness is used as a synonym for awareness, combining the clinical with the psychological. To a neuroscientist, for instance, consciousness simply refers to a state of arousal or attentiveness, as easily applicable to an earthworm as to a great ape. Most of us, however, think of consciousness in the psychological sense, as an attribute of a sentient being that is capable of reflecting on his actions and the actions of others.

Still, we continue to confuse the two, seeing consciousness where in fact lies something else, like a very well developed emotional attachment, or keen awareness, or intelligent behavior, or any form of the above qualities which we perhaps mistakenly call consciousness. And there's a very good reason for this.

It's simply astounding what can be accomplished without being conscious – the very consciousness which we now take for granted as our birthright.

WHAT IT TAKES TO BE CONSCIOUS

The trouble with consciousness is that we cannot be conscious of what we cannot be conscious of. Imagine a flashlight in a dark room. The room is the universe and all it holds. Consciousness is the flashlight. As Jaynes explains, consciousness is like a flashlight that you shine around in a dark room, searching for some spot that is completely in the dark, unlit. But because no matter where you point the flashlight you're going to find light, you would falsely conclude that every part of the room is bathed in light. Likewise, we conclude that whenever we turn on the flashlight (wake up), we are conscious of all around us.

The Impossibility of Consciousness Without Language

A well-developed language is a prerequisite to developing consciousness. And language itself is nothing more than the ability to make metaphors — that is, we use some term that is familiar to us to describe something that may be similar, but also appreciably different. So to a technologically more primitive culture with no word for airplane, I may describe an airplane as a bus (or people-carrying cart) that has wings. It is in this way that all language evolves, from the most primitive of beginnings to the hundred-thousand-plus-word dictionaries we have today. Metaphor generates new language "as it is needed, as human culture becomes more and more complex."

When we say we understand something, all we're really saying is that we have successfully created a metaphor for it by substituting a more familiar concept. This is particularly true when we get away from concrete things (carts, rocks, trees) and get into the realm of ideas and theories and meanings of life.

So language is a process of creating in our mind a metaphor for the real world. At some advanced stage in this process we begin to develop a 'consciousness' of what is really going on. Note, we do not suddenly *become* conscious. Like language itself, consciousness grows on us as a culture over the centuries. More importantly it grows on us as individuals.

None of us was born conscious.

Newborns and infants are not conscious, no matter how endearing their big eyes and ready smiles. Language they do not have, and do not begin to acquire until around two years of age. From there they gradually 'lose their innocence' — what some would call the innocence of the Garden of Eden — becoming progressively more conscious of the real world, and their place in it. And just as we cannot begin to recall how our unconscious ancestors perceived the world, so too we have no true memories of our earliest childhood years.

The criteria are very straightforward for determining when we are conscious, and we shouldn't shrink from using this same yardstick as a measure for all other living creatures.

Prerequisites to Joining the Club of Consciousness

1. Spatialization: We create spaces in our mind for things that don't have them in the real world. When we think of the Neanderthals as opposed to the time of Cleopatra as opposed to the Knights of the Round Table, we space them in our mind in a time-oriented order, something which is not to be found in the real world.

2. Excerption: We cannot possibly be aware of everything going on around us at every given moment. So we excerpt tiny portions, fully aware that there is much more to the bigger picture. If we were to envision New York City right now, it would not be of every soul living there, every street and building, every interaction. But it may well be of young children enjoying themselves at the Rockefeller Center outdoor rink.

3. An Analog 'I': Which is to say that we make a space in this metaphor world for ourselves to move around. In this way we can imagine ourselves cuddling rattlesnakes, and the consequences; climbing Mt. Everest without proper equipment, and the consequences; and dashing across a twelve-lane highway, and the consequences. None of this has happened in the real world, but we are none-the-less wiser for the exercise.

4. A Metaphor 'Me': The ability to see ourselves in the above scenes, from the outside, as others might see us. A truly extraordinary capability, given that it is not something that we can actually do in the real world. Even a camera is only excerpting a camera's point of view, not our own.

5. Narratization: We take all of the above and lay it out in a nice story, usually with our analog 'I' as the central figure. This is after all the story of *my* life which I am narrating, and the constant chatter in my mind isn't coming from anywhere else but me. (And thus the necessity of a well-developed language.) But of course the narratization also includes everything we have excerpted in consciousness.

6. Conciliation: Making sense out of what we perceive and what we imagine, even in daydreams. If we are asked to imagine children skating on a pond, and then asked to envision a large city, we will likely see them on a frozen pond in a city park, or on that frozen river wending its way through town. The world has to 'make sense,' even the metaphorical one in our mind.

To summarize his own criteria, Julian Jaynes writes, "Consciousness is an operation rather than a thing. It operates by way of analogy, by way of constructing an analog space with an analog 'I' that can observe that space, and move metaphorically in it."

When we can honestly attribute all of the above criteria to dolphins and chimpanzees and our pet dogs, then and only then can we begin to speak of them as being conscious beings.

8

BEING CONSCIOUS
OF THE UNCONSCIOUS

The long reign of the goddess culture was the long reign of the unconscious.

It was a time of intuition, of creating, of appreciating the poetry in life, of living as much as possible in harmony with nature, with the ebbs and flows of the natural world. A time where the dream world and the waking state intermingled freely — imagine not remembering whether people we met yesterday or things that happened to us were part of a dream or part of our awake world, and it not mattering to us in the least! A mystical time when mystery and magic 'explained' all that there was to know. History and progress and the rush of time did not exist. Mother Nature, author of the seasons and cycles of life, ruled supreme.

This idyllic setting is fondly remembered in the collective unconscious, described in ancient tales and myths, tales written long after this way of life was abandoned. It is nostalgically drawn, vaguely as through a dense mist, and pictured perhaps a little too idealistically, in stories like the Garden of Eden in Genesis. Man and woman in harmony with the rest of creation, enjoying its abundant harvest.

But then, as the allegory would have it, they went and ate the fruit of the tree of knowledge of good and evil. Or some other downfall in some other story, with the same results. People lost their innocence, the naive innocence of young children. They grew up, whether they wanted to or not, and were forced out of their Eden. Good and evil, right and wrong, love and hate. So many choices. Consciousness erupted and took command.

Nevertheless, the unconscious still underlies our consciousness at all times. Many theorists say it is the source of our intuition. That it is where those great ideas spring from, the kind that helps inventors and scientists while they sleep. That it is the fount of all creativity and artistic endeavor. That it is the wellspring of our dreams. And our nightmares.

It may be a moot point which came first, the chicken or the egg, but when it comes to consciousness versus the unconscious, the unconscious won the race into our mental life by several hundred thousand years.

According to Carl Jung, the unconscious is the mother of consciousness, the conscious mind resulting from an unconscious psyche which existed (as any mother does) prior to her offspring consciousness, and continues to function *with consciousness.* Consciousness as son. The 'mother' of consciousness. Images of mother and child abound – important images as we shall see in a moment.

Thus for a very long period of our human history we were not conscious, but lived as unconscious beings. We developed intricate societies, tools, farming, laws, deities, cities, art, song, and language — all while unconscious. The idea seems astonishing at first, but not really when we consider the above qualities of the unconscious — intuition, thinking, creativity, etc.

And when consciousness did finally assume command, the unconscious did not simply disappear. It is still here with us. Just sublimated; pushed down under the conscious mind (not to be confused with the Freudian concept of the repression of unwanted or powerfully painful memories). Consciousness, being the egotistical child that it is, so to speak, tries to deny the existence of its mother, but the unconscious remains steadfast, an integral part of our mental make-up. In order to get in touch with her, we need to nudge her young offspring aside.

As Jung said, "the ego was born in the conscious mind, and turns its back on the unconscious, seeking to deny it as best it can."

The Feminine Not the Female

The unconscious in this scenario is the abode of the feminine. The goddess, the feminine, the unconscious, all end up buried under the weight of the male god, the masculine principle, the conscious mind.

The feminine, of course, is not necessarily the female. Each sex encompasses both feminine and masculine aspects. *Animus, is the man in a woman. Anima, the woman in a man.* Jung described them as being at the very foundation of the unconscious. The animus and anima make up for each sex the inner personality, as contrasted with the conscious external personality. And out of these, over a period of thousands of years, blossomed all the gods and goddesses of ancient mythology.

Feminine intuition and feminine psychic abilities are neither imagined, nor sexist statements to divide the genders. The unconscious tends to exhibit what we call feminine characteristics, and the conscious mind so-called masculine traits.

"This psychic life is the mind of our ancient ancestors," Jung wrote, after his extensive studies of ancient legends and myths. The way in which our ancestors saw the world and felt towards it, the way in which they imagined life and the gods and their place as human beings, is to be found not only in these stories, but in our very own unconscious

9

CONSCIOUSNESS BY ANY OTHER NAME

The phenomenon of déjà vu may help us shed some light on this consciousness-unconsciousness conundrum. According to Webster's, déjà vu is "the illusion of remembering scenes and events *when experienced for the first time.*" That is, we are quite certain that we have never been in this situation before or, say, visited this particular island, yet we can amazingly predict what's going to happen next or what lies around the next corner. So what's really going on in our brain?

Déjà vu may be a remnant of a form of rapid cognition that was common in our pre-conscious days. That is, it may be a hint as to how our ancestors actually saw the world, day-to-day and hour-by-hour.

In 1844 a researcher by the name of Arthur Wigan suggested that since our two cerebral hemispheres, left and right, can act independently (amazing that science has known this fact for at least a century and a half, yet so few are aware of it today), then déjà vu is an incidence of one hemisphere momentarily not paying attention while the other is recording a new experience; then, when the other side catches up, seconds later, we record an eerie experience of having been through this before, though quite unable to fathom just when or how.

This isn't difficult to understand when we realize that our brain reaches conclusions in indirect ways, through often Byzantine channels. Most of the time 'we' are left pretty much in the dark as to how our own brain arrived at these conclusions, tending instead to the mopping up business of 'rationalizing' our conclusions, convincing others and ourselves that we arrived at them consciously.

Malcolm Gladwell in his recent bestseller *Blink: The Power of Thinking Without Thinking*, points out that psychologists have discovered that this form of leaping to conclusions takes place in our adaptive unconscious. It's a mental scenario in which we arrive at a very rapid conclusion about almost any novel situation.

"The power of knowing, in the first two seconds," Gladwell says of this ability to instantly decode the truth of any situation, "is not a gift given magically to a fortunate few. It is an ability that we can all cultivate for ourselves." As it is as available to us today as it was to our forefathers.

These intuitions can be so powerful that instead of spending hours in conscious deliberation, we can come to the right conclusion in a matter of two or three seconds. What a powerful mental ability, an ability which our unconscious ancestors used as their primary source of knowing!

The trouble (there's always a downside) is it's not always accurate. If we don't learn to identify the telltale signs of a 'bad hunch,' it can just as easily lead us astray — in the blink of an eye.

This is the main reason there is such a vast gap between what we know today and what our ancestors of three or four millennia ago managed to learn; we are no longer dependent on just this intuitive source of knowledge because we have added the incalculably greater universe of knowledge made possible by the questioning and analytic expertise of the conscious mind. It's also the reason why the ancient Egyptians could be so technologically advanced – intuiting what techniques would work, seeing in an instant the grand picture, being inspired to create incredible works – yet so ignorant of the science and principles that lay behind anything.

Both ways of thinking, the intuitive and the analytic, have their strengths and weaknesses. All snap decisions "rely on the thinnest slices of experience," are enormously fast, and all, without exception, spring from the unconscious. Yet without the awakened conscious sphere, there can be little meaningful questioning or stockpiling of discoveries that will lead to new truths.

10

A CHANGE OF MIND

Our unconscious self is not only capable of experiencing situations and coming to conclusions separate from our conscious self, but it also retains other powerful abilities, abilities which guided our ancestors in ways that at times seem foreign to us. We have difficulty imagining these complex ancient civilizations as being created and run by unconscious ancestors only because we insist that consciousness must be present for important decision-making to take place. Yet current brain science is telling us a different story.

It is in fact beginning to lend support to Jaynes' fascinating theory. In *The Split Brain Revisited* Michael Gazzaniga, director of the Center for Cognitive Neuroscience at Dartmouth College, reports that the right hemisphere apparently doesn't even try to interpret its experiences or find deeper meaning. In essence the right side of the brain tends to live almost exclusively in the present moment, and is very truthful — traits chiefly associated with the unsophisticated, innocent and non-questioning stages of early development.

By contrast, Gazzaniga says, "the left hemisphere seeks explanations for why events occur. *By going beyond the simple observation of events and asking why they happened, a brain can cope with these same events better, should they happen again.* (Italics added)" What could be a clearer description of the split between the unconscious person and the one who has entered consciousness — the one starting to ask serious questions about the nature of our existence?

Gazzaniga concludes that these findings have lead to a new appreciation of the origins of left and right specialization. Or as Anthony Campbell wrote in *The Philosopher's Magazine* (Spring, 2003), Jaynes is a man whose time may finally have come, that he may well have given us "an indispensable clue to understanding how and when the modern human mind developed."

The right hemisphere of the brain is privy to all those qualities that were associated with the unconscious era, the matriarchy, the goddess supreme. Perhaps all that really changed with the great upheaval that lead to the consciousness revolution, is the particular side of the brain that dominated. Which do I feel is *me*? Am I an unconscious, intuitive being — perhaps hearing commanding voices intruding from the other half of my brain? Or am I a conscious, intellectual being, blithely ignoring the intuitions and inspirations which tease and tempt me from this other hemisphere?

Is it possible, even, that the little voices which our ancestors purportedly heard are in fact none other than the little voices which we ourselves hear all the time – the 'monkey chatter' that invades every waking moment of our days? If for our ancestors the right (unconscious) hemisphere was the dominant side through which they perceived the world, then those little voices would indeed have appeared to have been coming from somewhere outside of what they considered to be themselves. Much as we, now dominated by the left (conscious) hemisphere, have no problem with this chatter, accepting it as an integral part of who we are, yet see inspiration and intuition as arising from outside of ourselves, and outside of our control.

The only real distinction, then, is that most of us today realize that these outside influences are in fact a product of our own mental processes, and not the work of some gods or muses, angels or demons.

At least in this scenario the idea of little voices in the head leaves the realm of exotic fantasy and becomes as familiar as our ever-instructive internal dialogue. Schizophrenics, in this understanding, would be those who periodically slip into right hemisphere dominance, hearing the inner voices as coming from other than who they feel themselves to be at that moment; then slipping back to the left side again. Artists, and those who find themselves inspired in one way or another, as well as the intuitive, are those who are able to, however briefly, lift the veil, or open the doors of perception to see reality in this different mode of perception, without releasing their left brain dominance. That is, not losing their 'sanity.'

In short, the people we are calling our unconscious ancestors are those whose awareness of the world was mediated by the right hemisphere. They were not 'right-brain conscious'; they were simply not capable of naratizing, of seeing their analog selves in a metaphorical world – as Gazzaniga said above, the right hemisphere doesn't even attempt to interpret its experiences. So in no way were they conscious as we know the experience to be, and thus the necessity, as I agree with Jaynes and others, of referring to them as 'un-conscious.'

If our unconscious ancestors were indeed right hemisphere dominant, then we should be able to find evidence in the archaeological records that the majority of them were left handed (as after having switched over, the majority of us today are right handed). It would certainly explain a lot about our history of anti left-handedness once we became conscious as a society — everything from tying back a child's left hand so he would learn to use his right (and thus not be associated with the unconscious past), to our denigration of all things left as 'sinister' and of the evil or dark side

11

AN INVISIBLE MATRIX

Just because we can't explain how something works, doesn't mean that it doesn't exist. It does force us, though, to rely heavily on circumstantial evidence. As in anecdotes. And although anecdotes can be entertaining, and sometimes packed with manipulative emotion, in the final analysis they don't 'prove' anything. (Try telling this to the millions who purchase self-help books that are filled with nothing but wall-to-wall anecdotes, often fictional.)

Several years ago, in the time we refer to as BC (before children), my wife and I were camping in New Brunswick. Sometime around ten at night we were standing on a beach, with our mouths literally wide open, in awe of the most enormous orange, full moon ascending from the distant sea. Suddenly Lili turned to me with an "oh my God!" She clutched at her chest, trying to catch her breath. We had to get to a phone right away, she insisted. Something had just happened to her younger sister, but she didn't know what. Just that it was bad. An accident.

We searched frantically throughout the near-deserted campsite for a payphone, for any phone, to no avail. I tried to assure her that it was just a random thought that popped into her head, that it didn't mean anything, that her sister was probably at home sound asleep in her bed. Thus spake the male. But she wouldn't have any of it. She *knew* she was right.

The next morning we headed straight for the nearest town, and Lili to the first phone booth. Her mother was, indeed, upset on the phone. Sure enough, her sister had been out the night before and had fallen down some dark concrete stairs and broken her leg. She was in a lot of pain.

What to make of this and several other similar incidents she has *known* over a distance. Does this have anything to do with intuition? Is she somehow connected to her sister through some invisible matrix? Is the unconscious at work here, trying to tell us something, while our conscious ego denies there is anything involved but coincidence?

Reincarnation – Collective Unconscious

Or to put it another way, there is a part of us which responds to our personal unconscious needs, what later we will call our daimon or soul, destiny or character. And there is another part, called our *collective unconscious*, which is somehow enveloped in our heredity of thousands of years past. Even Freud in his later years came to accept that somehow, mysteriously, we all share a greater unconscious.

In Jung's interpretation, the unconscious has tremendous staying power. This mother, so to speak, battles quite successfully with her son, consciousness, because she has "immensely deep roots in the past, in the phylogenetic substructures of the modern mind, the so-called *collective unconscious*." — a treasure chest of archetypes which, over thousands of years, were transformed into myths, fables, and legends. "Myths are first and foremost psychic manifestations that represent the nature of the psyche."

A collective unconscious would explain that feeling of having been through past lives, of remembering things we purportedly did in ancient times, in ancient places. I have for a long time sensed that when people talk about their memories of past life experiences, what they are recalling is not actual previous incarnations of their soul, but perhaps memory fragments somehow dredged up from their chromosomes whose genes have undergone many different life times — in the persons of thousands of generations of their ancestors.

Re-incarnation, after all, doesn't quite fit into a space/time continuum universe, where existence in eternity is simultaneous with each and every moment in time. As we will see in chapter 9 on Living in Time and Living in Eternity, for everything outside of this universe there is no passage of time. So all of our incarnations, if we had more than one, would be present side by side, from first to last, from our most disastrous appearance to our final attainment of Enlightenment. Why would we keep coming back? Just send the last one, the one that got it right!

It would also explain what we call instincts and other forms of knowing that aren't connected with anything we were taught in this lifetime. And about the conundrum of identical twins who though separated at birth, growing up in different families, in different cities, in different socioeconomic levels, etc., have so much in common, aside from their physical appearance. Could their identical DNA be carrying something mysterious, something invisible that has yet to be spotted in any laboratory gene experiment?

The Human Genome and the Collective Unconscious

The major problem with something as invisible and universal as the collective unconscious, is trying to understand how it could possibly work. If the collective unconscious is something that we all share as a species, how do we pass it on?

As far as we know, the only substance we inherit from our parents is the DNA in our chromosomes. So for this collective unconscious to be passed down from generation to generation, it would have to be entwined somehow in the double helices of our DNA. A possibility, yes, but how would it work?

The current Human Genome Project has made giant strides in nailing down a large portion of the somewhat 30,000-odd genes in each of our cells. Geneticists now know the functions of many of these genes, their weaknesses, which ones cause what diseases, and perhaps even which ones contribute to a buff body, or flabby thighs. But I suspect few of us dream that one day they might find a gene which stores our collective unconscious. And there is no evidence to seriously challenge this point of view.

Still, each generation finds itself stumbling upon new realities which just a few decades earlier weren't even conceivable. These same genome scientists have labeled over 95% of our genome as 'junk.' That is, it takes less than 5% of our genome to account for the 30,000 active genes. So what's the purpose of the rest? That 95% may indeed have no real function. Then again, we may simply be staring at something which we haven't yet learned how to see.

Already scientists have discovered that our genome is actually three books in one, each with a different story to tell: One, it's a history book showing humanity's migration throughout the ages (more about this later); two, it's a medical textbook, revealing things about biology which had never before been imagined; three, it's an owner's manual, complete with a detailed analysis of each and every one of our separate and personal working parts.

12

STREAM OF CONSCIOUSNESS

Can it really be that most people lie about their inner sanctum? Lie to themselves as well as to others? Lie about the incredible control they wield in the only kingdom in which they have any real power? Such is the conclusion of scientists who have been tracking the bits and bytes of our mental makeup.

"Consciousness researchers have long pointed out that most of us exaggerate the richness of our inner mental world," writes author, and broadcaster with Discovery Channel, Jay Ingram, "but never before had I seen numbers quite so shocking."

Shocking that is in how little we are actually aware of. Our stream of consciousness it turns out is but a trickle. We convince ourselves that we have a vivid imagination, which is as lord and master of a universe of our own making (our mind's imaginings), a private reclusive world where we question what we will, and command as we please. A created Eden of our fantasies, and a Hell where we torturously even the balance. But that too is a fabrication to hide the truth.

The human brain is not a computer, and vice versa, but the comparison is handy for gauging just how powerful our brain really is. Louis Scheffer, an engineer at Berkeley, used the bits and bytes of computer terminology to try and quantify the information package known as our brain. A bit is one piece of information; a byte is eight of these bits. Each time a neuron in our brain tries to communicate with a neighboring neuron, about one hundred bits of information are exchanged.

100 Billion Neurons Synapsing Through Our Brains

Now, there are something like 100 billion neurons in one brain. Each neuron makes contact with between 1,000 and 10,000 other neurons. Scheffer did the math and came up with an estimate of the information content of our brains. Due to the enormity of the number it is stated here in megabytes — eight bits to a byte, one million bytes to a 'megabyte.' The answer is 10,000,000,000,000 (ten trillion) megabytes.

To put these incredibly large numbers in a way we can envision, contrast that ten trillion megabytes with this bit of trivia from *The Sizesaurus: Making measures fit for human consumption*, by Stephen Strauss: It would require only 25 million megabytes of computer space to store all the information contained in the more than 70 million books, magazines, and newspapers in the Library of Congress – or about 1/400,000[th] of the brain's capacity.

"Here's the kicker," Ingram continues. "How much of that enormous bank of information are we aware of at any moment? How many of those bits and bytes can we bring into our conscious mind? Would we believe about 40 or 50 bits per second?"

Fifty *bits* per second out of ten trillion *megabytes*! This is what we envision as our vibrant stream of consciousness! This grain of sand in a Sahara storm.

The discrepancies between what we receive and what we use are truly astonishing. For instance, our eye sends ten million bits of information to the brain per second, and our skin a million bits; yet we use only 30 bits a second to read, and 23 a second to play a musical instrument.

"There are two bottom lines here," Ingram concludes. "The first is that the human brain is a huge repository of information. The second, and more important, is that at any moment we are only aware of a minuscule fraction of that information. The rest goes unnoticed."

We, the conscious human race, must humbly accept that we are conscious of so very little. So little of the world around us. So little of what goes on in our own minds and bodies. So little that we can subsequently question. *So little of what affects us and guides us and makes us do the things we do.*

How different was it, then, before our species became conscious?

13

THE ECHO OF POETRY

Lest our egos get carried away, remember: Our magnificent ancestors created incredible civilizations, erected architectural masterpieces, and laid the foundations for a vast and intricate Civilization, all while grounded in the right side of their brains. Since then this Civilization has leapt forward with an astonishing array of accomplishments, all grounded in the left side. Yet, each was limited by what it lacked from the other side.

Dare we imagine what could be accomplished if we dissolved the perceptual blockage dividing them, and used both brains with equal ease!

The muses were relics of this bygone era, seen as inspiration in all forms of the arts. Nowhere is this clearer than in a particularly unique form of expression – poetry, the rhythm perhaps in which unconscious humans heard the gods. The great epics of the past, like the Iliad and the Odyssey of Homer, were written down in poetic stanzas and read aloud in singsong fashion.

As Jaynes says, the first poets were the gods speaking within us, a clue maybe to our ancestors' ability to deal with their bicameral mentality

There were myths long before the dawn of consciousness, and there are myths after; there were gods before consciousness took hold, and there are gods (or God) afterward; and there were ways of reassuring our self that decisions reached were correct, both before and after. But each of those befores and afters had marked differences.

The quest for truth began in this cleavage between the old and the new ways, and it is this deeper questioning that led to the founding of all major modern religions, that led to the questioning of philosophic and scientific enquiry, and that led to a new form of myth and mythology that sought to understand the deeper issues of our existence.

And this fundamental fact is as true of the realm of Camelot as it is of the mythology of the 21st century.

III

THE MYTHOLOGY
OF MYTHS

Learning to question what we have always held sacred.

The quest for truth is a conscious undertaking to find meaning and purpose in our lives, to step out onto the path unknown in the company of all the great sages and Questers who have gone before.

What are the truths to be found in ancient myths, and what have they to teach us about ourselves? Unmasking the realities of our modern myths. Questing for Camelot, for a kung fu black belt, for a Master Po or Merlin.

The monomyth is exemplified in the Star Wars and Harry Potter series. They inform us of our innermost strengths and frailties.

What to expect along the path to wisdom:

- John Romer
- Thomas Moore
- Joseph Campbell
- Xenophanes
- TS Eliot
- John O'Donohue
- Sam Keen.

1

THE POWER OF BELIEF

♫ Don't let it be forgot, that once there was a spot,
For one brief shining moment that was known as Camelot ♫

Good King Arthur and the most fabled castle in all of medievaldom, Camelot. He, of the pure heart, crowned king by extracting the magic sword Excalibur from a rock. The call went out to the finest and noblest knights of all Europe. The bravest and most chivalrous of these he invited to Camelot, to be his Knights of the Round Table.

Merlin, the magician, shaman, wizard, astronomer and prophet, advised the young king in all matters of importance, and himself designed the famous Round Table so no knight should be superior to any other. All were considered equal in this elite brotherhood, though some dazzled brighter than others simply because they were better at what they did. The bravest and most skilled of all was Sir Lancelot, the most principled gentleman, fairest to all the ladies, undefeatable in battle by even scores of men.

The tales of the Kingdom of Camelot, reigned over by noble King Arthur and his fair Queen Guinevere, have been told and retold for centuries. The countless battles fought, of good triumphing over evil. Of the magical feats of a sword called Excalibur. Of the search for the Holy Grail. Of Merlin's wise tutelage, and omens of things yet to come. And in the end of an illicit love affair, of a love triangle involving Arthur and Guinevere and Lancelot. The Round Table breaking up, the castle being abandoned.

In the end, as the legend goes, there stood Camelot, noblest of human worlds, for *one brief shining moment*. Then all was at an end.

The mythology of Camelot and King Arthur and the Knights of the Round Table was written down over several centuries, though even then it referred to a much earlier time, before the Saxons invaded England. In the 12th century Chretien de Troyes wrote

Lancelot, and Geoffrey of Monmouth penned his *History of the Kings of Britain.* In the 15th century Sir Thomas Malory wrote perhaps the best remembered version, *Le Morte D'Arthur.*

Hollywood, being the modern purveyor of legends to the world, peppered the last century with numberless tales of noble knights and clanging armor, evil castles and hard-fought jousts, of magic and Merlin and a fairytale land where justice and truth ruled. I loved every moment of it, back in the gloomy Cold War 50s, when the movies offered an escape into a grander world of chivalry. I dressed up to look more or less like some knight, as we played out the tales in our backyard. The older kids took the juicier roles of the main heroes, but it didn't matter to me. I was a part of Camelot, and that was enough.

Years later, when an assassin's bullet brought the Kennedy White House to an end, the overwhelming sadness had little to do with politics or foreign policy or affairs of a more personal nature. Like the Camelot of legend, the Kennedy White House had opened up our collective aspirations to a more daring possibility, to a world enthused with nobler causes. Our grief was our recognition of this lost ideal.

From all over the world, each summer, visitors — or should we say pilgrims — descend on sites throughout the British Isles in search of the 'true' Camelot. Places in Wales and Cornwall, and especially Cadbury Castle overlooking the Vale of Avalon to Glastonbury. Medieval Faires are held, complete with mock battles, and tourists dressing up in armor and Merlin and Guinevere costumes. Stories are told of the *Once and Future King* Arthur who will return one day to rule a better world.

It is incredible, really, this need we have to touch as real and solid, that which we know is but a metaphor. Or perhaps more accurately, our craving is so strong for what the metaphor stands for, that we long to see it brought into flesh and blood. At the very least, to believe that it was so, somewhere back in our misty past, for at least one brief shining moment.

2

THE TRUTH ABOUT MYTHS

"The world and all its gods was explained in sacred stories. These stories of course were myths," archeologist John Romer explains in *Testament,* his acclaimed British TV series on the Bible. Myths, not in our modern take on the word, as being lies or fabrications, but in the sense of a story that "told of the underlying order of the world. Myths could explain the beauty of a spring or a fish, the mystery of a cave. It could explain your good fortune and your misfortune. It helped you feel secure, part of a sacred family, a universal order. All ancient people would have seen life in terms of myths."

To understand what our ancestors already knew about life, the noted Egyptologist and artist says we should take a closer look at their myths. "The truth you find in myths is not the sort of truth you find in history books." Far from being a series of historical dates and happenings, true myths are descriptions of the collective dreams of a particular culture. Originally they sprung from the minds of our unconscious ancestors, but as consciousness took hold they gradually morphed into vehicles of questioning and questing, exploring man's place in the world and our very reason for being. The obedient mind of the Iliad became the wily and demanding mind of the Odyssey.

Myths are exciting. They are a window into the minds of our ancestors as they grappled with their newfound consciousness. Most of the characters and gods and storylines came from an earlier pre-conscious time, but the emphasis shifted; fanciful descriptions of the heavens and man's lot on earth were no longer sufficient. There had to be good reasons for the way things were and why people should behave in a certain way; obedience now had to be won, over and over again.

Eventually every sort of character and character trait, and every sort of moral dilemma was covered by these tales that pointed the way for our ancestors on the consciousness frontier. These were moral tales wrapped in a fictitious world of fantastic beasts, capricious gods, and struggling everyman.

Thomas Moore calls myth a sacred story set in a time and place outside history, which in fictional terms describes the fundamental truths of nature and human life. It gives seeable form to what is essentially invisible. In this sense myths are very true because they reach to the depths of our being.

In Tom Harpur's description, myth "moves beyond history in that it deals with abiding, eternal verities rather than the flim-flam or transitory details of ordinary existence. Myth, then, gives the inner meaning to all history, personal or universal."

As such Campbell found that myth was infinitely more transformative and true than any history. What is historical is fleeting and open to a hundred viewpoints, but the meaning of a myth is always eternal.

In a beautiful few lines in *Before Philosophy,* Dutch anthropologist Henri Frankfort writes, "Myth is a form of poetry which transcends poetry in that it proclaims a truth; a form of reasoning which transcends reasoning in that it wants to bring about the truth it proclaims; a form of action, of ritual behavior, which does not find fulfillment in the act, but must proclaim and elaborate a poetic form of truth."

"Mythology is not a lie," Campbell said in response to those who dismiss it as fiction and fantasy. He saw it instead as poetry, as metaphor, as psychology which people often mistake for history or a description of the workings of the cosmos.

Meaning Beyond the Facts

In short, myth invites us to use our imagination, to push beyond the mere facts. All great mythological stories start from a simple set of facts, and end in illuminating revelations about the meaning and purpose of our lives. We forego all of this, to paraphrase Moore, the comprehension and wisdom, these insights into life and where we are headed, when we cannot imagine something other than the concrete at hand. "The facts, Ma'am, just the facts," as Sgt. Joe Friday of *Dragnet,* repeated ad nauseam. A sad summation of our modern obsession with data, to the exclusion of meaningful insight.

Every mythology has some sort of cosmology, some description of how the world was created and how it continues to function as it does. No different from where we stand today. It's not that we don't have a current mythology — we just don't call it that. We call it the truth. The scientific truth. The Big Bang-Quantum Uncertainty-Theory of Relativity. It's not incorrect. Its truths are its truths. But so too are the truths to be found in the mythologies of the past. They just can't be seen through the eyes of the Hubble telescope.

3

EMBARKING ON A MYTH

When it comes to discussing the true meaning of myths there is no finer expert than the late Joseph Campbell. He said that we currently find ourselves in a dilemma where the lines of communication between our unconscious self and our conscious self have been cut, that we have effectively been split in two. So we set out in an effort to perform a psychic bypass to restore the links. Our longing is for the "lost Atlantis of the co-ordinated soul."

Myths in a very real sense give voice to unconscious longings. This is why we look to them now, to reacquaint ourselves with the truths and knowings which are buried deep.

As we embark on this mythological journey, then, it is important to not confuse the literal with the metaphorical. This 'journey' need not necessarily entail traveling thousands of miles over treacherous terrain, climbing the highest peaks, and doing battle with formidable beasts — though there is a certain romantic appeal to this part of the quest, which is kind of hard to give up. Nor is this fascination with the literal something new to our time.

"Men have created the gods in their own image. They believe the gods were born and have bodies and clothes and language just as we have. Ethiopians believe that gods are black and flat-nosed; Thracians imagine them to be blue-eyed and fair-haired. If oxen, horses, and lions could draw, they would depict gods that look like oxen, horses, and lions." Thus spoke a perplexed Xenophanes, in 570 BC. The medium, then as now, has a way of becoming the message, in the process obscuring the message itself.

Everything is portrayed in symbols. Our ancestors who lived when our treasured holy books and great moral tales were first written down knew very well how to interpret the deeper truths behind the symbols, a skill which many have long since lost in a maze of surface and verbatim interpretations.

No Turning Back

So we step forward boldly, cross over the line from easy answers into the quicksand of troubling questions. There is no turning back.

"It is better to have begun a great journey than to have finished it," Edward Wilson notes, as it is better to discover something new and exciting than to put the final touches on a theory. The quest itself, as we are constantly reminded, is what life is all about, not the hoped for revelations at the end of our personal rainbow.

Recall the often-quoted verse by T.S. Eliot:

> *And the end of all our exploring*
> *Will be to arrive where we started*
> *And to know the place for the first time.*

The idea itself seems straightforward enough, about seeing things in a totally new light as a result of our vast life experiences. Nonetheless, it's often wrongly quoted as an example of what can be accomplished by the powers of belief. As an example, we hear of the good witch in *The Wizard of Oz*, who tells Dorothy at the end of the story that all she needs to do to get home is to click her heels three times and say 'I want to go home.' When she is asked why she didn't tell Dorothy this in the beginning, before she went through all her trials and adventures, the witch replies that she didn't tell her because Dorothy wouldn't have believed her at that time.

This implies, as several authors have insisted, that if only Dorothy had a strong enough belief in herself, she wouldn't have had to go on this journey. Belief alone, like some magic potion, would have brought her back home.

But this is not the message of all the great myths, or for that matter of *The Wizard of Oz*. The purpose of life is to live life, to awaken to and savor our day-to-day experiences, not to rush to the finish line — like fast forwarding a DVD of *Romeo and Juliet* from the moment the lovers meet to their death scenes. Cliché or no cliché, life *is* the journey.

It doesn't matter that we end up back where we started, or on the moon, or anywhere else. What matters, they tell us, is that we take the journey, for it is in the journey that we discover truths that even the most devout faith cannot reveal. The most powerful heroes of all ages could not forego this passage. The wisest philosophers and spiritual leaders alike had to take up their walking sticks and rice bowls and head out onto the path. As Jesus of Nazareth took up his cross long before he came in sight of Calvary. As Buddha ceased longing long before he found his bodhi tree.

4

ONE MYTH

What is seldom clear, and what in the end leads to a lot of confusion, is that not all myths are created equal. That is, there are different types of myths serving different purposes. Lumping them all together only leads to gross misunderstanding of what can be gained by studying them.

Essentially, there are four kinds. As Timothy Roberts, of Lincoln University, describes it in *The Encyclopedia of Mythology: Gods, Heroes, and Legends of the Greeks and Romans*:

"**First**, there is the true myth, the attempt to explain a natural event such as a rumbling volcano to a prescientific world that has no rational means of explaining natural phenomena." With our modern scientific understanding of the workings of nature we have little need of these myths, other than as insights into how our ancestors explained what was most terrifying and mysterious to them.

"**Second**, there are "the saga myths, essentially factual events from Greek (or any other) history that have been colored by the imaginations of numerous ancient storytellers." The siege of Troy is a good example of this type of myth, a real military encounter which happened sometime in the second millennium BC, but whose details are embellished by the participation of gods, and demi-gods, and humans who are more superhero than human.

"**Third**, there are fairy tales, "stories created simply for the delight they bring in the telling." Stories and fables which we all learned as children, through bedtime storybooks or Disney cartoons, which usually imparted a moral so we would grow to be good little girls and boys. Fantastic babysitters, and conjurers of untold recurrent nightmares.

"Fourth, there are the myths that are "psychological, designed to explain human behavior; the classic example is that of the self-love of Narcissus."

The subject matter of university courses on the mythologies of classic civilizations and shamanic societies. And of George Lucas' *Star Wars* sextuplet, and Joanne Rowling's *Harry Potter* series.

It's this fourth kind that's the focus of all modern talk about myths. It's the kind which Jung analyzed, the kind which psychology delves into in seeking a better understanding of the unconscious, the kind which starred in Joseph Campbell's acclaimed *The Hero With a Thousand Faces.*

Campbell's great insight was the universality of this fourth type of myth. What he called the 'Monomyth.' That is, the characters and names and details of the stories differed from location to location, but the underlying messages about humanity's place in the cosmos, about apprenticeship and discovery, about death and birth and resurrection, about the hero's journey and our relation to some divine unknown — these are surprisingly retold again and again right throughout the continents, even in cultures which have long been separated.

The Story Within the Story

Movies, TV dramas and comedies, novels and science fiction; music videos and pop songs; Broadway plays and mega musicals; just some of the ways in which we today bring to life our common concerns, and possible ways of handling them. We know that the characters are not real flesh and blood people like we are; they're just a fiction. Yet we still get emotionally caught up in their 'lives,' weeping and laughing at their ups and downs, worrying what's to befall them next, heaving a huge sigh of relief when some semblance of a 'good' end is finally found. The fact that we react this way is a sign that the story in question was well crafted. We see ourselves in the characters.

In much the same way, our ancestors saw the grand old myths. But instead of Clarice Starling in *The Silence of the Lambs* being a young FBI agent in search of a serial killer, they would have portrayed a minor god or demi-god struggling against formidable heavenly foes to help some powerless human live to a better day. In both cases the story is really about overcoming paralyzing fear, and facing one's personal demons in order to do the right thing. But today's versions are so down-to-earth and lifelike — not off in clouds of heavenly mystery, amidst god-like powers which none of us possesses — that we tend to get caught up in the details of the story, and miss the cultural tale altogether.

Ask most anyone what *The Silence of the Lambs* is all about and you'll likely hear something about a clever FBI rookie who, with the help of a mad psychiatrist who loves eating his enemies with fava beans and a nice Chianti, tracks down and nails a vicious serial killer who has a penchant for tailor-made suits.

Of course we don't really know if many of our ancestors also got caught up in the details, but given the 'other-worldly' nature of their stories, it seems more likely that the moral point of the myth got through; that there is more to the story than just the story.

Surprisingly enough it's precisely this story-within-the-story that we start off teaching our children to find. From the simplest tales about the Grinch who plotted to steal Christmas, and his motivations, to taking apart the inner workings of the psyche of *Hamlet,* and the tortured souls in *Heart of Darkness,* our educational system is a burning torch, lighting the way to true meaning and understanding.

But something happens to our critical sensibilities between the classroom and the real world. Between those plays and novels about characters in another time and in another place, and the TV commercials which overwhelm our 'down town,' and the action flicks which multiplex our senses.

Maybe that's why, despite all the knowledge available at our fingertips, our culture as a whole has so little depth of understanding. We follow the daily news; we pursue our careers and relationships and raise our families, all on a surprisingly superficial level, with virtually no time left to reflect on the deep currents at play in our lives: Issues like honor and calling, destiny and longing, good and evil.

Multiplexing our senses is the most effective – and pleasurable — drug we have yet developed for silencing the questioning mind. After an intense immersion of some twenty years, our offspring enter the workplace with sound-byte minds and an addiction for endless novel stimulation. No wonder sex is taking a backseat to Internet porn. How could the real thing compete with endless novelty? Is this where the sexual revolution has led?

THE BATTLE IS JOINED

Strangely enough, these deep currents become crystal clear when fashioned in the form of an exciting character in *Star Wars* — a modern myth, in its most recent and high-tech incarnation. Of course there is still the temptation to identify with the escapist lives of the heroes, but most of the settings and characters are so literally other-worldly — think of Jabba The Hut, or the exotic mix of creatures at the cantina on Tatooine — that the hero and his journey are as clear as the lightsabers before our eyes.

There is the call to action of the young Luke Skywalker (the same is repeated in the prequels, with young Anakin Skywalker). Like the young King Arthur, Luke is called to train to be a knight in the service of truth and justice. His mentor, the noble Jedi knight Obi-Wan Kenobi, teaches him how to fight on the side of good, and how in doing so to "let the force be with you". But there is a force of evil out there in the form of a fallen knight, by the name of Darth Vader (back to the future, as young Anakin above). Luke must summon all his courage and his inner strength in a battle to the death. All that is good is depending upon him.

Such is the hero's journey. Joanne Rowling has brought to life the same ideas for the young reading set in her incredible best-selling *Harry Potter* series. Young Harry Potter discovers that he has special wizard powers running through his veins, as the young Skywalkers learned that they were born with special powers (but then, weren't we all?) Young Harry is sent off to a secret sorcerer's school called Hogwarts School of Witchcraft and Wizardry, where he learns the tricks of the trade. But there is evil afoot. A former graduate of Hogwarts, Lord Voldemort, has gone over to the Dark Side. He in fact was responsible for the deaths of young Harry's parents. Can there be any escape from the final showdown?

The most fascinating take on all of this is that these stories are of greatest interest to children and adolescents — a time when the great call to adventure and heroic journeys are still a very real possibility in their uncharted lives, before the fear and uncertainty settles in.

Nevertheless, mythology is trying to tell us, perhaps too subtly, that this is not a child's game, even though we may first become interested in it when we are young. That in essence we are all called...not to do battle with lightsabers against evil wizards, but to a more difficult task. That if we don't answer the call, one day we will awaken in horror, decades having raced by, and we will see ourselves way back there through the mist, still stuck in the starting blocks.

The Path Whisks Us Away

So we begin again to seek the hero's path. The journey within, which can be a frightening maze of golden temptations, egocentric delusions, and humble prophecies of our unique greatness. All guarded by no one other than me, myself and I. Is it any wonder that many are called to this quintessential search, but few are chosen?

It's a one step program. The one step onto the path. Then the path whisks us away.

"You give yourself over with tremendous attention to the world," poet David Whyte cautions us. But not unconsciously. There is fierceness in the world that obligates us to stay awake. Pay attention as much as we can to all that is happening around us, because our life is at stake. The world in its own time and way will take care of the lessons we have to learn. Whyte points to the admonishing of Neruda, and all the great teachers; "but did you go your own way...and if you didn't, why didn't you go your own way?"

Yet all too often we shrink back from taking that all-important first step. Paulo Coelho touched on this trepidation in *The Alchemist: A Fable About Following Your Dream*. "People are afraid to pursue their most important dreams because they feel that they don't deserve them, or that they'll be unable to achieve them." Or more frightening still, that it may drag us out of our complacent comfortable old ways, thrusting us out into an unknown world, into a powerful current that "will carry you to places you never dreamed of when you first made the decision."

In actual life, of course, the failure to heed the call is very common, far more so than we will find in popular myths and tales. (But then, who would want to read about a stay-at-home 'hero' who didn't rise to the occasion, who didn't slay the dragon or come home with the Golden Fleece, who didn't save the damsel in distress or ever bother to search for the Holy Grail?)

In practiced avoidance, we wrap ourselves in all the trivia of daily life, and focus our attention away from what is most important to the very success of our lives. This is known as the Refusal of the Call, and it converts the great adventure into an enfeebling void. "Walled in boredom, hard work, or 'culture,'" Campbell laments, we lose the power to take action and instead become victims longing to be saved. Our promising world becomes a wasteland, and our life a meaningless grind.

Albert Schweitzer, the great humanitarian and philosopher, warned that our soul suffers in very real ways if we live at this superficial level. "It is tragic that most men have not achieved this feeling of self-awareness.... when they hear the inner voice, they do not want to listen anymore."

6

THE HERO'S JOURNEY

The heroic journey, quite simply, is the search for a profound truth which once it is found, the hero willingly shares with all humankind.

The first stage of the journey is what Campbell labels *the call to adventure* — that is, the hero has been summoned, she has accepted the call, and now her spiritual center of gravity has shifted "to a zone unknown." This metaphorical zone of course can be anywhere from a distant forest or kingdom beneath the waves, to a mysterious mountaintop or an altered state of being. Whatever its locale, Campbell assures that it will always be an unimaginable place of torments, superhuman deeds, and impossible delights.

This inward passage, we hope — or why else are we doing this — will bring to life a part of us we only vaguely knew existed. As John O'Donohue reminds us, there is an eternal essence within us, an essence we need to tap into in order to uncover our boundless potential. So the process of self-discovery, he reminds us, won't be an easy one, involving doubts, anguish and even suffering. But there is no way that we should allow ourselves to shrink back from it, no matter the trepidation. We are adventurers on the brink of discovering a land within we never even imagined. A small price to pay.

So we give up all attachment to our personal limitations, our idiosyncrasies, hopes and fears, and no longer resist, in Campbell's words, "the self-annihilation that is prerequisite to rebirth."

If there is any problem with the great myths it's that they've gone too far. Not just in the way they externalize our demons, giving the impression that we have to ride into battle against some ferocious dragon, in order to grow. But the great mythmakers were seldom happy to present the great heroes as anything less than ancient versions of Superman. Even though what they were talking about was just people like us, mere mortals who broke past the horizons that restrained others, and returned with treasures that were available to anyone who dared take the journey with dedication and courage, they instead clothed the hero with extraordinary powers, virgin births, auspicious omens, and magi and genies who guided their every step. Not exactly a role model for the average person.

In reality, the hero is the man or woman who can step outside the norm without falling prey to the very schemes which claim to be there for his or her assistance. That is, our carefully selected regimens can become an obsession in themselves, leading us away, not toward our inner longing. O'Donohue warns that we can so easily become addicted to the programs of religion and psychology themselves. In fact, we become so desperate to learn the 'how-to,' that in the process our lives slip by, and we never quite get the hang of just being.

Beyond the Veil of the Known into the Unknown

Reality, unfortunately, is rarely what we imagine it to be. Much more so for the heroic journey than any other. We head out on the path, hopefully when none other is watching, so we will not be dissuaded. But the exhilaration of departure soon gives way to darkness. We panic, if only momentarily. Nothing on the road ahead is even visible, let alone corresponding to our expectations. It's not too late to turn back. What a stupid idea! A heroic quest. Who am I kidding anyway?

The adventure is always a journey beyond the known into the realm of the unknown, what Campbell calls the *Crossing of the First Threshold.* Once the hero goes forward, the only way back is to complete the journey. That is, we will never again be content to live within the normal bounds of popular belief systems. But, like finding our true lover or soulmate, amidst the joy and ecstasy of discovery we must accept the reality that one day we could lose it all, that the greater the find, the greater the potential loss. And so it is for our life. We can lose our life in the trying. But this is the price we must pay. And anyone on the journey will have it no other way.

It's all a part of breaking through our personal limitations. To assist us in this — and it isn't a minor feat by a long shot — we may choose to use the help of art or literature or philosophy or bodhisattvas, or whatever esoteric disciplines we may find beneficial to help us over the humps and into an ever-expanding reality. In this manner we make our way forward, crossing threshold after threshold, as Campbell said, conquering dragon after dragon, until we find we are straddling what appears to be two very different worlds.

The Two Kingdoms

These two worlds, the eternal and the time-bound, the divine and the human, are for mysterious and not so mysterious reasons, portrayed as being as separate and distinct as night and day, as life and death. The hero's task is pictured as an adventure wherein he will either bridge the void, or fail in the trying. But there is one essential secret which we must keep at the back of our mind and before our eyes at all times. In the words of Joseph Campbell:

"Here is a great key to the understanding of myth and symbol — the two kingdoms are actually one. The realm of the gods is a forgotten dimension of the world we know." Exploring that other dimension is in essence what being a hero is all about.

The kingdom of the conscious and the kingdom of the unconscious. A journey of exploration and insight to arrive at a truer understanding of who we are. Mythology's heroic quest to bridge the gap.

7

1969

The *mythos* of an era is its theme or plot. As Webster's describes it, it's 'a pattern of beliefs expressing often symbolically the characteristic or prevalent attitudes in a group or culture.' Which is to say that at all times we are living in the mythos of our culture, whether we see it as such or not. Perhaps even three or four different ones at the same time.

Nineteen sixty-nine was one of the most exciting years of the 60s. For me, in a matter of months I traveled through such amazingly different 'themes' that I began to wonder just how schizophrenic our modern mythology could be.

In the spring I was working in Lahr, West Germany, at a NATO air force base as a civilian employee on a maximum three-month stint. The runway was being rebuilt, so during this period the pilots had to be driven around to the far side of the airfield to get to their jets. Each morning and afternoon I would drive them there and back for their twice-daily missions of taking reconnaissance photos on the far side of the iron curtain, of tiny bridges and troop movements and whatever else was considered important in those no-nonsense Cold War days. I guess they figured this cushy job was too soft to waste on an enlisted man.

At least once a month, without warning, the base would go on Red Alert drill. The sirens would blare all over the tiny town of Lahr, alerting everyone that regular business on the base was canceled for the day, as the soldiers got to play at being soldiers. All civilian employees were locked up in the truck barn, so we wouldn't see what only soldiers should be privy to. Such was the ironclad scenario for maintaining top secrecy. But ironclad and the military are rarely good bedfellows.

During one of these Red Alerts, a Master Sergeant (my boss) pulled me from the barn and sent me in my six-ton truck with a tiny package to be delivered to an address on the base where I had never been before. It seems all the soldier drivers were busy doing gun-wielding things, and this package had to get to this Colonel immediately, "in his hands only, no one else!"

I was stopped at several points along the way, but I reiterated my explicit instructions, and I was allowed (against all rules) to continue. In the end two heavily armed guards opened the door to a vast room, like a theater, aswarm in military insignia of the highest order. The War Room. My eyes just popped. I couldn't believe such a place actually existed. It was a scene right out of the movie *Dr. Strangelove or: How I Learned to Stop Worrying and Love the Bomb,* a scene which I had always assumed was a product of the writers' wild imaginations.

Here it was, in the flesh, everything except Peter Sellers and his uncontrollable saluting arm. A huge wall screen map of Europe, East and West, with flashing lights and trajectories launching off in every which direction, a buzz of telecommunications, officers rushing past me. All this...just a practice run. In how many similar rooms was this same scenario being played out, on both sides of the Iron Curtain? What were the odds on accidental launch?

I never did get to give the Colonel his package. A certain cheerless Major let me know that within seconds he would have either the package or my butt. I walked out of there in a daze, butt intact. Here was a vastly contrived and secretive world about which the average citizen knew precious little; citizens were after all but studied projections of likely casualties, given a controlled scenario. As always the military had the weapons, the bunkers, and the all-important red buttons.

Before I left the base for the last time my Master Sergeant friend sneaked me out to one of those top-secret areas where the bombers were *always* on alert. I ran my fingers slowly over the cold metal casing of the nuclear weapon attached to a surprisingly small jet. Face to face with the number one icon of the era. An oversized bullet capable of taking out hundreds of thousands of lives in an instant.

From the Moon to Woodstock

From the Cold War mythos of the air base to the macho male mythos of Ernest Hemingway. In July my friend Nick, from New Zealand, and I found ourselves on pilgrimage in northern Spain to the small town of Pamplona, for the annual running of the bulls through the streets. What could be more macho than young men dashing out in front of bulls, proving their bravery and readiness for a 'manly' existence?

Unfortunately, on this unbearably hot day, and amidst the clamoring of thousands of tourists, it was the young bulls who were terrified, trying their best not to go near anyone, just to get through this horrendous ordeal. The only trampling was of young men by young men as, upon seeing the snorting beasts, they scampered for the safety of the railings. Then everyone adjourned to the bullring in the heat of the late afternoon sun for the slaughtering of four of the five bulls — only one matador, worthy of that title, actually dispatched his prize in the prescribed non-butchering manner.

Still to this day, and likely for a long time yet to come, Hemingway's romanticism about the nobility of bull fighting and the goings on in Pamplona, is what draws people from all over the world to this otherwise nondescript spot in Spain. Despite all evidence to the fallacy of it, the mythos lives on. And it does so because people *want* to believe it.

A few nights later, in a dusty hamlet whose name I have long since forgotten, we watched on a flickering black and white television as Neil Armstrong set foot on the moon. The whole world was watching. This too was another mythos. The space race, astronauts, cosmonauts, trips to the moon, exploration of the cosmos. It wasn't Americans really who landed on the moon in July '69. It was the human race. And our worldwide watching of this singular event heralded the dawn of the Global Village.

A couple weeks later, in a rain-soaked field in New York State, the Woodstock festival became an instant legend. I wasn't there, but word of it quickly spread to those of us traveling through Europe. Similar get-togethers were happening in Europe and the British Isles, but Woodstock was the master of them all. It was the grand opus of the counter culture, a weekend summation of all the love and peace and drugs and music that the baby boomer generation stood for. At least at that time. The mythos of the 60s lingers still to this day for those who are young now, looking back fondly on it as some Golden Age, an Eden before their time.

A World of Phallic Symbols

What vastly different worlds to pass through in so short a span of time. It's interesting that the only one of these four that still survives in its '69 form is the running of the bulls in Pamplona. The cold war is over, the iron curtain but a newsreel memory. The manned exploration of the cosmos died an early death, a victim of governmental cutbacks to feed the 'me' generation's need for more personal possessions. And the 'me' generation itself warped into an unparalleled era of greed and every-man-for-himself mentality. Even recent attempts to revive the peace-loving spirit of Woodstock, at Woodstock, have ended in violence.

From another perspective, there are the symbols which each of these 'themes' had to represent them. If one was to apply the appellation 'sex' to any of these, I think that most people would point, perhaps disapprovingly, to Woodstock with its gratuitous sex and free love.

Yet I find far more interesting the phallic symbols — the extremely elongated intercontinental ballistic missiles of the cold war pointing threateningly from one hemisphere to another; the very hard and penetrating horns of the bulls of Pamplona chasing the young men's backsides; and the thrusting power of the mighty Saturn V rockets blasting off from Cape Canaveral into the dark void of space.

Myths and mythos. We live our daily lives little aware of just how much our perceptions are guided by mysterious underlying patterns and symbols.

BLACK BELT MYTHOLOGY

"*Everybody was Kung Fu fighting!*" Or so the hit song informed us in the 70s. Everywhere we turned it seemed there was someone high kicking at imaginary foes in the air, or daring us to grasp a coin from their open hand before they could close it. David Carradine was cloned on every street corner. The inscrutable East had at long last landed on the terra firma of the Wild West.

It's no coincidence that the 70s saw a huge interest in matters spiritual at the same time as enrollment in martial arts courses went right through the roof. Popular interest in mystical and/or spiritual powers which lie within the individual, powers that could be revealed if only one knew the secret to releasing them, had already been peaked by the best-selling Carlos Castaneda series of books. Downtown streets and airport terminals and city parks were a bazaar of countless cults and new religions, promising all the mystery and magic of the universe in a beggar's bowl. But whom could we trust? How could we know when we were on the right path?

Then David Carradine and his *Kung Fu* TV series strode into town. Or more correctly, Kwai Chang Caine. He was humble, very spiritual, and could whip the backside off the toughest, meanest and fastest hit men the Wild West could throw at him. And he showed us how we could do the same. Start by joining a monastery (ashram, dojo, karate club) and faithfully following the teachings of our instructors; the deeper we become as spiritual beings, the greater we perform as martial artists. The one rises hand in hand, or belt over belt, with the other.

Kung Fu Knighthood

The mythology is ever so enticing. How many of us dreamed we could become like Caine, spiritually at one with the cosmos, physically invincible, being of help to one and all, noble to a fault.

A 70s version of chivalrous knighthood, where Camelot was wherever we happened to park our bedroll.

But here in the real world, what Kung Fu Academy, or 7th or 8th or 9th Dan black belt instructor could possibly make good on these expectations? Caine's mentor, the blind Master Po, was only a fiction, a Merlin of the Shaolin Temple.

What most of us were left with was this fantasy that we could gauge our progress on the spiritual path in much the same way that we measure our martial arts skills, by the degree of our belt. In reality, no matter how many colored belts we piled up, or how many degrees our black belt went up, our spiritual growth stayed more or less where it was before. At the very least, growth in one had little to do with growth in the other.

Spiritual growth is not an easy thing to measure. It doesn't readily fit into a hierarchy of who is ahead of whom — even though there are a number of cult leaders who create exactly this type of 'progress chart,' shamelessly situating themselves right at the top of the pyramid.

A bishop, it should be remembered, is not necessarily more spiritual than a priest, nor a cardinal more so than a bishop, nor a pope more so than a cardinal. These are political rankings which have little to do with spiritual growth. Likewise, the chain of command in the military goes from five star general right on down to the lowest private. The steps themselves in no way reflect on who is the better person.

Grand Master of Egos

Which is what makes me instantly suspicious of any spiritual group, or martial arts system, which insists on our calling the teachers *Master*. Inevitably, somewhere behind all the Masters we will find some *Grand Master,* to whom all should respectfully bow. What we have here is nothing short of narcissism. As martial arts expert and author Joseph Svinth explains in *Martial Arts: The Real Story*, today "a lot of teachers like their students to call them Master. Some even demand it. Some even prefer Grand Master. This is ego."

I have a great fondness for the martial arts. I know there are martial artists who successfully improve their spiritual development in tandem with their art. This is reasonable, given as Svinth puts it, we can have a Kung Fu of almost anything..."you can have a Kung Fu of driving a car, you can have a Kung Fu of chopping lettuce."

So why not of spiritual growth? But the part of the Kwai Chang Caine myth that has not sunk into our culture is that the two do not come hand in hand. A great martial artist can as easily be a street thug, as a soulmate of Mahatma Gandhi.

Jon Bluming of the Netherlands, president of the International Budo Association, 10th Dan black belt in karate, 9th Dan black belt in judo (highest in the world), of all people comes closest to being worthy of the title *Master*. Yet he will stand for none of this nonsense. Nor does he find anything mystical about what is essentially an endless stream of techniques for defending against an opponent, and taking him out. In Budo — a blanket martial arts term covering Judo and Kung Fu and Karate and Jujutsu and Aikido — we are always learning. As we are on any spiritual path. So one could never in honesty declare oneself a Master, let alone a Grand Master. Such is the talk of those who have forgotten the primary clothing for the road to wisdom...a cloak of humility.

So it is this latter garment, not the fancy colored belts, we look for when entering a martial arts club (or a spiritual community). In university I studied judo for two years under Frank Hatashita, one of the highest-ranking black belts in the world at the time. He considered it such an honor to be teaching at a university that he refused to charge us for the lessons. He personally led all instructions, and regaled us with his stream of humorous stories, usually with himself as the butt of the joke. He asked for no special title, just to be referred to with the traditional *sensei* (teacher).

Years later my daughter ended up attending a Tae Kwon Do school on the recommendation of a friend. I went to the special session where students try out for a belt upgrading. There at the end of the hall was a dais built up in three levels with a virtual throne on top. Here the Grand Master presided over the contests, with the senior belts arrayed around his feet. My daughter got her new belt, but the Grand Master lost himself a student.

From then on I took martial arts classes along side my daughter, son and wife — Karate from a gifted university professor, Burt Konzak, who specialized in philosophy and black belts; Budo from Ron Yamanaka, a multi-talented teacher and holder of 8th and 9th Dan black belts in several martial arts disciplines. Each asked only that they be called sensei. Sensei as in teacher, rabbi, priest, minister. The one who knows something about a certain path, but who is wise enough to know that he is in no way the master of it.

9

THE MYTHOLOGY OF QUESTING

"Every culture, nation, tribe, family casts a spell over individual members," Sam Keen points out to those who still think they're not intimately enfolded in some pre-packaged mythology. That everything from who we think we are and our value system, to our outlook on the world and how we judge those who are different from us, is but an accident of birth, a geographical accident that brands us as Christians or Jews or Muslims or Hindus. From our very birth we are indoctrinated, twisted and formed by a corps of experts we did not choose. As he says, in order to free ourselves we must first engage our personal history.

Everyone is programmed to believe that their religion is the one true religion. (But then, if we believed that some other religion was the true one, why would we stay where we are?) Every religion claims to know the will of God, written down in their divinely inspired holy books, replete with sacred rituals and prayers especially tuned to the ear of God. What in essence the religion offers the follower is an official 'map of life' — everything we need to do, think and say for the rest of our lives. The rules, commandments and holy traditions to be honored, proscriptions to avoid, and the exemplary lives of saints and bodhisattvas to be imitated — all very comforting and reassuring. Heaven is where we're headed, and the holy book or religion has provided us with a day-planner, already filled in.

This is the way, the truth, the pilgrim's path. Yes, there will be backsliding and dark nights of the soul, moral struggles and inevitable disobedience and sins committed. But the path is well charted by the religion in question. The believer must simply submit.

That's a description of the religious quest.

A Spiritual Quest — Not a Religious One

However the quest for truth is a spiritual longing, not a religious one. As Keen says, "the spiritual quest is the reverse of the religious pilgrimage." It begins when we stumble into a spiritual 'black hole' in which everything that was once solid vaporizes. All certainties evaporate under a persistent onslaught of questions.

We're no longer certain that our faith is the one true faith or that we are a chosen people. We question the authorities, no longer taking their word for anything. We realize, one day, that we're no longer on that comfortable path. We are exploring in uncharted areas whose boundaries are not yet known. We begin to experiment. Our life becomes absorbed by the great mythic questions.

As Keen observes, a person on a spiritual quest makes a virtue of what religion considers a vice (and vice versa). Doubt replaces certainty, freedom is sought in the darkness of unknowing and the disillusionment lurking in the shadows. We need to enlist courage to dive into the depths of the unconscious, and to counter the common wisdom that places the sacramental in favor of the ordinary and the miraculous in place of the profane. The spiritual path is without hierarchy.

The spiritual path has no ready-made answers. There's nothing to submit to. There is no comfortable pew from which to listen to sermons. We must dig deep in places we had never even imagined, and find our own answers. Which is why we must stay awake and on our toes. And why this path is not for everyone. But it does provide incalculable freedom.

Beyond the Symbols of Myth

Joseph Campbell wrote that the enormous gulf between "those childishly blissful multitudes who fill the world with piety" and the considerably rarer individuals who are *truly free* is to be found at that precious point where symbols are broken open and transcended.

That is, when we are truly free our eyes can focus beyond the symbols of myth and mythology to the ineffable — the inexpressible, indescribable, unspeakable, nameless and transcendent.

The hero on the quest awakens to the depths beyond the symbols, to the eternal essence in the everyday moment. All the other kinds of truths, founded on observable facts and rational thinking and science can be demonstrated to be true, as we do when we question the verities of the media and big business and politicians and even our friends. These deeper truths, though, because they emanate from the eternal in the moment, cannot be measured in a time-bound way, but must be breathed in, in an all-at-once gestalt. As in discovering a tangible reality in what seems most unreal.

The path can be intimidating, though there is little reason to panic. Like a skilled martial artist, we must learn to remain calm in facing the unknown.

In the end, when we extract the gods and goddesses from their mythical trappings, what we discover is nothing other than our inner selves – our hopes and fears and chimerical possibilities, not to mention the wisdom and ways of knowing that have been largely overshadowed by our conscious mentality.

IV

SOPHIA
& THE GODDESS
WITHIN

Intuition, creativity, inspiration, compassion — all strengths from the feminine.

Reflecting on Bonobo chimpanzees and the different kind of human we might have become. We come face to face with matriarchy and all those great qualities that have faded from prominence as surely as Aphrodite, Demeter and Persephone, their archetypes known as the Goddess Within.

Exploring the 'feminine face' of God we discover the truth about the witch-hunts, and why women are portrayed as victims and not as sources of power.

We uncover the Gnostic knowings of Sophia, or feminine wisdom:

- Elaine Pagels
- Hildegard of Bingen
- Agapi Stassinopoulos
- Erica Jong
- Marija Gimbutas
- Gloria Steinem
- Umberto Eco
- Jean Shinoda Bolen
- Will Durant
- Frans de Waal

1

THE POWER OF THE FEMININE

To rival the men at this point, the women of the later periods resort to stiff corsets, and lift their bare breasts to the sun... no one seems to take offense...(There's) a grace of line, a delicacy of taste, that suggest a rich and luxurious civilization, already old in arts and wiles.

— Will Durant, *The Story of Civilization*

Bonobos are a type of chimpanzee, once called pygmy chimpanzees, which only in the 1930s were classed as a separate species on their own. Somewhat smaller than the average chimp, they are much rarer — living free today only in the dense rain forests of the Congo — and when they walk upright, in their awkward balancing act, tend to resemble what we imagine our early hominid ancestors to have looked like as they struggled to adjust to walking on two legs.

I only mention the bonobos here because they contrast so well with their cousins, the chimpanzees, in pointing out the different forms our human cultures may have taken through their many millennia of development. We easily forget that the current model of Homo sapiens was not the only version that could have emerged from the material at hand.

"Whereas chimpanzees are known for male power politics, cooperative hunting, and intergroup warfare," primate specialist Frans de Waal writes in *Bonobo: The Forgotten Ape*, "bonobo society is egalitarian and peaceful." Another major difference is that individual bonobos tend to be very sensitive to the feelings of others in their group. In contrast, as fellow primatologist Jane Goodall states in *In the Shadow of Man,* "Chimpanzees usually show a lack of consideration for each other's feelings which in some ways may represent the deepest part of the gulf between them and us."

Another obvious difference is that females play a central role in bonobo society, especially when they become mothers. "Bonobos form a gentle matriarchy," de Waal says, "offering a provocative alternative to the male-based model of human evolution that emphasizes man the hunter and tool maker." Indeed, they have become known as the 'make-love-not-war' primate. And they use erotic encounters, of every which variety, to resolve tensions. "The species is best characterized as female-centered and egalitarian, and as one that substitutes sex for aggression."

Not only female centered, but also female dominated. "If a male bonobo tried to harass a female, all females would band together to chase him off," he says. "Females may bond so as to outcompete members of the individually stronger sex." By contrast, both baboon and chimpanzee societies are supremely and exclusively commanded by males, often brutally.

Which raises some interesting questions about our human ancestry in the distant mists of time. What if we are wrong in imagining them as brutish and less refined forms of the way we are now. What if they followed a different model, one not based on 'might makes right.'

Making Love — Making War

"Just imagine that we had never heard of chimpanzees or baboons and had known bonobos first," de Waal summarizes. "We would at present most likely believe that early hominids lived in female-centered societies, in which sex served important social functions and in which warfare was rare or absent."

The picture primatologists draw of bonobo lifestyle is akin to some Garden of Earthly Delights. Only, in this Eden the inhabitants know how to party. Sex is the predominant preoccupation, and everyone indulges in it at every possible opportunity, in broad daylight, with anyone and everyone. And, far from being the pursued, the female is most often the initiator in this erotic playground. Rubbing, stroking, massaging, male to male, female to female, to form alliances, to appease, to blunt anger, to deflect aggression, to apologize and make up. Difficult to stay mad at someone who is pleasuring one in this most intimate and satisfying of ways.

When it comes to male-female relations, face-to-face intercourse, staring into each other's eyes, is preferred at least one third of the time — a position that not long ago was thought (by humans) to be the exclusive province of the human race. And similar to humans, instead of being receptive but a few days out of her cycle, "the female bonobo is almost continuously sexually attractive and active."

Our ancestors and the bonobos and chimpanzees broke along separate evolutionary paths some seven to eight million years ago, so it is wise to be cautious in what parallels we draw. Our human numbers and cultures and accomplishments far outstrip those of any bonobo or chimp. As we saw earlier, the price of becoming conscious and being capable of searching the heavens for wisdom is to abandon the idyllic Garden forever.

However, as the opening quote by Will Durant states so eloquently, at an earlier point in history there were at least some highly advanced human societies that had far more in common with the female-dominated bonobos than the male-dominated chimpanzees. And eroticism was an important and open part of that existence.

When he speaks of how they 'lift their bare breasts to the sun,' and no one takes offense, he's not describing a culture that is simply running around topless or half naked, but one where women deliberately choose to highlight their most powerfully erotic stance, much as men have long enjoyed publicly flexing their bulging biceps, pectorals, and buns of steel. In *Sanctuaries of the Goddess,* Peg Streep describes in similar words (perhaps viewing the same images) the strength pictured in goddess statuettes. "The complication of pattern and flounce endows them with a quiet *sense of grandeur* (italics added). Their breasts are pushed high by their bodices and in their prominence are clearly meant to be seen and admired."

Seen and admired by their male counterparts who are invited to crowd their waking hours with *thoughts* of making love, not war. This is difficult for a culture such as ours to envisage. We censor any hint of erotic sexuality out of TV programs for our children, while freely exposing them to a constant onslaught of shootings and brutal beatings, knifings and slit throats and mangled limbs. Instilling in them that the aggressive is fine, but the erotic is not. How different our world would be if it were the reverse.

Expressing Our Sexual Assets

It's not an invitation to promiscuity. It's a simple acknowledgment that women, like men, are free to dress and act according to their own dictates, and to employ their God-given strengths not only for their personal benefit but to profit their culture as a whole. To deny this to either sex is to throw the entire social structure out of whack. We have only to look to our world today to see how devastating this imbalance can be.

Nudity is not the issue, but the recognition of one half the population and its vital gifts to balance the scales of a healthy society. The cultures which most lack this equilibrium are, not surprisingly, the most repressive patriarchal regimes, where women are forced to cover-up from head to toe, to the point even of masking their faces — virtual walking shrouds — annihilating who they are as women, and as people.

From our earliest pre-human roots nature seems to be telling us that the 'female spirit' is one of love and freedom and equality. And where patriarchy rules, to the exclusion of women, the testosterone-fueled male spirit is funneled into ever increasing acts of aggression. And so we find in archaeological records and recorded histories in every part of the world, that the egalitarian make love, while the oppressors make war. Find a society where love and equality predominate over war and domination, and we will have discovered a land where the feminine is honored and free.

A sad comment on our world at the opening of the twenty-first century that we search high and low in vain.

2

THE GODDESS ARCHETYPE

It may not always have been so. Or at least we've come to envision in the
last few decades a more idealized and egalitarian world in the times of the goddess, back before consciousness leapt to the fore and patriarchy settled in. Most scholars today label this the time of matriarchy, although many say it's a misnomer in that it implies an era of 'women on top' – as opposed I guess to an era of the 'missionary position.' What records we have tend to show a period of considerable equality between the sexes. But then again, one of the great qualities of the matriarchal spirit is this very openness and compassion, listening to the viewpoints and concerns of all — as any nurturing mother would do.

The goddesses reigned supreme, not only over our mortal ancestors, but in many regions over the male gods as well. Yet, in the same breath we shouldn't forget that the goddesses and gods of antiquity were fabrications, metaphors for the hopes and fears of our dearly departed progenitors. It seems almost absurd to have to state what should be obvious, but it's incredible just how many people today mistake the metaphor of goddess for a literal being. That somewhere in the deep dark past there were actual goddesses ruling the world. That by extension these women today are goddesses — repressed goddesses, but goddesses nonetheless — eager to re-claim their regal thrones. So, before anyone starts polishing up their diamond tiaras or casting golden statues in their divine image, the obvious:

We never were goddesses! We never were gods!

Nor will we ever be. But then this should be a great relief, given the horrors and human sacrifices that have been committed in the names of these supposed deities. The goddess within is but an archetype.

When Carl Jung portrayed the idea of archetypes in modern psychology he described them as forms of behavior, instinctual forms, which lay deep in the collective unconscious. Joseph

Campbell further expounded on these archetypes, describing how they were an integral part of all mythologies, especially in regards to the Hero's Journey. However, perhaps because they were commenting on the historical record of the past three thousand plus years of patriarchy, their emphasis was very much on the masculine ideals in war and conquests and bravery and chivalry, and saving poor damsels in distress.

Envisioning the Goddess

To rectify this gender bias a host of women writers today have turned to ancient myths and tales of goddesses to discover just what these feminine archetypes might be. Of course, 'archetype' is a rather dull, academic sounding word, not the eye-catching titillation that sends books flying off the shelves; far sexier to refer to these visions of the feminine within as 'goddesses.' And thus the confusion mentioned above.

"The Greek goddesses are images of women that have lived in the human imagination for over three thousand years," Jean Shinoda Bolen writes in *Goddesses in Every Woman: A New Psychology of Women*. "The goddesses are patterns or representations of what women are like — with more power and diversity of behavior than women have historically been allowed to exercise. They are beautiful and strong."

That is, they speak to a woman far more realistically and with a far greater acknowledgment of her gifts and strengths than the role models so often portrayed in the media, starting right back, in my own personal imprinting, with *Leave it to Beaver* and *Father Knows Best*. June Cleaver, the Beaver's ever smiling, apron-clad mom, quite simply knew her place as wife and mother and keeper of the home, and beyond that there was no place. What other possibilities could there be for a woman? How could I imagine my ideal wife in any other likeness? And what we envision, if left unchallenged, inevitably shapes the kind of future we step into. Discovering these "inherent patterns or archetypes" will open up for every young girl a vast array of new and enticing alter egos.

Bolen describes every modern woman — starting with her rebellious counter-culture behavior in the 60s right up through the 90s and into the current 'o-zone' years struggling for a world more in tune with the feminine spirit — as a "woman-in-between," battling cultural stereotypes in the outside world (let alone with her husband and other family members), while being energized by the goddess archetypes within. The challenge of course is to become aware of which 'goddesses' are dominant within her, which traits are her strengths, and which she should concentrate on despite the sometimes dubious advice from well-wishers.

Archetypes of the Goddess

The major archetypes, out of a much larger pantheon, consist of the three Virgin Goddesses: *Artemis*, who personifies the independent woman, out to achieve great things on her own terms; Athena, the wise, logical woman who is self-assured and listens more to her head than to her heart; and *Hestia*, the steady one who enjoys solitude, wholeness, and a spiritual depth.

Then there are the three Vulnerable Goddesses: *Hera*, who values finding a husband and getting married ahead of professional or motherly concerns; Demeter, who is the great provider of physical and spiritual sustenance to her children, and generosity to all; and *Persephone*, the epitome of passivity and compliance, fulfilling her need to please others, while tuning in to the land of dreams and imagination.

And finally, the Alchemical Goddess, *Aphrodite*. The great embodiment of pleasure and beauty, she exudes genuine sexuality and sensuality, as she strives to balance both her creative and procreative sides.

These psychological thumbnail sketches are not meant to describe any one particular woman so she'll exclaim, 'Oh, yeah, that's me!' Every woman, as Bolen explains, holds within her all of these archetypes, to a lesser or greater extent exhibiting different aspects at different stages of her life. Menstruation can transform a predominantly Demeter type into a temporary Athena, and then back again. Marriage, puberty, and childbirth can all bring about similar alterations, as can career changes and emotional traumas. In this fashion, *shifting gears*, she "goes from one facet of herself to another."

June Cleaver can still be June Cleaver, yet not have to feel frightened that she has somehow become less of a woman, or is usurping the role of her hubby, when Athena or Artemis push through her social guise for a breath of fresh air.

In essence it's all part of the quest for wholeness, the union of opposites, incorporating in each individual both masculine and feminine aspects. "These are parts of ourselves that we can come to know through life experiences, parts that are inherent in all of us...symbolized by the Eastern image of yin and yang contained within a circle."

Which is to say, in a profound soulful sense, that we are all goddesses. We are all gods. We are all possessed of the personalities and cherished traits, the faults and the foibles, of the heroes and heroines of all mythologies.

Inherent in us, and struggling to get out, not only for our own personal health and sanity, but also for the benefit of society at large. But how to convince our society of this, let alone the global village, that balancing the male qualities with the female is not some conspiracy of the damned or the intrigues of an ungodly feminist plot.

3

BALANCING DEITIES

"Getting society as a whole to adopt what many people call feminine archetypal qualities," Naomi Wolf says, "is really a matter of getting them to look at the situation from a different angle." The author of *The Beauty Myth* is more than happy to remind them, especially certain feminism-shy fundamentalist believers, that Jesus was a great feminist. "I really think it's important to remember that some of the great role models of these qualities weren't women — Martin Luther King, Gandhi, Jesus — compassionate men who were serving others. And so I'd like to think of it as an archetypal human manifestation of service."

If anyone was guilty of suppressing the feminine take on life it was

undoubtedly Aristotle. For him a woman was but an 'unfinished man,'

her inferiority based on the then prevalent misconception about conception, that woman was but the soil, while man was the sower, contributing in his seed all the characteristics a child would need.

"In Aristotelian language, the man provides the form and the woman contributes the substance," Jostein Gaarder explained to Sophie, his young philosophy student, in *Sophie's World*. This patently false description of the sexes was particularly harmful to our collective view of women because it was this teaching from Aristotle, not the less misogynistic view of Plato that dominated throughout the Middle Ages. As a result, the church "inherited a view of women that is entirely without foundation in the Bible. Jesus was certainly no woman hater!"

No woman hater, but that didn't stop Christianity from being less than welcoming to the female spirit, even if it wasn't as wholeheartedly patriarchal as Islam and Judaism. Women were decidedly outside the gates of power, and despite the high esteem in which Mother Mary was held, her sex was undeniably a step down from the only gender that really counted: God, after all, was He; Jesus was He.

Still, there was a progression of sorts in the type of relationship between the creator and the created: Mesopotamian gods created humans to be their slaves; the God of Genesis created humans in his own image; the God of Christianity incarnated himself as human, to demonstrate his great love for mortals by dying on their behalf.

Umberto Eco, author of *The Name of the Rose*, sees a further unfolding of the sublime depths of human nature in this story. That even if he, Eco, did not believe in the existence of God, "I have to ask myself how a section of humanity possessed enough imagination to invent a God who was made man and who allowed himself to die for the love of humanity." That is, where did "this ideal of the sacrifice of love" spring from?

Unearthed, perhaps, from the unconscious memories of the ideal of love and compassion? Are we witnessing here the gentle infusions of the feminine, the softening of the harsh war-like God of old? Perhaps early steps to a true balancing.

God as Woman

The balance we need of course is not between genderized images of God or goddesses and gods, but between the so-called masculine and feminine qualities in our culture. Whether it was thousands or tens of thousands of years on one side, followed by thousands of years on the other side, it's more than evident from our quaking world that it's time to consolidate the two before we lose all sight of its credibility. As Joseph Campbell wrote in his foreword to Gimbutas' *The Language of the Goddess*, today there is a universally recognized need for a worldwide transformation of cultural consciousness.

We have for too long been lulled into thinking that the way we perceive the world and interact with each other, whether in business or in private encounters, is the way it has to be. That what we are faced with is called 'human nature,' and there's no changing it. When in fact what we are seeing may simply be a long running travesty, what James Joyce has termed the 'nightmare' (of wars and ethnic cleansings) from which it is now time for this planet to awaken.

What have we to lose, anyway? Are we afraid to imagine a better world, where compassion is as highly esteemed as self-interest, where love may assume a slight edge over hate, where insight and intuition are as prized as data and logic? We're not suggesting here that we go back to some old outmoded way of life; but that we harvest the best from our long forgotten past and marry this to the good we can glean from our current existence. It could be incredibly exciting.

"Sometimes I say to myself look, the last five to eight thousand years were an experiment that failed," Gloria Steinem (*Revolution from Within*) says of this grand epoch of the exclusion of the feminine spirit. "Okay, it's over. It was less than 5% of human history anyway. So I try to look at what is left of the original indigenous cultures."

Not surprisingly, it's in these ancient cultures — both the ones that survive in part today and those that can be known only by scattered remnants — that we find the greatest balance between men and women, between 'nature' and human. Which is not a desire to turn back the clock or to "romanticize the past," as Steinem says, "but I think it's helpful to know that it wasn't always like this."

4

GODDESS SPIRITUALITY

The 'Old European culture' is what Marija Gimbutas called the peace-loving civilization in Europe before the age of patriarchy. In her groundbreaking *Gods and Goddesses of Old Europe* she reports on an archaeological record that often contradicts the findings of previous accounts of human pre-history. That is, she found the goddesses and the feminine abounded amidst barely a trace of masculine influence.

"The Goddess in all her manifestations was a symbol of the unity of all life in Nature," Gimbutas writes in *The Language of the Goddess*, the "perception of the sacredness and mystery of all there is on earth." This celebration of life, the pervasive motif of both daily life and art, was in stark contrast to the barbaric warmongering and enslavements of the era yet to come. She describes this pre-patriarchal time as being one of great stability, creativity, and very little strife. "Their culture was a culture of art."

Gimbutas found in Malta and on the European mainland, as we did earlier in Crete and the lands around the eastern Mediterranean, that this more or less peaceful age came to an abrupt end with the invasions of a blood-thirsty lot. "The outcome of the clash of Old European with alien Indo-European religious forms is visible in the dethronement of Old European goddesses, the disappearance of temples, cult paraphernalia, and sacred signs, and the drastic reduction of religious images in the visual arts. ...The Goddess's religion went underground."

Underground to be found now, according to Carl Jung, in the collective unconscious and the dream world. And in the dusty ruins of archaeological digs. But what exactly is it they are finding in these digs; proof of a Golden Age of matriarchy? Or merely a re-reading of the record to support a particular point of view?

Archaeology has a long history of difficulties with the interpretations it makes, and in the past half century has made great strides in restricting what can and cannot be concluded from the evidence at hand. Prior to this, for example, a hundred and fifty years of expeditions to the Holy Land ended up with countless 'proofs' of Biblical incidents — which just happened to be what the expedition leaders set out to prove in the first place — only to have these overturned by the following generation of explorers of the past.

As such, Gimbutas and her followers are on the one hand being lauded for bringing to light this massive cache of statuettes and sculptures and Neolithic inscriptions and places of worship from our common pre-history, while on the other hand raising eyebrows as to just how far they are going in their interpretations of these artifacts.

"Where archaeology meets the Goddess," warns the British Museum publication, *Ancient Goddesses*, "is also where science meets religion and where mind meets body. They are not expected to brush shoulders comfortably in our society."

The Goddess in History

Comfortable or not, the shoulders do brush, sometimes quite forcefully. The now deceased former UCLA archaeologist, Gimbutas, has been hailed as the catalyst in raising goddess consciousness in our culture today. It's no surprise then that the Goddess plays a major role in a rapidly expanding religious movement which embraces both feminists and new-agers, each pointing to the archaeological record for its backing. So how sound is this backing?

Cynthia Eller is a scholar who has been studying feminine spirituality since the 80s and is quite sympathetic to a more woman-friendly religion. Yet at the same time she is appalled by the "sheer credulity they demonstrate toward their dubious version of what happened in western prehistory." In *The Myth of Matriarchy: Why An Invented Past Won't Give Women A Future*, she writes that the evidence supporting a Grand Age of Matriarchy is so sketchy and subject to biased interpreters with a political agenda, that it "leaves feminists open to charges of vacuousness and incompetence that we cannot afford to court."

That is, has this recent reinterpretation of the archaeological record merely replaced one set of biased assumptions with another set, reading into the imprecise details a paradise based on female principles and creativity in place of their male counterparts? This doesn't discount the possibility that a time of matriarchal, egalitarian, peace-loving, goddess-centered society existed before the time of the patriarchs. Just that when we choose to build our proofs on a scientific basis then we'd best make certain our facts are facts and not mere wishful thinking.

Or put another way, perhaps this great pre-consciousness era of art and peaceful co-existence wasn't just a feminine thing — if it was indeed an *egalitarian* time, as the records seem to indicate, then whatever greatness it had must be equally attributable to both the masculine and feminine spirits. Any claim to the contrary cannot help but be seen as spurious.

The Black Madonna

On the spiritual side, Goddess Spirituality has come to mean very specific things. "The contemporary renaissance of Goddess spirituality," Charlene Spretnak writes in *States of Grace*, "is not merely a protest demonstration against patriarchal hegemony ... It is the practice of an embodied way of knowing and being in the world."

According to Spretnak a hallmark of this spirituality is seeing the divine as immanent, at hand — "laced throughout the cosmic manifestations in and around us" — not transcendent, in some far off sky-heaven. There is also a shift in perception from "the death-based sense of existence that underlies patriarchal culture to a regeneration-based awareness, an embrace of life as a cycle of creative rebirths."

As such, it's crucial for women to link up with other like-minded women. Since the idea of spirituality is to strengthen connections with others, all the more important for women to get together and "honor the sense that we are deeply relational beings."

A part of this quality is a feeling of relationship to the divine. There's little point in arguing that God is without gender when all through a woman's life God is presented as He, and the males in her religion are enshrined as His intermediaries here on earth.

"Symbols communicate authority and power and shape people's lives," China Galland writes in *Longing For Darkness: Tara And The Black Madonna*. Tara, in the Tibetan tradition, is the female Buddha, the mother of compassion. "We need them, but if the symbols are devoid of a female presence we don't have anchors. The need for a female image of God is there."

However this doesn't mean that modern women must throw away their current religion or spiritual practice — be they Lutheran, Catholic, Jewish, Buddhist — and take up some ancient religion, worship the moon goddess or goddess of the dawn, and dance around Druid ruins during the solstice, all to show that they are in touch with the Feminine Face of God!

There's a lot of apprehension about this having to take up some pagan

(country, heathen) religion, scaring many women off from even contemplating this other face of divinity. And just what kind of rituals are safe and which anathema? Erica Jong writes in *What Do Women Want?*, that this has lead to growing confusion in the last few decades for many women about supporting women's causes — what is expected of them and to what lengths must they go — often ending in comedic conundrums. "Nobody could quite decide whether to be a white witch and do good with herbs or — more exciting — to be a bad witch and go to bed with devils."

The devils of course are the entry point of witchcraft into Europe and eventually America. Under a patriarchal sky there is, as Jong says, a harking back to a female sense of divinity. Nostalgia for the mother goddess is born. Excluding women from participation in the rites of the Church only sends women back to the privacy of the fields and their curtained kitchens to practice incantations that welcome them with open arms. 'Magic' is never suppressed, only driven underground.

Symbols of Evil

So throughout the ancient world, whether in partnership with gods or dominating them, goddesses reigned and were worshipped. They represented womanhood distilled to her essence. "Ishtar, Astoreth, Aphrodite," Jong says, "held sway over love, procreation, fecundity — and most of the gods obeyed her urgings." To this day even there remains within us an echo of those primeval times when Mother Nature was suffused with creative magic, and womanhood represented for us our intimate relationship with the creator of all.

The goddesses who once were parthenogenetic, creating life from themselves without the aid of male insemination, were gradually, in Gimbutas' words, transformed "into brides, wives, and daughters and were eroticized, linked with the principle of sexual love," a consequence of the new patriarchy. Still, for a long time her worship continued in Rome and Greece, in secret mystery cults — Eleusinian and Dionysiac — providing "a way to feel religious experiences in old ways."

But the old ways are inevitably transformed, reality performs an about face, and the gods of old morph into the devils of the new. "If serpents were once worshipped as symbols of magic power, they will later be despised as symbols of evil," Jong, succinctly summarizes this transfer of power. "The symbols remain, but their values are reversed." And so the sacred snake goes from being the revered goddess of ancient Crete to the despised devil himself in the tales of Genesis. As for Eve as representative of womankind, she tumbles from being the magical bringer of life to the prime cause of death and toil on the planet. "Good and evil are reversed. This is the way the politics of religion works."

5

THE BURNING TIMES

The Great European Witch Hunt. Witches burned at the stake; 9 million; 80 per cent women. A holocaust of the first order! A battle of the sexes wherein 'independent' women — especially older ones — were tortured and set afire for daring to go against patriarchy and the wishes of the Church.

This is the story I have read about, and heard preached from podiums, countless times over the past few decades. The figure doesn't vary: nine million is nine million. It must be right! Yet as hard as I search, even amid the writings of some highly respected writers who mention it, I cannot find any reference or footnote as to where the figure comes from. It's not as though this is some idle accusation, the slaughter of nine million human beings, and in this most torturous and meanest of ways. Surely there must be a responsible headcount somewhere.

I must admit that from the very beginning I've been suspicious of this claim. I mean, nine million human torches set ablaze, each upon their own bonfire? The highways and byways of Europe must have shone brightly night and day, not to mention the suffocating smoke and horrid stench of burning human flesh. And where did these women come from? Surely they were somebody's daughter, granddaughter, sister, mother, grandmother, wife? Did everyone, nine million families worth, just stand by and watch as their dearly loved ones shrieked in agony?

This was not an ignorant time. This was the time of Shakespeare and Cervantes, of Luther and the Protestant Reformation, of Michelangelo and Da Vinci and the Renaissance, of Columbus and voyages of discovery of brand new worlds. And these executions did not take place in the secrecy of concentration camps, under the cover of world war, in high-tech shower stalls and ovens. These were the result of individual public trials — open in examination, open in execution.

The enormity of the horror is that people actually were bound alive upon a mound of wood and screamed in agony as the wood was torched and the flames licked mercilessly at their flesh. And the torches were lit by fellow humans who acted in accord with the wishes of the many. Be there nine victims or nine thousand or nine million, the horror and guilt does not lessen one iota. So why this unbelievable number, this hyperbole, doing sacrilegious injustice to the memory of those who really did pay the price?

I dug further and discovered sources that present quite a different picture about these three hundred years of infamy. The *Malleus Maleficarum* (The Hammer of Witches), published by the Catholic Church in 1486 — "Women are by nature instruments of Satan" — was used by the Holy Inquisition as a guidebook for determining the guilt of witches. The Inquisition itself had been set up a couple hundred years earlier as a means of weeding out heretics within the church, not as a witch hunting organization. In fact, until the publication of the *Malleus*, almost no one in the hierarchy of the church took the existence of witches seriously — that is as dangerous souls who were in league with the devil, who could cast evil magic spells on the devout, and who posed a threat to the 'one true church.'

The witch of Medieval times was simply a direct descendent of the ancient goddess religions. And throughout the countryside of Europe these religions still had many followers, unlike the more educated towns and cities where official Christianity held sway. It's easy to see then how this latest weapon of the Inquisition could be employed to wipe out these final pockets of resistance. And how this innocent religion of the Wiccans could hold special appeal to women. As Erica Jong puts it plainly, when you disempower people they long for a sense of magic to set things right, "which explains why magic becomes the province of women in a sexist society."

Which explains in part where the witch trials came from, but not the source of the hyperbole. Jenny Gibbons, a scholar in medieval history with a particular interest in the Great Witch Hunt, places the blame for this misinformation on the types of sources which were accepted, until the mid 1970s, and on certain groups that continue today to publish this misleading propaganda about the 'burning times.'

The Truth about the Burning Times

In short, the inflated number of trials and deaths were the results of fakes, forgeries, and out and out hoaxes during the last couple of centuries of European scholarship. Most notably one Lamothe-

Langon who in 1829 published a history of the Inquisition in France filled with spectacular trials and massive slaughters — none of which ever happened. Turns out he was a known forger and hack writer, not an historian. Another was a certain Jules Michelet who played fast and free with the truth. These and others, unfortunately, were used as prime sources by historians, at least until the 70s when Norman Cohn and Richard Kieckhefer, through strenuous scholarship, set the record straight.

"A potent myth has become established, to the effect that 9 million women were burned as witches in Europe," Robin Briggs explains in *Witches & Neighbours*. "Gendercide rather than genocide (e.g. the witch-hunt documentary *The Burning Times)*. This is an overestimate by a factor of up to 200, for the most reasonable modern estimates suggest perhaps 100,000 trials between 1450 and 1750, with something between *40,000 and 50,000 executions* (italics added), of which 20 to 25 per cent were men."

Based on Brian Levack's work, *The Witch Hunt in Early Modern Europe*, Jenny Gibbons calculated roughly 110,000 witch trials, "48% of trials ended in an execution, therefore he estimated that 60,000 witches died." Ann Llewellyn Barstow (*Witchcraze*), in order to 'compensate for lost records,' increased the possible death toll to 100,000. Ronald Hutton (*Counting the Witch Hunt*), using a grid system to determine what happened in unknown areas, estimated a grand total of 40,000 dead.

Other interesting revelations are that women weren't always the predominant victims (men were 50% in Finland, 60% in Estonia, and 90% in Iceland); Catholic countries were far less likely to burn witches than the Protestant strongholds of Germany and Switzerland, and later on Britain; the vast majority of witches were condemned by secular courts, with local courts most noted for their zeal of persecution; and that mid-wives were as likely to be the accuser as the accused, using the trials as a way of eliminating the competition, all in all proving in the words of Deborah Willis (*Witch-hunting and Maternal Power in Early Modern England*) "that women were actively involved in making witchcraft accusations against their female neighbours".

Woman as Victim

All of which brings us at last to what in essence is reverberating beneath these myriad exaggerations — the 'victimization of women' — that women were the innocent victims of a Church-led male conspiracy to destroy them, to seize their property, and usurp whatever power they held as mid-wives and healers. Yet as Steven Katz notes in *The Holocaust in Historical Context,* "statistical evidence...makes clear that over 99.9-plus percent of all women who lived during the three centuries of the witch craze were not harmed directly by the police arm of either the state or the church, though both had the power to do so had the elites that controlled them so desired." At best, not a particularly efficient conspiracy.

The problem, I believe, lies in the therapeutic age in which we find ourselves entrenched. Not to put too simple a turn on it, but in modern psychotherapy we are encouraged to search for the root causes of whatever is currently holding us back from being the great person we know we can be; inevitably there are some events or persons in our past who sponsored these negative effects in us; thus we are victims — it wasn't our fault but we are nonetheless left with having to deal with the results.

Not only does this lead to an escalation of competing personal stories — and everyone it seems has their 'story' — but now masses of humanity feel obligated to portray their group (ethnic, religious, gender, race) as being even greater victims than others, in order to get attention. The benchmark they all look to is the six million Jews killed in the death camps, a truly massive number of human souls, victims to circumstances clearly beyond their control. But how grotesque and cold-blooded to enlist these chaste immolations in our need for one-upmanship. Do we really need 9 million human bodies burning at the stake to bring attention to the inequalities between the sexes? Were fifty or sixty thousand innocents not enough?

If we really must have victims to rally around we don't need to look to dubious records from the past. United Nations agencies remind us every year, as they have since at least 1990, that *30,000 children die each day* from complications and diseases resulting from malnutrition. Each day! Put in simple English, these children don't just die; they die from our collective neglect. And 'children' here are defined as four-year-olds and younger. Toddlers and infants; all these children are our collective responsibility. We are the human race; they are dependent upon us.

That's thirty thousand innocents condemned to death each day (some say the figure is even higher). Do the math. It comes to roughly eleven million deaths a year, every year — talk about a holocaust in our midst. Yet so many in our midst complain that if only they weren't such 'victims' they could do so much more with their lives.

"Victim is flip side of hero," archetypal psychologist James Hillman states. We cannot at the same time be both a victim of our culture and a hero in pursuit of its deeper truths. It's a tragedy of the first order that so many women today see their lot in life as that of victim.

The heroic awaits, a mere perceptual change away. The world is longing for the strengths of those multifarious feminine gifts. That is, for a blossoming in the arms of Sophia.

6

SOPHIA

Sophia is a Greek word meaning wisdom, from which we get philosopher, 'one who loves wisdom.' Sophia was a goddess, the feminine face (or side) of God. Bolen portrays her as the essence of feminine wisdom, a "knowledge that comes *through the heart* (italics added), a way of knowing that became discounted and devalued with patriarchy," which denigrated all knowledge that did not sprout from the state/religion.

So the wisdom that's associated with its namesake, Sophia, and by extension said to arise from the feminine spirit, is a different kind of wisdom than the one we associate with scholarship and learning. This wisdom doesn't spring from the intellect, but from some part wedged deeper in our emotional makeup.

Elaine Pagels is one of the leading lights in interpreting the beliefs and meanings of the near two thousand year old Nag Hammadi gospels which were discovered in Upper Egypt in December 1945. In *The Gnostic Gospels*, her book on these gnostic (Greek for 'knowledge') texts, she clearly identifies these two types of knowing, or wisdom. "Gnosis is not primarily rational knowledge. The Greek language distinguishes between scientific or reflective knowledge (He knows mathematics) and knowing through observation or experience (He knows me), which is gnosis." That is, the difference between knowing objectively (logos) and subjectively (gnosis).

Gnosticism as Insight

"As gnostics use the term, we could translate it as 'insight,' for gnosis involves an intuitive process of knowing oneself. And to know oneself, they claimed, is to know human nature and human destiny." This gnosis then (or noetic as it is sometimes written) is similar to the type of wisdom that we have all along been calling intuition, and the insights that inspire genius. Yet it is something decidedly more than that.

It's a way of getting to know ourselves profoundly, and "to know oneself, at the deepest level, is simultaneously to know God;" Pagels concludes. "This is the secret of gnosis."

And that is the basis of the beliefs of the ancient gnostics, beliefs which caused a rift in the early Christian church, leading to their followers eventually being banished from the official fold.

This mystic version of Christianity soon withered away, but individual mystics, especially women, have long played a prominent role in the church, even being declared saints. In medieval times alone there was Hildegard of Bingen, Teresa of Avila, Julian of Norwich, Clare of Assisi, Catherine of Siena, Catherine of Genoa. And their 'women's wisdom' wasn't as silent or ignored as is popularly believed.

In her wonderfully researched book *The Flowering of the Soul: A Book of Prayers by Women*, Lucinda Vardey demonstrates that no matter what the politics of the situation, wisdom will find a way. These are but some of her amazing findings.

Hildegard of Bingen (1098-1179) was a full fledged nun at fourteen, went on to found her own convent, was a personal advisor to the Pope and to the nobility, wrote extensively on natural science, medicine, ethics, cosmology, and mathematics, and published treatises on the divine nature of life. Established the first feminine imagery of the divine by using phrases such as the *cosmic egg*.

Teresa of Avila (1515-1582), born to a Spanish family of Jewish 'conversos', she reformed the Carmelite order of nuns by bringing it back to the basics of poverty and cloistered contemplation. A close friend of St. John of the Cross, she is known mainly for her spiritual masterpieces, *The Way of Perfection* and *The Interior Castle*, and her mystical teachings.

Julian of Norwich (1342-1416) was an English nun who lived a solitary life in a reclusive Benedictine cell. She was the first female mystical writer to refer to God and to Christ as Mother, and went on to promote feminine language and imagery in describing the Divine.

Catherine of Siena (1347-1380) was renowned far and wide as a woman of deep spiritual wisdom. She was a peace negotiator when the papacy split apart, and convinced Pope Gregory XI to return to Rome from Avignon. A Doctor of the Catholic Church and patron saint of Italy, her prayers are seen as works of theological genius.

As I said, these were medieval times, and a nunnery was one of the few places where a woman could make her mark. But that just makes it all the more amazing that her insights could still break through the darkness of these cloistered cells, emanating their clarity of vision. And that in the end is the thrust of these pages, to highlight the strengths of the so-called 'feminine qualities' that our society and world at large so lack.

And just what might these qualities be, qualities which Jung said lie submerged in the unconscious, and Campbell indicated are heralded in the great myths? Let's take a closer look at those seven goddesses mentioned above, and see if among their many attributes we can find characteristics particular to the matriarchy, to the unconscious times — a dose of which could go a long way to creating a saner balance today.

Feminine Archetypal Qualities

Aphrodite is the archetype of sensuality and beauty, and most widely honored as the goddess of love. Unfortunately, that's about as far as it goes for many people of a certain gender in considering the 'talents' and purpose of women. Women are on Earth for their beauty and sweet lovemaking, and that's the feminine spirit in a nutshell. But Aphrodite is just one of seven goddesses, and her attributes don't stop there.

She is known also for her playfulness, her richness and fullness, not to mention an elegance that goes beyond mere statuesque beauty. Above all, her love is a deep sensual love, sexually unrestrained, unafraid to let go, to be passionately full of emotion, fully alive. According to Agapi Stassinopoulos in *Conversations with the Goddesses: Revealing the Divine Power within You*, her gifts to the world are an "all-consuming passion, charisma, self-assurance, laughter, radiance, grace, and vulnerability."

Artemis is the heart and soul of independence. Swift to act, she symbolizes the "direct force that turns ambition into action." She is warm, protectful of the young, and compassionate, yet at the same time is vindictive and destructive. An avid adventurer and hunter, she invariably puts her intuition before logic. She represents the renewal of the cycles of life and death and life again. Above all, Artemis is single-minded, confident and focused, and encourages women to assume their strengths and to express their feelings honestly, especially in their dealings with men.

Athena is first and foremost the goddess of wisdom. One of the most powerful of gods, her influence "extends beyond wisdom and leadership to include war and peace, civilization and cities, and arts and literature." She is patron of all arts and crafts, as well as of woman's arts and cooking. A great mediator in war and disputes (she is the goddess of war), her judgments reveal keen wisdom, demonstrating heartfelt compassion and mercy. Patient and erudite, she is the protectress who helps us vanquish our deepest fears. Shrewd, resourceful and inventive, "she gives women permission to travel in male territory without guilt, fear, or anxiety."

Demeter is the goddess of fertility and harvesting the bounty of nature's fruits. She reigns over the earth's agricultural productivity, providing generously for all forms of life. She symbolizes hope and faith and eternal love. Demeter and her daughter Persephone together represent the unbreakable bond between mother and daughter. With an abundant love and a generous heart, "women who personify the Demeter archetype are usually great spiritual leaders who offer strong emotional support." Her contributions are not to herself, but to humanity.

Hera, the goddess of marriage, is the wife and twin sister of Zeus, the king of the gods, and is herself the 'Queen of Heaven.' Despite her being quite vain and vengeful (her symbol is the peacock), she had a large following among humans because she possessed "the power to confer the gift of prophecy on man or beast." Strong and unpredictable, she represented the unifying strength and permanence of the marriage bond — this despite her husband's unrelenting infidelity. She represents the ideal that can be accomplished when both husband and wife respect and acknowledge each other's strengths, accepting one another on an equal footing.

Hestia is the goddess of the home and hearth. More importantly she is goddess of the fire within the hearth, providing the home with warmth and happiness, and hospitality to all. That is, "this fire symbolizes the inner light that burns within each of us, recharging and rekindling our spirits." She is the sacred essence of things, symbolizing spiritual purity and integrity. In her presence we feel at home with ourselves, secure and tranquil. Hestia knows the importance of having a sacred space. As Joseph Campbell described it, she is adept at finding a private hour or so in the day where she can retreat to her special place, a space devoid of newspapers or TV or the intrusion of friends, a space where she can "simply experience and bring forth what you are and what you might be."

Persephone is the goddess of death, renewal, and transformation. To Agapi Stassinopoulos, she reflects the alternating light and dark elements of life; "Persephone shows us that we can grow and transform ourselves as we adapt to these experiences, steering us into awareness and wholeness." Gates are one of her great symbols, indicating an entranceway to the afterlife, or to another realm of power, or to the unconscious. She is the goddess of spring, the season of renewal. To journey with Persephone is to travel on the road to transformation.

The great wisdoms of the female spirit are here laid before us. Some we are quite familiar with, others are rather distant from our everyday experience; like the necessity of art and beauty to feed the inner landscape; the wisdom of not always letting logic lead the way, but allowing intuition to also have its say; the importance of being playful and sensual and passionate; the strengths to be found in being kind and merciful, and being generous to a fault; and the importance of grace and laughter and equality. Perhaps the one that is most dearly missed is the ability to place ourselves in another's shoes, to be more tolerant; that is, the wisdom of compassion.

Compassion, amazingly, works strikingly like a truth serum – an antidote very much in the spirit of this book — stripping away all the masks, forcing open our reluctant eyes, exposing the stark reality. Without it we can even kid ourselves that all is well with the world. And this is the true beauty of the feminine spirit – a deep longing for an inner truth that can balance the material world with the spiritual, in the process being captivated by the intriguing nature of a human soul.

PART 2

A MASTERWORK IN PROGRESS

The kind of creature we are:

- *How our ever-evolving consciousness must be seen as just one player alongside our unconscious, spiritual cravings, and sensual longings.*
- *"Our purpose in life" — not as the result of some preordained destiny, or pinball cause-and-effect, but the unfolding of our acorn and our strength of character.*
- *How to perceive with new eyes, and how to create great art, scientific inventions, and an astonishing reality in which to live, just by using the mind tools at our disposal.*
- *The essential truths behind a maze of claims for longevity, health, and forever-young schemes, and the only ones that will help us achieve all of the above.*

We are rapidly evolving beings. To prosper and to insure the success of our offspring, we need to seize these incredible advances as they emerge.

V

CONSCIOUSNESS, SOUL & SENSUALITY

Our inner landscape craves spontaneity, surprises, humor, and sensuality — the antithesis of the mind-numbing sameness we are fed daily.

Of what is our mysterious inner landscape made? What's going on in our minds when we are torn between two apparently opposing sets of instructions from within? Where has evolution delivered us today in the realm of soul, spirit, mind and consciousness?

Spirituality pictured not as some religious safety net, but as that part of us that is not material. Great art as the soul's greatest feast. How our concepts of soul and spirit differ. How the soul craves spontaneity, surprises and humor.

The importance of having a sensuous soul:

- Thomas Moore
- James Hillman
- Descartes
- Democritus
- John O'Donohue

1

THE POWER OF SOUL FOOD

Because we cannot be conscious of what we're not conscious of, it's virtually impossible for us to imagine what it was like to live without being conscious at all. Or to imagine daily life without the companionship of our friendly narrator, that constant inner chitchat which we like to think we control, but which in fact wanders off in a myriad of directions unless, through practiced personal discipline, we keep a tight leash on it.

Attempts to control it, or temporarily put it in pause mode, have come down through the ages in the form of often-exotic esoteric systems and mystical practices. Succinctly, "Be here, now!" That only by silencing our inner dialogue, however briefly, can we get to enjoy the 'moment' unencumbered by musings about past choices and future repercussions.

The one thing all these practices have in common is to teach us how 'not to think.' Silence the mind. Learn to listen.

But listen to what?

Finding that still, quiet space is a great way to clear the mind and get rid of the day's tensions – accomplished through deep breathing, meditation, yoga, exercise, etc. But clearing away this chatter may also reveal hitherto unknown voices that may not sound at all like voices, but come in the form of silent inspirations or intuitions or fortuitous guidance. It's these inner voices that our cultures and religions have variously labeled as divinely inspired or evil, the devil or guardian angel, to be heeded or banished.

Visibility is viability. What the mind's eye can see becomes reality. Whether we see malevolent influences as being witches or the devil or some unresolved trauma from our childhood, very much depends on the cultural milieu in which we live. The same for the benevolent 'voices' that seek to guide the course of our lives. The question is, who or what is it that's being guided – mind, consciousness, soul, spirit, personality? Or are these just fabrications to help spread responsibility when lives go astray?

All evolution is characterized by change, which applies as equally to our mental make-up as to any other aspect of nature. Except that our mental prowess seems in recent centuries to have taken off in exponential leaps. Consciousness is no exception. The consciousness acquired by our ancestors when they first became conscious was not at all like the lens through which Shakespeare wrote Hamlet, nor was Lincoln's consciousness quite like the one we have today. Each of these eras developed vastly different worldviews, perceiving possibilities that simply weren't visible before.

As cognitive archaeologist Cameron Smith wrote in *Scientific American Mind*, September 2006, "Getting closer to our ancestors – closer to the minds that created the artifacts – requires us to apply everything we know about evolution to the study of consciousness itself."

Of what then is this mysterious inner landscape made? What's going on in our minds when we are torn between two apparently opposing sets of instructions from within? More importantly, how do we decide which to listen to, which will promote our best interests in health or career or relationships?

We'll start by diving deep within that mysterious alternate reality that often feels more our true selves than any physical attribute we glance in a mirror, and see where evolution has delivered us today in the realm of soul, spirit, mind and consciousness.

2

THE SOUL OF SPIRIT

I heard the following amazing statement proclaimed recently by the guest speaker in a large ballroom: "Whether you call it the collective unconscious, or soul, or spirit, God, the great Tao, it's really all the same thing... what we're trying to get in touch with."

It was one of those Whole Life/Health get-togethers in an upscale Manhattan hotel, where spirituality mixes freely with pop psychology, Eastern religious paraphernalia, and aura readings. The speaker is a well-known author and a very much down-to-earth sort of guy. He was simply trying to reach as many people as possible with his message of how small are our differences, how universal our concerns. Yet he inadvertently contributed further to the massive confusion about just what in the world we're talking about when discussing spiritual matters.

On the one hand we have *soul* food and *soul* music and *soul* brother. There's the *soul* of a nation and a *soul*ful experience. I can be touched by her *soul*, or go in search of my *soul*mate.

On the other hand there is the *spirit* of St. Louis, the *spirit* of Christmas past, and the Holy *Spirit*. She may be full of *spirit,* or numbed by the *spirit* in the bottle. A *spirit*ed dance in the *spirit* of fun won't let your *spirit*s down.

We use these words so casually in speech. Are they interchangeable? Is our personal quest one of the spirit, or of the soul?

As my philosophy professor in Logic 101 was fond of reminding us, words have to have meanings that we all more or less agree upon, or communication is impossible. A table is not a shoe, is not a cow, is not an orgasm — though if they were this would be a considerably more interesting world, in an Alice in Wonderland sort of way. Consciousness and soul and spirit are all part of the same inner landscape, but they are not synonyms. Each has distinctly different meanings, though what these are is very much a matter of debate.

Before we can begin to grasp the nature of our spiritual quest, we need to understand the meaning of spiritual and quest, and a host of other terms rendered more than slightly vague by popular writing. Distinction and clarity are fundamental if we're to avoid blowing hot air, as in the above statement.

It's one of our major failings in these postmodernist times. We confuse and confound by default. It's almost become a religious practice in itself. We are so eager to take it all in, to give equal validity and space to every known belief system, culture, religious practice, and mythology, that we quickly befuddle any real distinction that exists between them. And the only things of worth *are* the distinctions.

Yes, classical and jazz and country are all types of music, but it is in their differences that the music lover will discover the unique rhythms he cherishes. So it is important when a North American Indian shaman speaks of the Great Spirit, that I know whether he is referring to God, or to spirit as the medieval church meant it, or the way Thomas Moore defines it in *Care of the Soul,* or something more like the spirit of the Yankees as the winningest professional sports team.

To further confuse matters, there is 'spiritual' and 'spirituality' — which do not necessarily refer to spirit. A *Spiritual* experience can be either a soul event or a spirit event. It is often used interchangeably with *religious,* though technically a religious person is one who follows a particular religion, whereas a spiritual person doesn't have to follow any particular code. Spiritual can also mean sacred. *Spirituality,* of course, is simply anything to do with the above.

"The word *spirit* originally referred to breathing or breath," Sam Keen writes in *Hymns to an Unknown God.* It referred to what animated a living being, human or animal, in contrast to its physical material.

Soul has for the most part been seen as a spiritual entity which is distinct from the body. And immortal. Yet, he adds, while animating both animals and humans, soul also grants a unique capacity to humans that help them transcend their mere animalness. Perplexing, to say the least.

Both spirit and soul can refer to what animates (gives us life), both came from words meaning breath, both are without substance and distinct from the physical body, and both can sometimes refer to animal as well as human. Then there are the words 'consciousness,' 'psyche,' and 'mind,' which are quite frequently used as substitutes for soul and spirit.

In short, there is no clear-cut way of defining them. These simple words — soul, spirit — carry far too much baggage with them, from different cultures and languages, each of which took stabs at pinning them down, mostly to little avail. The words themselves stayed the same while their meanings morphed wildly through the ages.

So the only way to help clear the air is to see just how they have been used in the past, building an inner scaffolding of sense rather than precision. When definition doesn't work, look to the attributes.

Distinguishing Soul from Spirit

Spirit, in Thomas Moore's attempt at clarification, is "a dimension that wants to transcend, that would like to know where it all came from." It's the part of us that asks 'What's it all about, Alfie?' It's the inquisitive part of us. The spirit wants to know every little detail of what happens in the universe.

So our education system is very spirited, because we want to know everything. And our moral sense is a spirit quality, because with it we think we know right from wrong. It's all part of the 'spirit' of wanting to do the right thing, of being fair and just, of not hurting others. The spirit has to do with these higher aspirations.

Soul, though not quite aspiring to our baser instincts, is motivated by love and by intimacy — not by knowledge. The soul quietly instructs us to be here and fully present, with our senses wide open — that is, to be sensuous. The soul is the passionate side of our life — which sometimes, distressingly, the moral principles of the spirit too readily dampen.

Soul is having an imagination. Soul is being able to tell stories, and being entranced by a concert or a dance. Soul is seeing life as poetry and not just as a series of events. Soul is climbing into the landscape of a work of art and being there present with the artist and his vision.

So the soul world is very sensual, while the spirit world is more interested in quiet meditation, sequestered contemplation, and closing the door on the outside world to sit alone and concentrate on our studies.

Moore offers that when we encounter a soul-filled person, we immediately sense richness in her character. As for an extremely spiritual person, we may be impressed by his discipline and want to learn from him, but we might have second thoughts about having dinner with him, or indeed wanting him to cook dinner, because "he may be too removed from the life of food."

Or maybe it's just that his spirituality lacks a good dose of soul.

3

A SOULFUL EXISTENCE

Spiritual schemes in our time have become obsessed with separating the needs of our inner selves from the life of our senses, when perhaps what the spiritual craves is to get in closer touch with the tactile world of sense. The early Platonists taught that there were numerous ways to nourish our soul; a walk in the woods, stopping on the sidewalk to listen to birds, very sensual yet simple spiritual acts which feed the soul.

I remember with great warmth the four years I spent in a particular Catholic seminary. Yet it's only now that I am beginning to understand why. And why my fifth year at seminary — a different place, different Order — was not memorable at all. (More than thirty years ago I said a fond farewell to all formal religious ties, my questioning having opened an ever widening gap between traditional myths and my dawning personal ones.)

The seminary in question was located some miles outside of Edmonton, Alberta, on 176 acres of rolling land on the banks of the North Saskatchewan River. An incredible 'retreat' with an invigorating view no matter what the season, and all the amenities — sporting, cultural, educational — that a young man requires to grow into a well-rounded adult. But none of this is what made this experience so special.

To begin with, most people I know have a very constricted notion of what seminary life is like. They see it as a place of indoctrination, where students learn the rules and the rituals and the fine points of the theology of their faith. And do a lot of praying. And I guess in many seminaries, whether they churn out priests or ministers or rabbis, this is more or less the case. I come to this conclusion from meeting a number of these graduates in person, or hearing them preach on TV, or reading their books. They tend to be strident, goal oriented; they have discovered 'the truth.' Nothing but the *spirit* side of spirituality.

However I have also come to know a good many who had a seminary experience similar to my own. What makes this type of adventure so special is the almost imperceptible insinuation of an education in soul.

Once, someone donated something like ten thousand saplings to the seminary. They had to be planted within days, each in its own separate hole. Yes, it was backbreaking hard labor, and yes we got calluses in all sorts of places. But what was astonishing was the joy in each of our faces as we trudged back to the showers, the joy of getting down in the mud, of getting our hands on those little trees and tiny roots. Even more intense than when we harvested our crop of carrots and potatoes by hand each October.

There is something about intensity that the soul just thrives on. We can't really intellectualize it. We can't readily explain it, even to ourselves. We just feel it. Like being fully in the present.

The Great Intensifier

Silence is a great intensifier. It's been used in monasteries for this very purpose for centuries. In my experience, the first two hours of every day, beginning at 6:15, were in complete silence. Forty-five minutes in chapel, feeding the spirit; forty-five minutes in study hall, feeding the intellect; and a half hour over breakfast, feeding the body that would take us through the day. Without the distraction of conversation or interruption of another's thoughts, we were left in virtual solitude with each of these tasks. What an incredible foundation upon which to build our day. And it wasn't yet eight thirty.

Of course it didn't always work out this idealistically. We were young and human, and very much inclined to break the rules if for no other reason than we enjoyed getting into mischief. But that too is the soul speaking. We were goaded constantly by our mentors, the priests, to question. To question the academic matters we were taught in class, to question the religious principles being laid before us, to question why we were put on left wing in hockey when we thought we were better at defense. In such a milieu, how could we not hanker to let loose when those inner urges cried to break out?

The biggest crime we could commit at the seminary was to be a hypocrite. A hypocrite is a deceiver. Mainly, when we're hypocrites we deceive ourselves. We deceive ourselves into believing what we don't really believe, into supporting what we don't really care for, into lending our spirit to something that gnaws at our innards.

We were constantly reminded that this was a lifelong career we were preparing for, so if we ever felt we had to fake it in any way, the priests were only too happy to help us pack our bags and point us to a life more appropriate to our longings.

This was a soul-filled environment. Sam Keen writes similarly of the workaday life of a Trappist monastery he visited, where the daily routine alternated between prayer and chanting on the one hand and farming and baking bread on the other. As he says, this point/counterpoint between the act of doing and the act of contemplating is a balance that is essential for each of our lives.

And after a vigorous game of football we would clean up and head to chapel for an hour of singing Gregorian chant. The medieval monks who created these incredible tones knew what they were doing. The chant transports us as little else can. As we add our voices to the group we feel the reverberations in our own bodies, while simultaneously hearing the thunderous combined sound bouncing off the rafters. We don't even have to understand the words — it's not an intellectual exercise. Tibetan monks accomplish the same thing with their ever-elongating deep resonance of the sound "aum". This is the life of soul.

That was life in the seminary. Unfortunately, here in the 'real' world, to the great detriment of our health and sanity, there are all too few of such soul-sustaining moments in the goal-driven angst of our workaday lives.

"The more compulsively materialist we are, the more neurotic our spirituality," Moore writes. "To heal the split we need to establish the soul in the middle, between spirit and body."

4

BETWEEN SPIRIT AND A HARD PLACE

Which is to assume that there is a split between body and soul, or body and spirit, or body and mind. These modern distinctions were in fact quite foreign to our ancestors, as O'Donohue found in the early inhabitants of Ireland. There was no dualism in the cosmology of the Celtic mind. They made no distinction between the divine and the human, between the eternal and the time-bound, or between what was visible and what was not.

The dualist point of view, so some claim, originated with René Descartes (1596-1650) and his division of all things into either thought (mind) and extension (matter). But this isn't greatly different from St. Augustine (354-430) who saw mankind as being composed of a body, like all animals, and a soul, like the angels. But even he could look back further to the teachings of Heraclitus and others around 500 BC, who described the conscious mind-space as something separate and distinct from the material body.

On the other hand there are the materialists who believe that there is no such thing as soul or spirit or whatever we want to call it, at least not something that is capable of existing on its own, separate from the body. Materialists see this phantom entity as a fairytale, a Santa Claus or Easter Bunny for the grown up. There is in this universe only atoms and their constituent parts. Everything happens mechanically, and there is no spiritual force in life. What we call soul is just a byproduct of chemical reactions in our body. And there is certainly no immortal soul which will live on once our bodies die. Psychologist Ken Wilber refers to them as 'flatlanders,' for their inability to see beyond the material at hand.

Many scientists today adhere to this materialist view. Their patron saint is Democritus (460-370 BC). He first propounded the theory that everything is made out of atoms (the original atomic theory), declaring that what we perceive as soul is also made out of atoms, round smooth ones. This materialist point of view has been so successful in our culture that the whole idea of spirit has been relegated to the realm of phantasms, excised from our overall being as though we consisted of nothing but our material bodies. Any talk of spirit or soul is quickly dispatched to the fringes of unscientific speculation, along with religion and myth and ancient fantasies. This uniquely Western outlook was born of a centuries-old European myopia that chose to recognize only what it could see and measure, in true experimental/materialist fashion.

In fact, there came a point in the not too distant past when our culture began to even doubt the existence of a spiritual realm. Moore says of the ascendance of this materialist viewpoint, that "We became enchanted with the physical domain and our ability to measure it and manipulate it." So the spirit was tolerated as an area of concern for religion, while the viewpoint of the materialists took center stage.

Western culture proceeded to separate the one from the other, then set about denying the existence of the 'other' altogether.

Contrary to these materialists, Socrates was not only a confirmed dualist but he established dualism on its surest footing. He said that the soul is something separate from the body, incorporeal. The soul is an entity that is not born, and therefore cannot die. It is immortal.

Plato followed in his mentor's footsteps. He saw man as a dual creature. We learn from our senses, he said, which are based in the body, and we learn from our reason, which inhabits the soul. He in fact believed that the soul exists in some heavenly realm of perfect ideas, long before it takes up residence in the flesh. But once it is born to body, it forgets all that it has known. Only the longing remains. And thus our human quest to return to the realm of perfection.

Soul in Modern Psychology

In modern psychology there is precious little room for soul. Which is rather ironic since the operative word form in psychology — psyche — is an ancient Greek word meaning breath, principle of life, soul. Yet modern psychology, in its desperate mission to be accepted as a hard science, has virtually abandoned soul.

James Hillman, a prominent psychologist, has campaigned for most of his career to reinstate soul back into his field. As the founder of archetypal psychology, he sees soul as being at the very core of who we are. And, he says, it's unfortunate that we're stuck with the above dualistic view of ourselves, since that splits us into just body and spirit. Why not three parts?

Where Freudians reduced spirit to soul, Jungians reversed the process, reducing soul to spirit. What Hillman aims for is to give both soul and spirit there equal due — to change the perception into a being divided into three parts: body, soul, and spirit. This is vital, he says, because "we must first access the soul in order to gain access to the spirit."

Of course we only make these distinctions in order to better understand what makes us tick. In the reality of our space/time universe we cannot separate our body from our soul from our spirit from our conscious mind. We are a gestalt that only works when all the parts are not parts, but are one.

5

THE SENSUOUS SOUL

In the poetic tradition the human face is the mirror of the soul. The eyes light up and sparkle when the soul is captivated. "Love is the deepest language and presence of the soul," writes poet O'Donohue. That when we awaken our passion, our soul has no choice but to become young again and free. And where there is no passion, the soul is absent, neglected, starved for attention. There should be no doubt when our soul awakens — we become markedly passionate, our life suffused with creativity.

The poetics of the soul call for a trusting that things will work out without strict planning. Harsh spiritual disciplines have a knack of getting in the way and can block up channels which otherwise would allow soul a place in our day-to-day life. The soul stays hidden in the face of intense voracious searches.

If I'm a cruel taskmaster, if I constantly jump on my own case, if I beat up on myself as a form of daily workout, hoping that somehow this will make me a better person, I will never come close to knowing what soul is all about.

"Negative introspection damages the soul," O'Donohue warns, holding us trapped in a grip that, ironically, will never allow us the change we so crave. Whereas real soul relishes irony and humor and punching holes in our own self-seriousness. It runs from the tedious and repetitive.

Soul is drawn toward surprises — think for a moment of those old commercials from a certain hotel chain and a fast food franchise that bragged 'there are no surprises,' and then guess why the accommodations and 'dining experience' were so soulless. Soul craves spontaneity and freshness.

Moore's remembrances from his seminary days and the many retreats he went on have little to do with lofty thoughts or theological teachings. Instead he recalls the smell of flowers on certain walkways and the taste of grapes that grew on the paths where he meditated, much as I have resurrected memories of planting young saplings, harvesting potatoes and singing Gregorian chants.

"I don't remember a single idea or lesson from those retreats," he writes in *The Soul's Religion*, "but I would want to go back on retreat just for the sensuousness of it all."

It's this very sensuousness which is missing from so many of the so-called spiritual schemes that are common in our culture these days, schemes that amount to little more than mind-numbing self aggrandizement. As Moore sees it, if a spiritual system concentrates on our ego-driven needs for self-improvement, it's completely missing the point. That is, our culture today is obsessed with self improvement – physical, mental, financial, spiritual. This Narcissism or self love has bumped aside soul. "We have substituted self for soul. That's almost a definition of narcissism."

The end result is we over-identify with our personalities and get caught up in lofty spiritual quests, pushing aside the very real physical nature of our universe and the genuine contact with it we experience through our bodies.

Only our senses can deliver these remarkable gifts: the erotic touch of our bare skin against the skin of another; the sound of children's laughter and the moving chords of a cherished piece of music; the haunting beauty of a misty sunset across a still lake and the silent gaze of Michelangelo's *David*; the enveloping aroma of home-cooked soup on a chilly day and the enticing attraction of the scent of a lover; the sweet juicy taste of a fat ripe mango and the elixir of a cold mountain stream after a long tough hike.

So lofty ideas and spiritual schemes are wonderful guiding lights, but if we don't get down in the mud, as it were, we soon find ourselves in the grasp of neurosis. Mind and reasoning are only part of the equation; reality is to be found in the details, the details revealed by our senses.

As the tastes, smells and feel of real life become more abstract and distant from us thanks to the Internet, TV and a myriad of video simulations, there is a growing danger that the truths obtained through our senses will be deemed second class. Yet it is important to remember, as Moore states, that it is only when we absorb the world through our raw senses that we are able to take in what "an artist has beheld in trance," the cold facts of the universe as well as the deep secrets of the spirit.

Perhaps it would help if we imagined soul as this sensuous lover whose passion is everything the universe has to offer, and whose embrace is the exquisite touch of our body's senses.

6

THE WORLD SOUL

The *anima mundi* is literally the soul of the world. The anima mundi is not something abstract floating about up there in the atmosphere, but refers to the soul in each and every thing. It's never about what a thing does but about its shape and beauty. Moore writes. "In a world where soul is neglected, beauty is placed last on its lists of priorities."

We are all too familiar with school boards pushing the hard sciences and math — the very lifeblood of technology. When it comes to making cutbacks it's always the arts, music, drama — the soul food — that's slashed from our children's lives. Cold comfort for a cold world.

Antiques and old buildings are another interesting dish of soul food. They act as a gateway to the soul of our ancestors. The soul needs to capture a sense of history, of who we are and where we came from. This is as true for the modern world as it was for ancient and tribal societies. Any culture that sweeps away the past in favor of a pristine present is depriving itself of this essential part of the anima mundi. As we need to dream of a brighter future, so we need to taste the wisdom of the old ways. The Platonists envisioned the soul, in fact, as transcending the everyday, embracing in an instant an awareness of past, present and future.

This all-encompassing description of soul is in direct contrast to the type of spirituality that is all too common today. A spirituality caught up in its own self-importance and righteousness. An addiction to eating only a specific diet, to chanting or meditating in a prescribed fashion, to mouthing platitudes about the ecology and animal rights and love and peace for all mankind.

Nourishing the Soul Every Day

The problem is never spirituality itself, as Moore says, but the special sort of narrow fundamentalism that takes over when spirituality and soul are split apart. "When spirituality loses contact with soul and these values, it can become rigid, simplistic, moralistic, and authoritarian."

The next time we ponder joining a group — *any* group, be they academic, religious, philosophic, whatever — we'd best first check out how many of the above adjectives apply to them. We might find our soul can't afford the cost of admission.

It's important that we care for the soul and nourish it every day. And this is not some mysterious ritual that we need indulge in. We do it in various ways already without being aware of it. As Moore asks, when we speak of the Orient Express, do we rave about it efficiently arriving on time, or is there not something more intangible that draws us to it? Do we try to recapture the magic of grandma's cooking because it was low in fat? Or for that matter do we sit in awe of a sunset because we need to be reassured that the earth is still rotating?

Ultimately, the spirit strives to do what is right, while the soul longs to be captivated.

A soulful existence is one of intensity and attention to the moment, valuing the sensual as highly as the intellectual. Soul is about feeling and poetry and letting go, while spirit leads us on to higher goals and learning. Each imparts truths about who we are and what we get out of life.

7

THE SEAT OF CONSCIOUSNESS

When asked to locate where consciousness resides in a person most people will point to the head, though a few suggest the heart or the chest area in general. There is of course the oft repeated experience of hovering in the upper corner of a room looking down on oneself, whether this be when seriously ill in a hospital bed, or 'high' in the arms of a recreational drug of choice. What this implies about the location of consciousness is difficult to say, though it does hint at a certain degree of mobility.

In general though, when we really want to get through to someone we tend to stare them right in the eye, as though assuming that the real conscious person is right there behind the forehead. Recent studies on the brain appear to confirm this ancient habit; that the prefrontal lobes (the part behind the forehead) are an important contributor to consciousness. But this no more proves the location of consciousness as being behind the forehead, the mysterious 'third eye' territory of certain esoteric systems, than finding the area of our brain that registers pain when a pin pricks our index finger. The pin, and the pain, are still in our finger.

René Descartes, that famous dualist, placed consciousness in the pineal gland. He envisioned it as some sort of screening room where we 'viewed' our stream of consciousness. But modern brain science has found no such Roxy cinema — just billions of neurons inputting billions of bits of data, with no one, or no place to sort them all out.

According to most scientists and philosophers, the mind and what we call consciousness are simply the brain at work. Further, as Edward Wilson notes, these thinkers have not only rejected the dualism of Descartes and its belief that the mind could exist without the body, but they've totally rejected his location for consciousness.

Far from being a screening room, the pineal gland has been found by medical science to regulate our body's biological clock and rhythms, and secrete the hormone melatonin, known today as an antidote to insomnia and major stress.

So who or what is monitoring all this activity in the brain? "No one. Nothing," Wilson answers. There simply is no part of the brain that screens all the neuron input and decides what to go with. "They just are. Consciousness is the virtual world composed by the scenarios."

Far from being an overseer filtering all the information that comes in, consciousness is simply a part of the system itself. "There is no single stream of consciousness in which all information is brought together by an executive ego."

Which then leaves the problem of just how the hundred billion nerve cells in our heads manage to create and sustain consciousness at all. Or is 'in the head' too narrow a scope?

Consciousness Without Emotion Cannot Exist

Consciousness and emotion are intimately entwined. In fact it is now believed that without emotion, the rational mind would slow to a crawl, and eventually disintegrate.

Rational mind dependent on emotion? So much for those imagined scientifically-advanced civilizations who have dispensed with all need of bodies and their accompanying senses, existing as pure brains hooked up to an oxygenating source. So too for the ideal of *Star Trek*'s Vulcan culture of advanced emotionless intellect!

This 'brain-in-the-vat' depiction is not at all likely to be the next step in evolution, liberating the superior brain from the constraints of flesh. The evidence in real science, Wilson assures, points to quite a different scenario for the disembodied brain, "to a waiting coffin-bound hell of the wakened dead, where the remembered and imagined world decays until chaos mercifully grants oblivion."

Consciousness needs an emotional life, needs an advanced language, needs to be learned anew by each generation? Funny thing this consciousness. A far more complex and convoluted labyrinth than mere awareness could ever imagine.

8

BEING CONSCIOUS
OF BEING CONSCIOUS

I recently dusted off my old acoustic guitar with the intention of giving my teenage son a few introductory lessons. I hadn't played on the guitar in quite a number of years, and I was amazed at how readily it all came back to me, with no real effort on my part. I thought back to some old favorite tune from when I first met my wife, and lo and behold the fingers of my left hand smoothly changed position from fret to fret as the chords required. My right hand alternately strummed in rhythm and plucked at individual strings. My voice changed from hesitant humming to singing (more or less in key) the actual words of this many-versed song, words somehow retrieved from long forgotten memories.

What part of this was I conscious of, while all this was happening? None of it, really. What I *was* conscious of was my boy and his reaction to what he was hearing. Was he impressed, was he discovering a different side of his dad, would he be interested in taking up the guitar, too? I could just as easily have been wondering what we were going to have for dinner. Somehow, the words and music would have continued to flow.

I think most of us know that we don't have to be conscious to ride a bicycle. And that if we pay conscious attention to our foot movements as we rush up and down the stairs, we will soon stumble. And that the far more complicated task of driving a car in traffic is accomplished with little conscious attention at all. The radio is playing some old pop tune which has our fingers tapping, as we point out some passing building to the kids, while we're still going over that tough meeting we had this morning and are planning how to handle the situation tomorrow. Meanwhile we are safely changing lanes, keeping an eye out for pedestrians, stopping for red lights, staying more or less within the speed limits, and navigating our way through the maze of streets to our intended destination. And when we get there we find that with few exceptions, we don't remember the drive at all!

In fact, we are not conscious while doing most things that we think consciousness is necessary for. The complexities of playing a musical instrument are but one example. How about learning difficult tasks? Not necessary. How about that most sacred of human behaviors, thinking? Not necessary. Then surely we must require consciousness for those higher intellectual accomplishments, like reasoning? Not necessary.

Such is the conclusion of much of modern psychology, which has been devising tests for a long time to decipher just exactly what consciousness is. Julian Jaynes points out that most learning is accomplished by repeating basic steps in a certain pattern over and over again, as in the above examples of walking and playing the guitar.

We are Conscious of so Very Little

Most thinking is done before we even know what we think. We need only try opening our mouth and see what comes out. "When we speak, we are not really conscious either of the search for words, or of putting the words together in phrases, or putting the phrases into sentences," Jaynes writes. What we are conscious of is a constant stream of subtle instructions that we produce to guide what we want to say, which then amazingly, without our conscious input, results in speech. If we did in fact try to become conscious of each and every word we were about to say, we would soon all be mute.

And the popular image of a scientist sitting down with his problems and using rational thought to come up with the great discoveries is as mythical as a unicorn. The greatest insights in history have come about quite mysteriously. As in Archimedes shouting 'eureka' in his bathtub when it suddenly dawned on him how to discern the purity of gold. Or Stephen Hawking, while working with difficulty to get into bed, realizing the profound limitations of a black hole. As one physicist put it, "We often talk about the three B's, the Bus, the Bath, and the Bed" as places where some of the greatest discoveries of science have been made.

Which is to say they are rarely the result of conscious reasoning.

Our Mind Has A Mind Of Its Own

"Never forget that your unconscious is smarter than you, faster than you, and more powerful than you," Australian psychologist Cordelia Fine writes in *A Mind of its Own: How Your Brain*

Distorts and Deceives. "It may even control you. You will never know all its secrets."

According to recent studies, our brain is so adamant about protecting 'our' cherished beliefs that it regularly warps perceptions to match our emotional bias. What's even more astonishing is that this is done on the quiet, without alerting our consciousness to this nifty neurological sleight of hand.

In a study using M.R.I. scanners, neuroscientists tested politically committed adults (card carrying Republicans and Democrats) to see what their reactions would be to negative criticisms of their Party's favorite candidates. What they found, surprisingly, was that their responses were almost entirely emotional and unconscious, even to the point of the brain's pleasure centers getting excited as they rejected bad criticism.

"Everything we know about cognition suggests that, when faced with a contradiction, we use the rational regions of our brain to think about it," reports Emory psychologist Drew Westen. "But that was not the case here."

While the Republicans in the study were extremely harsh with John Kerry, they readily let George Bush off the hook, no matter how damning the evidence. And the Democrats were just as illogically biased in reversing the equation. Even-headed logical reasoning had nothing to do with either side's conclusions, a fact long exploited by campaign slogan writers.

Questioning the why and the wherefore of everything we think we believe is the first step in getting to know the truth of who we really are. Our unconscious is very clever at convincing us that we are rational beings in total control of our decision making, while it goes on promoting a hidden agenda based largely on emotional ties, much of which go counter to our conscious desires.

So whether we strive to do the right thing, in the spirit sense of things, or long to be sensuously captivated in the depths of our soul, very much depends on underlying aspects of who we are. The 'character' we present to the world pretty much unfolds unconsciously.

VI

DESTINY, CHARACTER & AN ACORN

If your life has a destiny, then how can you have a free will?

Unraveling the conundrum of destiny versus free will. How can we claim to have free will and at the same time believe that we are fulfilling some greater plan? Can we believe we are responsible for our lives if our fate is already written in some book, or in the stars, or in the palms of our hands?

The nature of genius, daimon, and character.

The implications of our place in a cause-effect universe, and whether we have the freedom to change anything at all:

- Kant
- Laplace
- James Hillman
- Plato
- David Whyte
- Neruda

1

THE POWER OF FREE WILL

*Destiny rules! Why obey the Ten Commandments? Or the golden rule? Or the thou shalts and thou shalt nots of whatever system? Think of all we could get away with, cut corners for immense personal profit, if we didn't have to worry about the eternal consequences. Since God wrote the script of our life from beginning to end, the script **has** to be played out. There's nothing we can do about it, so why fret?*

Is there a direction to life? Is the universe unfolding to fulfill some deeper purpose? Is there such a thing as destiny? Is everything predetermined from creation to the final curtain?

Better still, when things go really sour, can we blame it on fate? 'It wasn't my fault; it was written in the stars.' That is, do we have free will? Or is everything determined for us by some cosmic plan?

The great French mathematician, Pierre-Simon Laplace (1749-1827), summed up the view of determinists by proposing that if, at any point in time we were given knowledge of the position of all particles of matter throughout the universe, *nothing would be unknown to us. The past and future would be laid bare before our eyes.* Everything, in a way, all that was and will be, is written in the stars. Everything is predetermined.

Can't get more straightforward than that. A simple cause and effect world, every reaction the result of a prior action; nothing just happens on its own. God alone in his heaven enjoys that privileged omniscient view of each and every particle, and that is why he knows everything that will be, while we live in a fog of what ifs. It's all been laid out before hand. St. Augustine and Thomas Aquinas, those two great fountainheads of Christian doctrine, accepted predestination as real, and so placed their faith in God's mercy.

The Stoics of ancient Greece were determinists. Contrary to popular belief, their stiff-upper-lip philosophy didn't mean they were trying to prove their courage, or to do penance for some noble cause. They simply believed that everything happened out of necessity, that everything was predetermined. So we shouldn't get carried away by feelings, whether it's something wonderful that happens to us, or something disastrous. Whatever is going to happen to us is going to happen, and there's nothing we can do about it. So be stoical!

In fact many great thinkers of the West have been of this mind, including scientists and philosophers like Isaac Newton and Thomas Hobbes, who saw the universe unfolding in a very mechanistic manner, in keeping with the clockwork age in which they lived.

Is Everything Predetermined?

There is a catch however to all this determinism. If everything is predetermined, what does this say for all that I speak, think, and do in my life? Where lies my responsibility, and my *sense* of responsibility, in a cosmos controlled in its every action from the Big Bang to the final Big Whimper? As Edward Wilson framed it, if our minds are subject to the laws of physics, and as such can be read like fine calligraphy, how can we claim to have a free will?

Free will, indeed. Without it there can be no meaning to responsibility. And without responsibility there can be no choosing between right and wrong. No moral sense, the very moral sense upon which modern civilization is built. Without free will, the whole supra-structure of our high-principled lives comes tumbling down. Yet the entire mechanism of the universe seems to be telling us that, due to cause and effect, everything is predetermined.

We're speaking here not of free will in the simplistic sense — to choose, say, that we agree or disagree with what we just read, or to think a happy thought right now, or to scratch the back of our head. We're questioning that much deeper level, where because of all of our life's experiences, and all of the inputs from our culture and our learning, and every chemical reaction that has ever coursed through our body, and the replication accidents in our DNA — how can we say that we had a choice to make a choice at all? We scratched our head simply because it was the end result of all that has gone on before, right back to the dawn of time. We only *think* we made the choice?

Strangely enough, current experiments on the intricate workings of the brain seem to back this up. As Wilson says, because of the hidden nature of the mental activity that goes on in our minds, we only have the illusion of free will. "We make decisions for reasons we often sense only vaguely, and seldom if ever understand fully."

Milliseconds before we become aware of it, our brain makes the decision, and then our conscious self sets about devising a logic to back up our decision. Our freedom of choice resides in the logic we choose to back up the decision, not in making the decision itself.

2

KISMET

*F**atalism*, or kismet, is the belief that whatever happens is predestined. Believing in this can have dire consequences for both the individual and society as a whole. Its dark side can be lethal. Depression and despair are constant companions to those who see their lives as a quirk of fate, a bad role of the dice. Their lives are a misery, they believe, not because of anything they may have done, but because of some mysterious twist of fate. They end up drowning in lethargy and hopelessness.

On the other hand, if fate has been kinder to us, leaving us with a more optimistic disposition, we may seek out those who make their living discovering our fortune in the cards. Or the crystal gazers who see our future lover in a globe of quartz. Or those who read the ups and downs of life in our palm, or scan the stars for our prospects with a new job.

There is however another side to this flip of the coin. There is a way of both seeing ourselves as determined beings, and at the same time as possessing a free will. That is, a fate or destiny which is not predetermined, but buffeted by free choice.

Immanuel Kant (1724-1804) made a distinction between humans as material beings, where we belong to the material world, and thus subject to the laws of cause and effect; and humans as rational beings, where we have a part in what Kant calls 'das Ding an sich' — as Jostein Gaarder explains it, "the world as it exists in itself," independent of our sensory impressions. In the former we have no free will, in the latter we do. Kant said that only when we follow our 'practical reason' — which enables us to make moral choices — do we exercise our free will.

He believed that it was essential for morality (and for the smooth running of society) to presuppose three essential elements — that man has an immortal soul, that God exists, and that man has a free will. These are what he called his 'practical postulates.'

151

A Passionate Belief in Free Will

That is, there is no way we can possibly know the world as it really is in itself (das Ding an sich), but only as it appears to us, through our very fallible senses. And that leaves us with rather obvious limitations, both in what we perceive to be reality, and how we choose to exercise our free will.

As such, "there can be no simple determinism of human thought," Wilson summarizes, at least not in cause and effect way the universe functions on the galactic scale, as well as on the atomic.

And so in plain language, we can go on justifiably believing that we have free will. And that's a good thing for our survival. If we all felt doomed to some fate beyond our control we would hardly make the Promethean efforts that have given us the cultures, arts, sciences and technologies of our world.

In short, we need to know that we can make a difference. Without this confidence we would slowly succumb to the prison of fatalism, and simply give up trying. Thus in organismic time and space (that is, for living creatures as opposed to particle physics), Wilson concludes, "in every operational sense that applies to the knowable self, the mind *does* have free will."

Or as Michael Gazzaniga states in *The Ethical Brain*, "the brain is determined, but the person is free." Brains are automatic, but people in their choice-riddled interactions in the social world are surprisingly free.

And what do the 'hard' sciences have to say about all this? Quantum Theory and its uncertainty principle cast a whole different light on the topic of determinism and free will.

The uncertainty principle creates quite an anomaly for physics. It states that even if we knew the position of every particle in the universe — as Laplace suggested above — we still could not with certainty predict the position *of even one particle* in the next moment (let alone everything in the universe), because its next whereabouts will always be just a probability, never a certainty. Not only that, but we cannot in the same instant know both the *position* and the *speed* of any one particle. And if we cannot know these simple basics, like taking those first teetering baby steps to prognostication, then how can anyone presume to determine where *anything* is going to be at any given time, or what *anyone* is going to do?

Whereby, if even the most minute of particle interactions cannot be predicted with any certainty, then what can be said of the larger encounters of the lives composed of billions of these particles?

These same limitations on predictability, in turn, sound a ringing death knell to the claims of palm reading, crystal gazing, and horoscope predictions. Our individual lives may indeed have a unique direction; it's just that we're a lot more certain of predicting where our lives have been, than we are at unraveling the uncertainties of where they are heading.

3

DAIMON IN THE MIND

To wit, is there a sense of calling at the core of each human life? A destiny? Destiny not in the sense that everything is predetermined, but as a preferred path. As in, if we follow this path we will fulfill the 'purpose' of our existence, and be a success. If we choose not to follow this path, for whatever reason, our life will be an endless series of frustrations, and ultimate failings.

This alternate and more commonly held view of destiny has been with us since the earliest philosophies and has worn many different labels — character, image, calling, genius, fate, daimon, soul. To this list we can add James Hillman's term 'acorn,' which he elaborates on in his book *The Soul's Code*.

Hillman describes the age we're living in as the direct opposite of the heroic ages of the past, those ages of the self-made man/woman. Today, he says, we identify with the idea of being victims, not because we choose to, but because the 'experts' have told us we are victims.

"Victim is flip side of hero." This victimization, he says, is largely due to the therapeutic and scientistic age we live in, limiting paradigms which blithely ignore that mysterious "sense of calling" that's to be found at the core of each human life.

That is, much of our therapeutic society is focused on ridding us of our demons, of bringing us back to some supposed norm. But what if those 'demons' are simply our daimon trying to break out, our 'calling' trying to make itself known to us and to the world? Especially troublesome if we happen to be heading in a totally different direction than expected.

Children these days are often labeled as uncontrollable and antisocial, and given Ritalin and other psychotropic drugs to mold their behavior. Might it simply be that the world around them is trying to reshape some young oak into an apple tree?

The Myth of Er

That sense of calling is at the core of the 'acorn theory', which regards each individual as being unique, not just in their physical make-up, but in their pattern or character that must be played out, a pattern established before birth. The acorn or daimon, according to the theory, holds the map of the path we were born to follow, just as the acorn holds the code to the grand oak tree that may one day grow to full maturity.

The roots of this theory he found planted in Plato's *Myth of Er*, where each person is given a unique daimon, or soul companion, prior to their birth. Like the acorn it contains a specific pattern that is a guide for our life. It seems that our soul was involved in the selection of this particular pattern, but in the process of making the journey into this life we have forgotten all about it and come to believe that we arrived with a clean slate. Our daimon, Hillman says, remembers our unique mission and as such is the carrier of our destiny, as it has our best interests at heart when it tries to nudge us back on course.

Plato tells us that we forget what our mission is because before we are born we are forced to drink from the River of Forgetfulness. Some of us are thirstier than others, and lacking the wisdom to know when to stop drinking, we become so overwhelmed by this amnesiac drug that we remain quite clueless throughout our life. This of course is a myth, but its message of a calling is unmistakable. It is to awaken to this calling that many religious practices work toward. As do certain archetypal therapies.

4

PILGRIM'S PROGRESS

What, after all, is the mid-life crisis/change-of-life scenario all about but waking up one day terrified that we're on the wrong path, that we missed the boat, that we will never reach the horizon of our true genius.

It is not so much that our lives are dull or lack importance, but we do "dull our lives by the way we conceive them. We have stopped imagining them with any sort of romance, any fictional flair." And an important part of this imagining is seeing some *noble* reason for our being here.

As Hillman says, there is our biography, which starts with our date of birth and ends with the day we die; and there is that other biography which traces the progress of the pilgrim within.

This progress is through an interminable sea of obstacles, yet there is often a mysterious, invisible hand helping us along the way. Or so it seems. It keeps us from stepping off the curb as a car flies by; from tripping down the stairs no matter how distracted we are; from going down that dark alley on a particular night.

Too much can be made of these incidents. Most can be attributed to mere coincidence, or good luck. Nonetheless, some people seem to be a lot luckier than others. Over the centuries we have come to name what preserves us as "instinct, self-preservation, sixth sense, subliminal awareness." Those with a magical bent might call it a genie. The religious will see the guiding light as their guardian angel.

The Mysterious Ways of the Daimon

The daimon, we are told, works in mysterious ways. If we look for it, we will start to see the happenings and compulsions in our own life in quite a different way. Chance and luck will assume a totally new meaning. Not only in our life, but we will start to see the eccentricities and foibles of others in an entirely new light. A lot less negative light at that.

156

When our children were six and two years of age, my wife and I were headed off for an incredible two week tour through India. We had a dozen years earlier made our way through the Indian subcontinent as young travelers, staying at the cheapest of places, soaking up the culture and the ancient ways as best we could. But on this occasion we were being hosted by the Indian Tourist Board. We were travel writers, earmarked to stay at the premier spots, including a luxurious few days on a 'houseboat' in Kashmir, in the style of the Rajas of old.

The details took some seven months to iron out, but we were on our way. Twelve nights before the flight I had this most vivid dream, something I rarely have. In this dream I saw these two East Indian men at an airline check-in booth. They finished with their customer, and then they pointed to me, motioning me to come forward. I froze where I was. They continued to motion me forward, mouthing words to the effect, 'come on, you're next.' But I didn't move. I didn't see my wife to my right side, though the feeling was certainly that she was there. Suddenly, as they continued calling me forth, 'we' started telescoping backward, like a special effects scene in some science fiction movie. They faded farther and farther into the distance. I woke up.

It was nearly a week before I told Lili of this. We both laughed it off as nothing more than a silly dream.

The flight was scheduled to leave on a Saturday evening at 6 PM. On Friday evening we were in the Tourist Board chief's office to collect our visa- stamped passports and tickets. But there was a problem. He could not get the authorization from London, England to release our tickets.

It seems there was a weight problem. An engine from an earlier 747 jumbo jet was in need of major repair, and had to be returned to home base in Delhi. In such cases the extra engine is strapped onto one of the wings of the current jet. This is standard procedure. However, it requires the removal of 100 passengers and their luggage in order to compensate for the weight difference. A hundred passengers had to be bumped from the once-weekly flight.

Our Tourist Board representative fought tirelessly to ensure that we would be on the flight. After all, this operation had taken more than half a year to set up. There were hotel rooms booked, taxis waiting, tour guides. But money speaks louder than other considerations. We were, in the final analysis, flying for free. Surely the paying customers stood in front of us, as did the full-fare flyers beat out those who were flying excursion rates.

Lili stayed on with him, trying desperately to work out a solution to our dilemma. I went home to relay the bad news to our children, and their grandparents who would be looking after them in our absence. As soon as my father heard that we were bumped from the flight, my father said "the plane's going down."

This was not like my father. He was a warm loving man with his arms open to the whole world. I was shocked. But he reiterated. Something informed him at that moment, he couldn't describe what it was, that the flight was doomed. There were several family members present (witnesses as it were), all countering his doom-like prediction. But in the end he would not be moved.

When Lili got home later that night I told her about my father's premonition. She confessed that she had had the exact same feeling. We must alert the airline, she insisted. The plane is going down! But I wouldn't have any of it. Without any kind of 'proof,' they would simply see us as quacks, and make it more difficult to get on flights in the future. Besides, everything was going to be all right, I told her. Our plans would just be delayed a little.

The following day Lili and I finally accepted that our great trip just wasn't going to happen. We went off to see some friends in a nearby town. On the way back we passed the airport, and only glanced at the runway that was not to take us away. We barely spoke for the rest of the night.

At six Sunday morning the phone rang. We both startled awake. We looked at each other in utter sadness, something I don't believe we had ever done before. It was a long time before she finally took the phone from its cradle. *We knew* what had happened. It was her father on the phone, a baker, working on early morning baker's hours. Somehow in the mix of the day before he hadn't been told that we weren't on the flight. He broke into tears at hearing her voice. He had just heard on the morning news that 'our' flight had gone down in the Irish Sea. No known survivors.

Does this have anything at all to do with one's daimon, with destiny or calling? Were the premonitions, my father's and Lili's alike, my distinctly foreboding dream, and the fatal crash linked merely by coincidence?

It's too easy to dismiss these types of 'knowing' as belonging to the lunatic fringe or as a result of after-the-fact fabrications, despite the obvious difficulties when there are several witnesses to the forebodings before the tragedy. Who's to know how many of the 329 victims had similar thoughts and dreams which are now buried with them? Perhaps instead of discounting these incidents as mere coincidences we should approach the phenomenon with a little more respect and serious inquiry.

In Chapter IX we will enter the eternal moment, wherein we will see that all things happen at the same instant in eternity. Is it not feasible then that under extraordinary circumstances the eternal and the time-bound might momentarily interact, leaving us with snippets of memory of things that have not yet happened (in our temporal mode)?

Then again, maybe this has nothing at all to do with daimon. These brief encounters with the eternal moment may in fact be nothing other than a very intense experience of intuition.

5

INTUITION

The silent voice within, the companion and source of inspiration. Can we know in fact when we are on the right track, in the groove, going with the right flow, following our bliss?

"The answer as I see it is getting in touch with that still silent voice inside that opens you up to your intuition, your true voice of power," says Judith Orloff, a psychiatrist and life-long psychic. She has ventured rather stridently and bravely into the realm of intuition, an area pretty much ignored by the scientific community, largely because of the difficulty of proving that it even exists — proving its existence, at least, to the conscious part of the brain.

It is after all a slippery ability to pin down. Put simply, intuition is 'the power of attaining direct knowledge without evident rational thought and inference.' Sounds rather suspicious, doesn't it, like getting a free lunch, or even Samantha in *Bewitched* twitching her nose for personal gain. If nothing else, we're informed, it too is one of those mysterious qualities from the right side of the brain.

Intuition is the sparkplug to original thought, the royal gateway to creativity. Intuition is not just some hunch we may have about the outcome of a sporting event or a role of the dice, nor is it a mysterious psychic force available to a privileged few. It's an ability we use daily, though mostly unconsciously. In fact, in a healthy society it should be displayed prominently. It's just that as educated, rational, scientifically oriented people we are coerced to outwardly deny its existence.

In *On Equilibrium*, his book on how to translate profound ideas into action, John Ralston Saul describes intuition as an impulse to action, a seizing of truth from amidst a racing imagination. "It helps us to act by seizing the swirl of uncertainty of which imagination and civilization are made. It allows us to express the organic nature of our world and our existence in it."

Intuition tells us that something is right, or wrong, a good idea, or definitely to be avoided, without there being any sensible reason for coming to this conclusion; that is, other than a vague gut feeling. It's a subtle form of perception. Yet at the same time, if we tune in to it, we find it is infused with passion, just as creativity is infused with passion, as any true artist is known to be passionate. And those who are passionate are those who are open to some innate force driving them from within.

When we listen to this voice, Orloff insists, there's no such thing as leading a passionless life; locating our intuitive thread will lead us back to a passion that is requisite for mental health. "And I think so many people have lost touch with this. I work with a lot of people who are very brilliant in their minds — corporate attorneys, stockbrokers, bankers — and they all swear they can't get in touch with this part of themselves. And this is not true. Everybody can. Anyone who wants to get in touch with the silent voice can find it and rekindle the passion within them."

The passion, it may be added, of being in a very wild uncensored moment — the seeding ground of intuition. And it's very important, Orloff says, not to try and censor this moment. "When you're in the intuitive state, you're allowing everything to flow freely in sync with spirit, as it was meant to be. And this is the essence of wildness. Spirit is wild when you get into the essence of it."

As Laurence Boldt summarizes in *Zen and the Art of Making a Living*, "intuitions, and not facts — imaginations, and not data banks, are the beginnings of creations." Or as Einstein concluded in assessing the creative process, be it artistic or scientific, global or personal, "the only really valuable thing is *intuition*" (italics added).

6

PUSH ME, PULL ME

Did fate destine me to believe in free will, or can I choose to be a fatalist? Was I meant to die in a plane crash, or to write about the conundrum of predicting one?

If 'life is determined' means we are pushed along from behind, like a billiard ball through the simple process of cause and effect, then 'teleology' means we are being pulled from the other end, towards some mysterious goal or purposeful end. Teleology is a term not often heard these days in general speech, though perhaps it should be. It is after all an attempt to put a logical spin on our life, to make sense of its ups and downs.

As Hillman describes the distinction, causality (determinism) wants to know who or what started something, what in the past pushed this event to happen in the present? Whereas teleology asks, 'What's the point? What's the purpose?', that things don't just happen for no good reason; they must be aiming towards some specific target. "Teleology reads whatever happens in life as confirming this long-range vision — for instance, God's will, some divine plan."

So, whenever we talk about there being a good reason for something or other happening to us, we're talking teleology. Thy will be done, as it is so often stated, indicating a profound belief in a Greater Plan, one which may not necessarily come to the desired conclusion.

The big question, of course, is where does evolution fit into this picture? Materialists see our existence as the result of accidental natural causes, and our destiny nothing more than the effects of things done today on things that happen tomorrow. Cause and effect and nothing more. No greater plan being worked out.

There are others though who sight this very 'progress' as proof positive of a master plan, that there is a purpose and reason for our creation, that it is not just some accident that we, the human race, became conscious and capable of asking questions about the why and the wherefore of the universe, and our place in it. That the universe is evolving for a purpose.

Or put another way, what if the 'accident' known as we (the conscious human race) never happened. What if this 'accident' happened nowhere in the universe. The cosmos would at no point be conscious of itself. It would burst into existence at some point, and at some other point be extinguished. All for naught. No Creator. No purpose. Our cosmos but a 'quantum fluctuation,' an accidental burp of un-created matter, serving no purpose, and going nowhere. There is no plan, there is no way.

Daimon as Our Genius

Daimon is said to know the way, at least a small portion of the way, that part which individually affects each of us. It knows the path we are supposed to be following, despite all of our tugging this way and that to avoid the very reason for our being. It is in effect our genius, the original meaning of *genius.*

It's only in the 18th century that the word genius took on the meaning of *extraordinary intellectual power*, as in an Einstein or da Vinci. But in ancient Rome genius simply meant the personification of our natural desires. That is, when we allow our daimon to show its true colors, we are displaying our genius before the world.

So it's no exaggeration to say that we have a genius within us. But before we lift it from potentiality to a real part of the world, we must first become convinced that it is there. Yet so many of us are convinced there's nothing there at all. Like some Doubting Thomas, if we can't put our finger on it then it doesn't exist. If we can't see a daimon, or whatever other name we may want to give it, then our daimon is no more real than a leprechaun.

7

A CHARACTER OF PURPOSE

Daimons and genii and acorns may all sound rather esoteric, so a change in terminology may help to clear the air. Another way of looking at this calling in one's life is simply as a matter of character.

Many are called, few are chosen; many have talent, few have the *character* that can realize the talent. Character is the mystery, and it is individual.

According to Hillman, psychology uses other words for character, such as *personality, ego, self, identity* and *temperament.* But character itself implies a bundle of traits and qualities...about which ego, self, etc. are but abstractions, telling us nothing of the human essence. They fall far short of the fuller meaning of character.

"If we regard character as more than a collection of traits or an accumulation of habits, virtues and vices, but rather as an active force, then character may be the forming principle in the body's aging." As the years pass we develop a history and a style, and a set of traits. But it is our character that molds us and guides us toward a particular destiny.

Young people, for instance, are often told that they must build character. But maybe it's not so much a building process as a flushing out, or blossoming of what is already there. Picasso for his part insisted that he did not develop — he just was the way he was.

Hillman calls his greatest detractors 'hustlers of materialism.' To materialists, he says, there is no soul or daimon interacting with our physical being. In this depiction the mind is seen as an array of computational organs designed by evolution to get our ancestors through the problems of hunting and foraging and defending themselves. In short, "the mind is what the brain does," processing information like any other advanced calculator.

Taking Responsibility Over Victimhood

As Hillman notes though, this outlook portrays a very limited idea of life, leading easily to the concept of victimhood. That is, when we accept the idea that we are just the end result of our personal heredity, or that we are just the creation of environmental effects on our personal history, we are describing ourselves as a species of hapless victims.

"The more my life is accounted for by what already occurred in my chromosomes, by what my parents did or didn't do, or by my early years now long past," he says, "the more my biography is the story of a victim. I am living a plot written by my genetic code, ancestral heredity, traumatic occasions, parental unconsciousness, societal accidents."

Which, oddly enough, seems to infer that to declare oneself a materialist is to define oneself as a victim, the end result of circumstances beyond one's control and responsibility.

THE COURAGE TO FAIL

" *No one can fall on their face the way you can fall on your face.*
No one can fail like you can fail."

Such is the incisive poetry of David Whyte, mocking our hesitancy to take a stand and get on with the task at hand. Much of this hesitancy is based on our fear of failure, that we could lose everything in the trying. As in, if we tried our life and it didn't work, where would we go, what would we do? So we turn a deaf ear to our daimon, our genius, our path.

Despite the fact that after several million years of evolution on this planet there is no one quite like you or I anywhere, we stubbornly fail to rejoice in this uniqueness. If I am who I am, am I not a success at being who I am? Is a bear a success or a failure? How about a mosquito?

The success and failure of our lives hardly seems like it should be an issue at all. Of course we want our lives to be a success in terms of the things we try, or why else would we try them. *I* want to be a success, whether in business or as a parent or as a lover or as a questioning being.

Nonetheless it is frightening at times to face up to the real person smiling back at us from the mirror, to look our talents straight in the eye and evaluate what if anything we have done with them. Far easier to curl up on the couch in front of the TV and disappear into a void.

That Burning Fire

In the parable of the landowner who, before traveling abroad, gave his servants five talents, three talents, and one talent respectively, Jesus relates how upon returning a year later he commended the two who had put their talents to good use in his absence, and how he cast out of his household the one who had cowardly hidden his for fear it may be lost. It takes courage to follow our unique path. But there is no other way. Rewards are not given which are not earned.

Pablo Neruda wrote, "And something ignited in my soul, fever or unremembered wings, and I went my own way, deciphering that burning fire." This priceless line about going your own way and deciphering the burning fire is what Whyte calls a perfect description of our lives. That burning, that fire in the belly is our path calling to us in desperation, nudging and pricking and shoving us to pick up the mantle and set out. It isn't easy. Of course it isn't, because if it were, we would for certain know that we were on the wrong path, on someone else's path.

All the great myths tell us that we must climb the highest mountains, cross the raging seas, struggle through hell fires to get to where we must go. That without doing so, we have truly failed.

Now is the Only Time

"Your own life, you make every step of the way," Whyte says with his typical clarity. Your own life is just the moment when your feet touch the ground. "That's your path, and you only know it in the moment of contact." Or as the great spiritual traditions of the world state simply, 'now, now is the only time.'

Which is why it is so important to follow our own path, not someone else's. Not some guru's, not some know-it-all's who would have us give up all our desires in order to listen to his. All the great traditions have warned us of these false prophets whether they be secular or religious, have cautioned us to seek our own way, to take whatever step we must take so long as it is our own.

"And that's the moment of faith," Whyte says. There are gifts on the path, and if it's your path you will find them, and that's when you discover that now you have something to give, "something that's really yours that you can give later, not something you've borrowed in order to follow a path."

Even the smallest step so long as it is true to who we are. The smallest step to telling our truth – not some postmodernist fabrication of what our personal take on reality is – but the truth we have discovered using all the mind tools and perceptions our world has provided for us.

VII

CREATIVITY, PERCEPTION
&
OTHER MIND TOOLS

The brain works on so many different levels, left and right hemispheres, amphibian through cerebral cortex. What we perceive is far beyond what our five senses take in.

Time to listen more closely to intuitions and inspirations and 'mind tools,' like the words we choose to speak and the attitude with which we start our day. The eyes of perception through which we stare out at the world. Our artist within creates, not just art, but our day-to-day existence.

In two generations we have learned more than in the previous million years. The pace is accelerating:

- Schopenhauer
- Roger Sperry
- Daniel Dennett
- Aldous Huxley
- William Blake
- Joseph Campbell
- Will Durant

1

THE POWER OF MIND TOOLS

<table>
<tr>
<td width="50%" valign="top">

Love in the right hemisphere:

Immerse our being. The warm glow of candlelight, soft music, a sumptuous dinner, heightened senses, bouquets of exotic fragrances, whispered words of endearment, silky sheets grazing across freshly bared skin, physical give and take and give, total abandonment, ahh ... ahhh ... ahhhh. The flush. The glow. The tingly feeling all over. Utter contentment ... Let's do it again!

</td>
<td width="50%" valign="top">

Love in the left hemisphere:

Oh, yeah, bring it on! I could do this all night. More! More! ... ahhhh. One more time ... zzzzzzz.

</td>
</tr>
</table>

Sex and creativity, to borrow from an old song, go together 'like love and marriage, like a horse and carriage.' Creative energy is sexual energy. Not that we have to be sexually aroused in order to create. Nor that every time we have sex we take on the guise of Michelangelo or Rodin. It's just that the same energy — the libido — is engine to both.

Life, in short, is an ongoing act of creativity, an integral part of who we are as human beings, not just the realm of 'artists.' In the Biblical view, God is the great creator and we are formed in His image. We are each created through the specific energy of a separate sexual act, and throughout our lives we call upon this same energy to create the day-to-day reality of who we are —though far be it for us to exhibit the exuberance of the God of Genesis in his six-day burst of energy.

Adding to the Vast Canvas of Life

We come into this world as little creators, ready to add our unique strokes to the vast canvas of life. But then, sadly, something happens somewhere along the path of childhood. Our peers, our schools, our parents, douse the flame. They convince us, all too thoroughly, that we can't sing or write or compose or draw worth a damn; that our efforts are a joke in comparison to the real thing.

Of course it's rarely done with malice aforethought — just plain old lack of thinking. The result however is just as devastating — we clam up, shy away from any unique demonstrations of 'what we see,' and are loathe to shine our light again where it may be viewed — and belittled — by others.

"By the time the child can draw more than a scribble, by age three or four years, an already well-formed body of conceptual knowledge formulated in language dominates his memory and controls his graphic work," wrote psychologist Karl Buhler. "As an essentially verbal education gains control, the child abandons his graphic efforts and relies almost entirely on words."

For 'graphic efforts,' of course, we can substitute any and all forms of creativity, including original thinking. As Betty Edwards writes in her delightfully instructive book on creativity, *Drawing on the Right Side of the Brain*, words are the way we have learned to see things and to remember them. We start by giving a thing a name, then adding facts about it.

However, due to the incredible onslaught of information coming at our brain in any given moment, it stands to reason that one of the functions of the brain is to screen out a large part of our new perceptions. The side doing the screening of course is the dominant hemisphere of the brain, the left side, or verbal realm. As most forms of creativity emerge from the non-verbal right hemisphere, it's little wonder that we so effortlessly slide into the all too common rut of being 'creatively blocked.'

That is, our lives continue to be an ongoing act of creativity, but like some never-ending assembly line of the damned we churn out day after day of more or less the same imprint of an existence, with only minor variations on the theme. We leave it to artists and inventors — the truly inspired — to come up with anything that is actually new — creative.

2

BRAIN GEOGRAPHY

In physical terms, the human brain or cerebrum is divided into two hemispheres, the right side controlling the left side of the body, and the left hemisphere the right side. But more than this, the two hemispheres have distinctly different ways of perceiving the world. It's as though each of us has two separate brains simultaneously processing information about the world around us. Being creative or inspired or filled with insight is very much dependent upon which brain we listen to. That is, who's running the show?

Serious research into the differences between the left and right sides of the brain began in the 1950s and 60s. "The main theme to emerge," wrote Roger Sperry, after he and his team at Cal Tech spearheaded much of the pioneering work, "is that there appear to be two modes of thinking, verbal and nonverbal, represented rather separately in left and right hemispheres, respectively." In sum, the brain has areas of specialty on one side which do not exist on the other.

"The (left) speaking major hemisphere seems to operate in a more logical, analytic, computer-like fashion. Its language is inadequate for the rapid complex syntheses achieved by the minor hemisphere." In contrast, "the minor hemisphere (right side) is specialized for Gestalt perception."

Left Brain — Right Perception

In short, the right side of the brain is associated with the unconscious, emotion, intuition, holistic, and feminine; what in the East is called the Yin side of our nature. The left side is seen as the seat of the conscious, reason, intellect, linear, and masculine; the Yang side of our being. More recently, studies have found that the split between the two sides is not as clear cut as these earlier studies showed, but still the left side has a decided 'local bias,' as in focusing on the trees, whereas the right side is definitely forest-oriented as it tilts toward a more global perspective.

Unfortunately, our modern world seems very much content to value the one side almost to the exclusion of the other. "Our educational system, as well as science in general, tends to neglect the nonverbal form of intellect," psychologist Sperry wrote in '73. "What it comes down to is that modern society discriminates against the right hemisphere." A discrimination, as we have seen, that began in the early days after the birth of consciousness.

Betty Edwards, creativity instructor and professor at the California State University at Long Beach, bemoans, "the dreamer, the artificer, the artist — is lost in our school system."

Those little voices which each of us hear — that ongoing interior dialogue which ceaselessly informs our waking hours — does not emerge from the 'artistic' side. Quite to the contrary, they are the main form of control which the verbal side uses to keep its viewpoint dominant. It's this very 'monkey chatter' which we try to still in our efforts to get in touch with the other side of our being, to hush it to silence so we may better hear those faint whispers. It's why we meditate, or chant repetitively, or take an evening course in sketching the human form. Or simply sit quietly concentrating on nothing but our breath.

3

TAKING SEXUAL SIDES

A sexually arousing situation — what a woman sees in a man's eyes, what a man sees in a woman's halter-top. Hormones rage, glands are aroused. And the great divide drops right down the middle of the brain.

Both testosterone and estrogen are released in both sexes when something sexy appears to get a rise out of him or her. A woman's sex drive is as much dependent on testosterone as is a man's. And a man cannot in fact get an erection without the help of estrogen. Yet once these hormones are released, in women they tend to converge on the right side of the brain far more than on the left. And naturally enough, the opposite is true for men.

This hormonal spread is sometimes serendipitously overcome, the ideal being reached when both man and woman allow each hemisphere to have its say, permitting the free exchange of energy between both hemispheres. It's a rare treasure called ecstasy. For the most part, though, men and women go on having sex 'together,' inhabiting two vastly different worlds.

This energy that unites them is a psychic energy known as the libido. In ancient times it was often associated with Eros, the Greek god of erotic love. At first Eros was depicted as the embodiment of our frankly sexual urges, which is what we nowadays refer to as our 'erotic' desires. Over the centuries, however, Eros morphed into a far more romantic and less carnal figure — a pudgy cherub called Cupid who litters St. Valentine's Day with millions of love-tipped arrows.

Eros — Linking the Sensual with the Creative

It was Plato who somewhere in the early stages introduced the idea of Eros as being a fundamental creative impulse, thus linking the sensual with the creative. And with the creative, eventually the whole process was linked to the divine.

John O'Donohue goes so far as to say that all of creation is resplendent with Eros. And in that primal sense Eros is revealed as

174

an integral part of divinity. It's an energy that we all possess, and because every thing and every human in the universe is created in this image, we feel the call of Eros.

This libido energy is essential in connecting consciousness with the unconscious, the masculine with the feminine, and thinking with feeling.

Eros works its magic. In the throes of sexual arousal a woman will tend to see things intuitively, in a nonverbal holistic 'picture," and be more relational and emotional. Man, by contrast, will be far more rational — linear and goal oriented.

Which doesn't mean that women are right-brained and men left-brained. Just that in matters of sexual attraction and behavior, the hormonal mix tends to engage opposite sides of the brain, resulting in quite different behaviors — and expectations. Considering, then, how often thoughts of sex enter our minds on any given day — like hyped-up pinballs the sexes daily collide with each other in never ending dances on the sidewalk, on the subway, in the office, at the store, on the phone, and in the bars, theaters, cinemas and night clubs which gather in our over-stimulated erotic zones.

In brief, our libidos are nothing short of throbbing. Throbbing with the creative fires that beg to be stoked, stroked and released. Or, barring release, threaten to smolder on as an unfanned and ever enfeebling ache in the belly.

Or was that ache somewhat lower down? If the libido energy is as likely to be sexual as it is to be creative, then perhaps their expressions can be substituted one for the other, as in our youthful tendency to channel all this energy into sexual outlets. What happens then when our sexual ardor wanes, as it inevitably does? Are we able to successfully transfer this energy to creative outlets?

4

THE ARTIST WITHIN

Where most of us seem to get stuck on the surface, artists have an uncanny ability to perceive and portray the essence of a person or a scene. Easy to understand, really, when we remember that the dominant side of the brain is the verbal, the very side from which artists manage to escape, at least temporarily, in order to be inspired. The question is how can we do the same — get inspired, and take temporary trips to that wonderland beyond the doors of perception?

Quite simply, by convincing ourselves that it's a most pleasurable place to be. Any creative benefits are simply a bonus on the side. "You may hear the sounds of speech, but you do not decode the sounds into meaningful words," Edwards writes of finding ourselves in this altered state. "If someone speaks to you, it seems as though it would take a great effort to cross back, think again *in words*, and answer."

Not only that, but whatever we are doing then, no matter what it is, grabs our interest intensely. "You are attentive and concentrated and feel 'at one' with the thing you are concentrating on." We feel a euphoric blend of high energy with calm, activity without anxiety. There is no doubt that we can accomplish the task at hand. Our thinking is composed of images not words, and while drawing an object our "thinking is 'locked on' to the object you perceive. The state is very pleasurable. On leaving it, you do not feel tired, but refreshed."

One could hardly be faulted for mistaking this as a description of the enthrallment of passionate lovemaking.

So whatever the form of creative activity, be it with words or paints or musical notes, it's not some mysterious ability available only to a few privileged and gifted people. This degree of creativity is available to anyone who can alter their state of awareness just enough so that they feel transported, 'at one with the work.' The passage of time fades away, words desert us; we feel strangely both alert and relaxed in the same moment. It's very akin to the mystical.

"The life of Zen begins with the opening of *satori,*" wrote the great interpreter of Zen to the West, Daisetz Suzuki. *"Satori* may be defined as intuitive looking into, in contradistinction to intellectual and logical understanding..... (It) means the unfolding of a new world hitherto unperceived."

Opening the Doors of Perception

This same unperceived world was well explored by Aldous Huxley. In *The Doors of Perception* he wrote, "To be shaken out of the ruts of ordinary perception, to be shown for a few timeless hours the outer and the inner world, not as they appear to an animal obsessed with words and notions, but as they are apprehended, directly and unconditionally, by Mind at Large — this is an experience of inestimable value to everyone."

It's when we become capable of opening ourselves up to the right side of our brain that we gradually develop a 'talent' for uncovering the deeper nature of things. As Edwards describes it, if we begin to look at people and objects in general as though we were about to draw them, then we will certainly see *differently.* We will begin to see with an awakened eye, the artist's perception that resides within us all.

Or to put it another way, most people never learn to draw because they never learn to *see* well enough to draw. And remarkably it's a two-way street. The more we open up to the right side of the brain, the better we will create; and the more we learn to create at will, the more we will be able to tap into those incredible abilities on the right side of the brain, and get in touch with those remarkable talents which our unconscious ancestors used on a daily basis.

The key to learning to draw, Edwards instructs, "is to *set up* conditions that cause you to make a mental shift to a different mode of information processing." Those conditions are what allow us to enter that slightly altered state of consciousness where 'seeing' takes on a whole different perspective.

She offers this very practical rationale for working on our right side brain. "Trying to draw a perceived form by using the verbal left mode is like trying to use a foot to thread a needle. It doesn't work." What we need to do is to temporarily tone down the dominance of the left hemisphere and let the right side show us a different point of view. As Aldous Huxley phrased it, it requires "opening the Door in the Wall."

So too, we should not try to use the 'foot' of the rational side of our brain to thread the mysteries of creativity and intuition. Just shift and see the difference.

Through the Looking Glass

Stepping through this door in the wall is similar to Alice in Wonderland stepping through the looking glass: We're not quite certain what we'll find there, but in a strange sort of way we're already looking at it. Half our brain, after all, is quite aware of something which 'we' don't know. Or as the Gnostic *Gospel of Thomas* states it, "Recognize what is before your eyes, and what is hidden will be revealed to you."

5

MIND TOOLS

C reativity is as much about perception as it is about doing.
For its part, perception is as much about language as it is about seeing.

All the books and courses in the world on art and creativity, though they will undoubtedly improve our technique, are not likely to make us more creative. Of what use is technique without something of value to express?

Which brings us back to the left side of the brain, the conscious, talkative, reasoning side of our existence. Just as it is important to get in touch with our right hemisphere to 'see' what it has unconsciously been perceiving, it's equally as important to 'see' what the left side has to offer. The trouble is, as the old saying has it, we can't make a silk purse out of a sow's ear. Any gastronomic recipe or educational system stands witness to this adage. Garbage in one end, garbage out the other.

Language as an Organ of Perception

Speaking from this left side, then, we find that the treasures from our depths can only be exposed to the world by the richness of our thoughts. And these thoughts cannot exist without words; the more meaningful the one the more expressive the other. So to speak realistically of creativity, we must begin at the beginning, with the word. *In the beginning was the word.*

The simplest way to see how different our perceptions can be is to look in the area of the everyday colors which we see around us. Where some people perceive an amazing kaleidoscope of scores of different shades and hues — chartreuse, magenta, burgundy, fuchsia, aquamarine, to name just a few — the vast majority see only reds and blues and yellows. Much like the often-repeated example of people like the Inuit in the high Arctic having more than twenty separate words for 'snow,' whereas most other languages of the world have but one. These people of course found it a matter of life and death to be extremely precise as to exactly what type of snow they were talking about. As do students of art and interior decorators need a similar precision with color.

What's important is not that Michelangelo likely had an extensive vocabulary in colors, but that this very vocabulary enabled him to see nuances of difference that just weren't 'seeable' to the average eye. As Julian Jaynes explains it, "Language is an organ of perception, not simply a means of communication." We learn a new word to describe a new piece of knowledge. But then that word itself opens up for us a new perception, a new way of seeing things that we did not have before.

Language is a tool to help us define our reality. All language is metaphor, and depending on the metaphors we choose, our perceptions of the world around us will change. Much of the clash between cultures, in fact, is due to each side's differing descriptions of the world around them. What we see is very much what we set out to see. And naturally enough, we set out to see what everyone in our immediate circle claims to see. This is the whole learning process for the child. It's no accident that a child learns his language and his perceptions of the world at the same time.

European explorers in the last few centuries often returned home with stories of cultures that didn't seem to understand the concept of possessions. Everything these people had, from food to pots to artifacts, was simply there, for everyone to use as need be. To the delight of these male explorers, wives were sometimes included in the list. And when missionaries came along and started translating the local language, they were astonished that they had no words for possessiveness, as in 'these are mine, not yours.' Similarly, when these same Europeans used racist and pejorative terms to describe these people, they couldn't help but then perceive them in racist and disparaging ways.

The Power of Words

So the power of words goes well beyond just our ability to describe what we experience. A limited vocabulary makes for a very limited experience of life, as any good educator tries to relay to her students. Don't expect to go very far in life, she will say, with a string of "well, you know" and "It's like, sorta" and "Like cool and stuff." We seem to know instinctively that a *smart* person is one who perceives the world much clearer than most, and we know they are smart because of the precision of their vocabulary.

Consciousness theorist, Richard Gregory, describes words as *mind tools* — the most important tools ever invented. They are the essence of what has given our minds their greatest power. Professor of philosophy, Daniel Dennett, puts this idea in sharp focus by comparing the introduction of language to the advent of high-speed still photography — where suddenly we could freeze-frame virtually any activity and see it in astonishing new ways never before possible. Like the way a horse's four hooves are all in the air at the same instant when in full gallop, the way a cat manages to twist its body in mid fall so that it will land on all fours, the explosive patterns generated by a single drop of water on a still pond. This new wealth of information profoundly changed our understanding of the universe and how it works.

"The advent of language was an exactly parallel boon for human beings," Dennett writes, "a technology that created a whole new class of objects-to-contemplate..." In effect, words are surrogates for the real thing, and can be brought to mind long after our encounter with the real thing.

But it doesn't stop there. In all other species the individual's learning is limited to what they can observe around them in the behavior of others. With language we are informed by a much larger community, yes, but even more so we are able to hear of the wisdom passed on to us from generations and generations of people who are long since dead. Where would our nearest relatives, the chimpanzees, be today if they had such a store of information, and the perceptions it makes possible?

"Our human brains, and only human brains, have been armed by habits and methods, mind-tools and information, drawn from millions of other brains to which we are not genetically related," Dennett summarizes. The end result is that this "process of enhancement has become so swift and powerful" that the knowledge we are acquiring in a single generation now dwarfs what our ancestors were able to accomplish in millions of years.

Dennett concludes, "a proper application of Darwinian thinking suggests that if we survive our current self-induced environmental crises, our capacity to comprehend will continue to grow by increments that are now incomprehensible to us."

Mind-Boggling Intelligence

These increments have indeed been mind-boggling. Our most brilliant scholars, Ph.D. candidates, and leading scientists at the turn of the nineteenth into the twentieth century could not understand concepts that are now routinely taught in high school. As Dennett observes, "When comparing the time scales of genetic and cultural evolution, it is useful to bear in mind that we here today — every one of us — can easily understand many ideas that were simply unthinkable by the geniuses in our grandparents' generation!"

I remember my own high school science teacher not being able to wrap his mind around certain aspects of Einstein's relativity theory, and thus unable to explain them to us — ideas which my children and their friends had little trouble with while in the latter years of elementary school. Which is not to hint that smart people perhaps weren't so smart in the past. But rather, as pointed out above, the more we learn the more we are capable of learning. Each new learning opens up new vocabulary which opens up new concepts, which in turn we use as new organs of perception of the enormity of all that there is to learn.

As Dennett says, anthropologists have long recognized that when early mankind began using tools there was a giant leap in their intelligence. Tools are embedded with incredible stores of information, and the better it is designed the greater the potential intelligence it bestows on its user.

Take a simple pair of scissors. Echoing Gregory, Dennett observes that when you give someone a pair of scissors you not only up their intelligence in regards to the use of scissors, but you "enhance their potential to arrive more safely and swiftly at Smart Moves." Any tool, be it scissors or car or computer, thus increases our intelligence and our power of perception — in its own right becoming yet another organ of perception.

Where, in his day, my grandfather picked up the telephone receiver and asked the operator to connect him with the general store a few blocks away, my children today press a few buttons to connect them to a web of world-wide possibilities.

That same grandfather was born, literally, in the back of a covered wagon, one chilly November in the late1880s near Pembina, North Dakota. When he died in our home eighty years later, his organs of perception had vastly changed from those he received in that old ox cart. The introduction of the light bulb, a kitchen full of electric appliances, automobiles, airplanes, jets, helicopters, radio, television, movies, recorded music, two world wars worth of inventions in weapons and tanks and bombs and aircraft-carriers and submarines, rockets, atomic bombs, spacecraft

— not to mention astronauts, humans but a generation or so removed from that oxcart, probing the mysteries of the moon. But a few of the ways in which his world changed in a mere four score years. And quite an addition to his original powers of perception.

What will yet be said about my generation's perceptual endowments, or that of my children's?

So both the everyday worlds we create for ourselves to live in, and the artistic creations that we may or may not choose to share with the world, are very much the result of our own perceptions. The fuller our perceptions, and the more varied they are, the more interesting and enlightening an existence we create for ourselves. Perception, in the final analysis, is what it's all about.

How we perceive and with what we perceive is obviously not as simple as looking to our five senses.

6

MANY BRAINS

My brain is really made up of three separate brains, one sitting atop the other, atop the other. If we were to peer through my scalp, looking from the top down, we would first see a pinkish-grey convoluted mass of soft tissue. This is my cerebral cortex, the quarter-inch outer layer of my cerebrum, often called the reasoning or 'human' brain. Below this is the mostly white-matter cerebrum which enfolds structures such as the amygdala, hippocampus, and hypothalamus — collectively known as the limbic system, or 'mammalian' brain. Finally, beneath all this we would discover the quite small brain stem at the top of my spinal column, the so-called 'reptilian' brain.

As I grew in my mother's womb, from fertilized egg to embryo to fetus, each of these brains grew atop the other, from most primitive to most recent, mimicking in less than nine months the long progression of our evolutionary history.

From Lizards to Super Mario

The Reptilian brain, as neuroscientist Paul MacLean explains, "is devoted to basic life support, characteristics you will see in any snake or lizard. The regulation of breathing, heartbeat, and muscle movements; and covering basic drives such as eating, self-protection, and sex. The reptile brain does not really have much more to offer these creatures. Of course all of these life support systems are firmly in place in all 'higher' forms of life."

The Mammalian brain, the second brain, is considerably more complex, adding to one's life fascinating qualities (and perceptions) which snakes and lizards couldn't begin to imagine. Our behavior is now informed by emotions, the "ability to snarl, skulk, cringe, purr, growl, yelp, to nuzzle, to show fear, to teach their young, to perform tricks for rewards, to wag tails in appreciation, to show affection, even to looking ashamed or guilty when having done something wrong." In fact, this mammalian brain is responsible for so much of what we humans consider to be 'human' qualities that we forget that we share this level of brain with virtually all the animals with which we come into everyday contact.

These fellow mammals, however, can go no further. They only have these two levels of brain. For we humans this level of brain evolution has for millions of years now been topped by the "massive cerebral cortex, that highly ridged and folded gray matter, which is responsible for all those attributes which we see to be so uniquely human..." Things like writing and language and rational thought and imagination and planning for the future. And yes, there are areas of it that are essential for consciousness.

And it's this third level, 'Human' brain, divided into two separate hemispheres right down through the cerebrum, which gives us such vastly different perceptions. Add to this all the perceptions we receive from our Reptilian level brain as it takes care of our life-sustaining functions, not to mention goading us on to get more food, to get more sex, and to fight to the death to protect ourselves. Add to this all the perceptions we receive from our Mammalian level brain, running the whole gamut of emotions imaginable, as well as the abilities to teach our young, and to fake our intentions, and to plan, and to show affection, and to appreciate, and to feel guilt and shame, and feel a part of something greater to the point even of giving our lives for it.

We are extremely complicated and multi-faceted organs of perception on so many different levels. Somehow, just opening my eyes and saying, 'I see,' sounds awfully naive and simplistic.

7

PERCEPTION – THE GIFT OF LIFE

The world in which a man lives shapes itself
chiefly by the way in which he looks at it
— Schopenhauer

Igor Stravinsky elaborated, "The faculty of creating is never given to us all by itself. It always goes hand in hand with *the gift of observation*. And the true creator may be recognized by his ability always to find about him, in the commonest and humblest thing, items worthy of note. He does not have to concern himself with a beautiful landscape; he does not need to surround himself with rare and precious objects. He does not have to put forth in search of discoveries: they are always within his reach."

The Irish philosopher and bishop, George Berkeley (1685-1753), long before the invention of Quantum theory, wrote "To be is to be perceived." We exist because we are perceived, and we bestow existence by perceiving. Or as James Hillman said, perception is a means of bringing into being whatever is perceived.

That is, creating does not begin with a magic wand or a burning bush or the incantation of some mysterious words, or for that matter with a paintbrush or a mound of clay. It begins with what we see in the mind's eye. It's incredible, then, how nonchalantly we are taught to regard the whole process of perceiving. If we only knew the extraordinary potency involved in the simple act of focusing our attention.

Perception Is Reality

The way you look at things can be the most powerful force in shaping your life. John O'Donohue says that "in a vital sense, perception *is* reality." So much so that when we really look deeply at something, it no longer is just something outside of us, but becomes a part of us.

"Visualize the mind as a tower of windows" as seen, perhaps, while ascending a spiral staircase in an old lighthouse. Sadly, he

186

says, most of us sit immobile staring out that same window, day after day without change. In this pose there is no chance for growth, for creativity, for altered perceptions, because all we're doing is taking in the same information day after day.

Real growth can occur only when we turn away from that one window and explore the inner tower of our soul and see all the incredible views that await our gaze. Only through these different windows can we come to know vastly new vistas, and new possibilities for our lives.

It's this very type of perception which is so crucial to our understanding of the world, because the way in which we see the world will very much determine how we will be in it. Reality results from the type of lens we choose to see through. The way in which we perceive things affects the way we perceive these things behaving towards us.

We all know of at least one acquaintance who is a sour puss, a person who is always searching for storm clouds on a sunny day, or fault to find no matter how perfect a thing appears to be. Hers is the judgmental eye. This eye is obsessed with separating and excluding: it lacks the will to see anything "in a compassionate or celebratory way." Sadly, its harsh and facile judgments prove to be most severe and unforgiving on the beholder herself.

To see where we stand, then, O'Donohue suggests we explore our particular style of seeing. That is, with what kind of eye do *we* look out into the world? How limiting are our own powers of perception?

"To the fearful eye, all is threatening. To the greedy eye, everything can be possessed." The problem with greed is that we can never actually enjoy what we have because we are always focused on all that we don't yet possess. As to the resentful eye, it begrudges everything it casts its vision upon.

And with an indifferent eye, there is nothing that can awaken its interest or call it into action. Indifference can swiftly place us right outside the bounds of love and compassion. "When you become indifferent, you give all your power away."

To the loving eye, however, everything is real. And it's this kind of open and accepting perception — like the euphoric and non-judgmental way we felt when Cupid's arrow first wedged its heart-shaped point deep within us — that speaks straight to the creator within.

And to be an effective creator we must welcome to out inner world a more courageous imagination.

Shaping the Future

Meister Eckhart (1260-1327) said that *thoughts are our inner senses*. To O'Donohue this simply means that when there is something wrong with one of our outer senses, the world is no longer quite as present to us as it was before. If our eyesight turns poor, then the world comes at us in a blur. Music and people's voices likewise become silenced or unintelligible when our hearing is damaged. And so too if our thoughts are impaired, if we allow them to become impoverished, then the wealth of our inner being can never emerge into the light of day.

Each day, each moment of every day, we step into the future. How we view this future will in large part actually shape what we step into. Often the troubles we discover there we have in fact drawn upon ourselves by our attitudes.

From ancient times our elders have warned us that the way we act toward life will very much affect how life in turn will come back to greet us. So to procure the things we think we really need we can start by changing our attitude to one of hope and compassion.

8

WILL

Is there a force or a power or an esoteric knowledge which we may employ to get the things we really want? That is, if we sandwich our eyes shut tight enough and concentrate until our muscles quiver, will we get what we wish for? Creating something by willing it to happen?

Most of us, since earliest childhood, have used some version of this wishing technique in everything from picturing ourselves as some larger than life hero, to being gifted with special powers, to landing our ideal spouse. Or to the everyday, as in getting that promotion or passing that math exam or speeding down the road in that shiny new sportscar convertible.

There's really no limit to the number of things we wish we could make come about. And we keep on wishing over and over again, regardless of whether or not it has worked for the last twenty or thirty or forty times. Anyone batting a thousand? Somehow we seem to think that if we keep at it long enough we'll finally get the hang of it, and then the world will be ours for the taking.

This of course is the appeal of such fantasy alter egos as the genie in *I Dream of Jeannie*, and Samantha, the witch in *Bewitched*. With a mere twitching of the nose or a folding of arms, and "abracadabra," your wish is at your command.

In short, when we 'will' something to happen we are trying to use our creative powers to bring into reality something that was not there before. The only question is, does it work? Do we possess such creative abilities? (Or like King Midas, should our greatest fear be that we might actually get what we wished for?)

Creating What We Visualize

Creative visualization is a good example of how we might realistically put that magical twitch into our nose. It's a straightforward magus technique that goes back to earliest recorded times. The idea is to draw, in our mind's eye, a clear picture of what we want. Don't just say in so many words that we want a new 3

GHz personal computer with all the bells and whistles — we have to actually picture it in a specific spot on our home desk or kitchen counter.

Then go ahead and work towards it; several times a day, and day after day for weeks or months or whatever it takes, actually visualizing that particular computer on our desk. And when we're not visualizing, we're thinking about, and talking to our friends about, and working towards actually making that vision a reality in our home. And lo and behold, that beautiful power tool is quite likely to take up residence in our home. The same applies to more private matters, such as wishing to be a more caring or loving person, or relinquishing our fear of failure.

Critics will quickly object that it's not the visualization but the added concentration and time spent on this desire that make it come true. To which the sages answer, "Ah ha, then it does work." The more fanciful and naive amongst us, needless to say, will actually expect the computer to appear, as if by magic, or as if Barbara Eden had just folded her arms and replied, "As you wish, Master." But then some people expect to become President one day, or meet their ideal mate, by reading their daily horoscope and waiting by the phone for it to ring. As one joker sarcastically commented, they seem to have missed the nuance that things are brought into being not by a passive of creation, but by an *act* of creation.

Using our will in this way has variations both subtle and not so subtle. As in projecting our thoughts and desires onto others. Or employing the power of suggestion, or the technique of repeating certain problems to ourselves before going to sleep, virtually willing our unconscious to come up with the solution.

What's in a Miracle?

On the broader stage, we find miracles and 'non-medical' healing. Miracle is such a catch-all word that it can apply as easily to a fielding play in last night's baseball game, as to the founding of a nation. 'They discovered a new miracle cure! It's a miracle no one was killed in that explosion. She made a miraculous recovery! The miracle of walking on water was awesome.'

Does a miracle go against the laws of science, or is it merely an unlikelihood? What kind of special powers do we need to perform one — a saintly existence, extreme asceticism, detachment from the world? *A Course In Miracles* is a best selling book which many have sworn by since its appearance in the 70s. One of its better-known graduates, Marianne Williamson, claims it certainly turned her life around. I have no doubt that it did, but having successfully completed the course, can she perform miracles? Is the title of the book merely a metaphor for changing our lives in ways we didn't think possible? (Actually, the book itself describes a miracle as a shift in perception, allowing one to see the spirit behind all things — *A Course in Shifting Perception*, perhaps.)

Are we just kidding ourselves with our cavalier use of such terms, that we are tapping into some unique creative source, or is a miracle just another name for more down-to-earth capabilities?

The universe is without doubt a very clever and often paradoxical milieu in which to navigate, as miracles are an enigmatic part of this description. Whenever we try to create a miracle we 'intend' a certain thing to happen, yet intention is wrapped in paradox, a paradox not to be toyed with lightly.

9

PARADOXICAL INTENTION

*Ironically enough, in the same way that fear brings to pass
what one is afraid of, likewise a forced intention
makes impossible what one forcibly wishes.*

— Viktor Frankl

T his is the peculiar nature of willing or wishing or desiring, known as the *paradox of intention*. The more we intend something to happen, the less likely it is to come about. It's as though we have to take a sideways glance at it. At first we concentrate on what we want, then we look away, not really caring whether we get it or not. In the East this is known as *wei wu wei*, or 'action no action,' or as Ken Wilber translates it, 'active inactivity.'

Just how this fits into the mechanics of how our mind and body work together is difficult to say. It certainly sounds more mystical than anything we found above in the topography of our brain. Yet any number of researchers into the inner functioning of our being insist that it's this caring/not caring attitude that gives will its power.

Perhaps 'will' is too strident an approach to take. John O'Donohue suggests that the far more creative and less strident tact is simply to be more mindful of what we'd like. We too often try to beat our life into shape, wielding will like it was some kind of hammer.

Using the hammer sounds like a tactic of that despot known as our consciousness, demanding that things be done its way and only its way, sublimely ignoring the input of all other parts of our being.

In *The Power of Myth* Joseph Campbell speaks about consciousness somehow thinking that it's running the shop, where in fact it is just a secondary organ of our much larger interior landscape. It should never be allowed to seize control but must submit to the humanity of the whole. When it does take control, "you get a man like Darth Vader in *Star Wars*, the man who goes over to the consciously intentional side."

It's a bizarre manner of looking at ourselves, almost as if we have to play office politics with 'ourselves,' but then we have to remind ourselves (in the plural), that consciousness is not the sole participant in the dominion that is me. As Schopenhauer suggested, our whole life is composed by a will deep within us, a depth far beyond the reach of our conscious grasp. Or as Blaise Pascal wrote, "The heart has its reasons that the mind knows nothing of."

The Pursuit of Happiness

So this sideways approach, this caring while not caring about the results, appears to act as some kind of diplomatic code, engaging all aspects of our being. Take for instance the pursuit of pleasure, or happiness, or success. Attacked head-on, these quickly become vanishing chimeras, mirages evaporating in the shimmering hot air of who we envision ourselves to be.

"Pleasure, too, is a side-effect or by-product," Viktor Frankl cautions, "and is destroyed and spoiled to the degree to which it is made a goal in itself. Anticipatory anxiety has to be counteracted by paradoxical intention." The more we make one of these our target, the more we are going to miss the target.

"Success, like happiness, cannot be pursued…you have to let it happen by

not caring about it. Success will follow you precisely because you had *forgotten* to think of it."

In the late 18th century the men who became the founding fathers of America must have had something similar in mind. The American Constitution, after all, does not guarantee the right to happiness, but the right to the *pursuit* of happiness. How each individual goes about pursuing it will very much determine their rate of success. It's a *rate* of success, of course, because happiness is not a commodity which we grab hold of and thence possess for the rest of our lives. It's a fleeting, passing feeling which we must purchase over and over again by our actions and attitudes.

10

ART

Paul Klee wrote of art's magic, "Art does not reproduce what we see. Rather, it makes us see… (it's) a journey into the land of greater insight."

In *The Re-Enchantment of Everyday Life* Thomas Moore points out that museums and art galleries and artist studios are not the only place where art should be on display, but that everyday places such as stores and work places and our homes should also incorporate works of art as a necessary part of the scenario. When art is seen only in professional venues, "a dangerous gulf develops between the fine arts and the everyday arts."

The tragedy is that by banishing art to these special places, the museums and art galleries, we as a culture come to accept that this is art's proper place, and so "fail to give it a place in ordinary life." Not only does the gulf widen, but our everyday existence soon becomes bereft of any sense of art, and the truth and beauty it bestows on our lives.

William Blake had a similar take on the widening abyss between industry and the fine arts. Around the time the nineteenth century eclipsed the Age of Napoleon he cautioned, "When nations grow old, the arts grow cold, and commerce settles on every tree." A wise thought to keep in mind as we watch every athlete's butt, back, and helmet grow increasingly smothered in brand marks and corporate slogans. Not to mention school buses and software programs designed specifically 'for the classroom.' Come to think of it, it's hard to imagine any aspect of our lives today that isn't up to its proverbial eyeballs in commercials of one sort or another.

How vastly different our world would be if this utter crassness were replaced, even in some small part, by true art. It's a sad comment on our society, but who among us would not be astonished to see city buses and public places covered in blowup copies of Monets and Rembrandts and Van Goghs, for no other reason than the expression of their truth, their beauty? Philosopher

Ananda Coomaraswamy pulled no punches when he wrote, "Industry without art is brutality."

Bad Art Copies, Good Art Creates, Great Art Transcends

Psychologist Ken Wilber in *Grace and Grit* writes with passion about the necessity of art in our lives. "Schopenhauer had a theory of art that said, in effect: bad art copies, good art creates, great art transcends. And by 'transcends,' he meant 'transcends the subject and object duality'."

What all great art has in common, he says, is this ability to pull the viewer out of himself right into the art, so completely, that at least for a few moments our separate self seems to disappear, and we experience a sort of *timeless awareness.*

No matter what the subject matter, great art in this way transcends the everyday perception, introducing the beholder to the mystical. "I never believed art had that power until I saw a van Gogh. It was simply stunning. Take your breath away, take your self away, all at once."

Arthur Schopenhauer (1788-1860) not only championed the value of art to the soul of a society, but of how necessary genius was in order to bring about the best of it. Art alleviates the ills of life, he said, by showing us *the eternal essence in what is otherwise but a passing moment.*

This eternity in the everyday is the food our souls crave. Which is why a great work of art is one that can convey through a single figure or scene some essential and universal quality of humankind.

To be fully creative then we must, like an accomplished artist, re-acquaint ourselves with those inner longings that smolder deep inside. Switch to the right side of the brain. Become passionate about what we do. The artist within whispers to be set free.

Su Dongpo (1036-1101), the great Chinese poet, long ago wrote about the role of perception in the creative process, of the depth of perception required, and of the necessity of acting upon it swiftly. "Before you can paint a bamboo, the bamboo must have grown deep inside you. It is then that, brush in hand gazing intently, you will see the vision rise up before you. Capture the vision at once by the strokes of your brush, for it may vanish as suddenly as a hare at the approach of the hunter.

11

THE TRUE ARTIST

German novelist, Thomas Mann, spoke of art as "the spirit in matter, the natural instinct toward humanization." In *Zen and the Art of Making a Living* Laurence Boldt adds, "The understanding is that the *impulse to humanity*, the movement 'toward the spiritualization of life' is the origin of art, the progenitor of all that is noble in the creative arts."

Noble indeed, and egalitarian. Art is in everyone, as intuition is in everyone. And creativity is our birthright. Art is simply a natural expression of who we are as human beings. When we allow our creativity to be stifled, we sell out our humanity.

"In many traditional cultures," Boldt reminds us, "it was expected that all people were, or ought to be, artists. (We can see remnants of such a culture today in Bali.) In regaining our naturalness, we regain our humanity and our art."

In *The Power of Myth* Joseph Campbell describes the real artist as the one who can portray what Joyce called the 'radiance' of all things, a way of showing its inner truth.

James Joyce, author of *A Portrait of the Artist as a Young Man*, explained that when we are truly affected by a work of art our reaction is not to want to go out and buy it, to in some way want to possess the object, but merely to wish to behold it. And while beholding we are entranced. A resonance is struck within. "You experience a radiance. You are held in aesthetic arrest. That is the epiphany."

The *radiance* of a work of art is what's responsible for stopping us in our tracks, for the arresting of time, where we are as if by magic pulled into the canvas or music or writing, to be a part of the creation. And there we linger, astonished and joyous, for the experience fashioned by the artist has struck a knowing and soulful response deep within.

Transcendent Bliss of the Mystics

The ultimate pleasure and benefit derived from art is the surreal sense of the mind being arrested. That's where we lose ourselves in art. It's in this deep state of contemplation, as Schopenhauer noted, that great art switches off that sense of 'other.' As our consciousness merges with the art it is beholding, we lose all sense of ourselves "as a thing apart." This 'loss of self' is extremely pleasurable — echoing the transcendent bliss of the mystics."

Transcendent bliss. Radiant epiphanies. Arresting time. It seems we have come a very long way in tracing the course of libido energy through our being. From our reptilian sexual arousals that draw the sexes together (so low on the evolutionary scale), to the mystical highs that help us transcend our mere conscious awareness, we find our creative/sexual energy is an effusive cornucopia of unexpected delights.

It short, we have to pay acute attention to a far more complex creature than we ever imagined ourselves to be. To the inputs from all three levels of our brain. To the differing agendas of the right and left hemispheres. To the ways in which we use our five senses to perceive the world around us, especially the inner landscapes of those people within it. To what we wish for, and how we intend and will things to happen. To waking up to inspirations and intuitions. To improving our techniques and embracing our inventions. To choosing our vocabulary with greater precision, leading to an ever mushrooming field of perception.

Mind tools and creativity; we have both in virtually limitless abundance, yet we stare out the same old window of our personal lighthouse as though it were all the cosmos had to offer. Still, it's not a conscious choice, but one that we effortlessly slide into because it's the rut our human condition has conveniently prepared for us.

There is great survival wisdom for our species in this rut. Can we just imagine the sheer panic and chaos in society if we were all at the same time at our feverish creative best, all the time?

Passing Through the Doors of Perception

The difference between our everyday living and living in those ecstatic moments, as Campbell explained about getting in touch with this level of creativity, is like the difference between being inside the Garden of Eden and outside. What we learn here is to conceive of our life as being deeper and encompassing a much greater scope than the usual narrow breadth of our daily focus, this 'fractional inkling' of what we can be. Somewhere deep inside we long to live at these depths.

A fractional inkling? Inside the Garden? Makes me want to run out and buy some paints. Or pick up that old guitar again. Are his words casting some magical spell on me, or is there something deep inside me hearing itself being addressed, and called to action? The work of shamans, mystics and artists are but variations on the same theme. Their canvas is a mirror which they hold up to our soul, revealing what has all along been buried deep within.

Silence the internal dialogue. Listen to the faint whispers of inspiration. Pass through the doors of perception. Open up.

In the end, to be human is to create. It's the most precious expression of who we are, the most truly spiritual and sacred offering we bestow on one another. In breathing in the essence of a fine work of art, Boldt says, we can't help but feel that we have received a precious gift. "A conscious spirit has moved over this form, in turn evoking the spirit of the beholder."

The greatest creation of our lives is in fact the very sculpting of our day-to-day existence. Its vocabulary is the degree of consciousness we bring to living on a daily basis, and accepting with passion that a part of living is aging, and the more successfully we age the more we have to contribute to the tapestry of life.

The art of living is a course whose final exam is taken bit by bit, every day.

VIII

THE AGING FOUNTAIN OF YOUTH

Living longer is one thing. Enjoying in optimum health and vitality the bonus years that modern science has bestowed upon us is quite another.

What does it mean to get the most out of every stage of life, and the years to be added to our lives by thumbing our nose with impunity at the plea to 'act your age?' What about the importance of distinguishing psychological age from chronological age and biological age?

Stepping gingerly through a smorgasbord of pills and supplements, mind-body connections, and willful intents to track down the secrets of longevity.

Imbibing the elixir known as a 'passion for life':

- Sam Keen
- Jane Goodall
- Stephen Covey
- Larry Dossey
- Stephen Levine
- Ken Wilber
- Hippocrates
- Anita Roddick
- Paul McCartney

1

THE POWER OF LIVING PASSIONATELY

et's get old! Let's age. Heaven knows we've all been too long obsessed with youth. Wrinkles are groovy. Shiny heads are the new standard of brilliance. Memories are piling up even faster than old scrapbooks. The clock is tick tick ticking away, and it's a good thing. The only way to stop aging — is to die.

Pithy. Ironic. The generation once dedicated to eternal youth — 'don't trust anyone over 30!' — will soon be declaring the 'silver standard of beauty.' Some 76 million boomers have zealously re-defined each decade of their existence. So we shouldn't be surprised when they start identifying their fifties and sixties as the age of wisdom, as a time of seasoned creativity and spiritual vision, as the blossoming of a mature perspective. In short, as the best of all times.

The first thing the baby boomers had to deal with as they grew up in the '60s and '70s was sexual freedom, and the body beautiful. Then along came a wave of mystical contortions and yogic-like practices to lend variety to the repertoire, and strengthen their performance. Next appeared a long succession of health and nutrient-conscious diets, combined with a myriad of aerobic and jogging and body building schemes — all designed to add stamina and suppleness to the ever-aging body personal. Spandex could do just so much.

So, as we skip through the opening years of this century it comes as no surprise that this massive number of aging souls is on the one hand declaring its dedication to overthrowing all of society's antiquated and largely negative ideas about aging and the elderly — while on the other hand working valiantly to discover ways to reverse the aging process, to live longer and prosper, and to tuck those eye-lines behind their ears. If not eternal youth, then perhaps the illusion of it.

"In most pre-modern cultures there was good news," Sam Keen states with tongue firmly planted in cheek. "Good news was people didn't have mid-life crises. Bad news was they died at mid life." And so most of us today will likely live twice, or even three times as long as the average citizen in our ancestors' time. It's important, however, to remember that single word 'average,' and not get carried away with some illusory personal accomplishment.

Medical scientists are fond of reminding us of how superlatively well we are doing in the longevity stakes. During the height of the Roman Empire, they tell us, life expectancy was a mere 28 years. And those were relatively good times. For parts of the Dark Ages that figure would be closer to the low twenties.

Even nearer to our own era, a hundred years ago, with all the advances of the Industrial Revolution, the average European or North American could look forward to no more than 48 to 50 years on this planet. Which makes it absolutely amazing that today's life expectancy is nudging the 80-year mark, and in another fifty years is predicted to push 95-100.

And so, as I heard one woman declare recently upon turning 55, "Wow, I would be ancient if I lived back then." Actually, no. (Unless of course she was alive back 'then' and still living today.)

The Frontiers of Longevity

Socrates was 71 and Plato 80 when they died some 2,400 years ago, and they weren't particularly famous for their longevity. Tolstoy was of a similar age and George Bernard Shaw lived to 94, both contributing significant works well into their final years. As did Leonardo da Vinci and Michelangelo during the Renaissance.

When Europeans first arrived in the jungles of South America in the middle 1500s they were surprised to find that these 'primitive' naked inhabitants of Eden were in far better shape than they were. Jean de Lery, in his Voyage in Brazil (1578), reported that it wasn't uncommon for the local Tupi Indians to live to a hundred years, never growing whitened hair.

It's not that the world hasn't known octogenarians from various cultures throughout the past few millennia. It's simply a matter of probability. Given the number of lethal diseases and plagues and natural disasters and mass slaughters and famine and infant mortality and poor hygienic conditions and lack of refrigeration for food storage and the non existence of life-saving drugs and advanced surgical procedures — how long a life would an odds maker put on one of us if we were born in 250 BC, as opposed to AD 1950?

My grandfather of the covered-wagon, though born a dozen years before the turn of the last century, lived to be eighty, and five of his siblings made it into their nineties. Still they had an equal number of brothers and sisters who succumbed in infancy to mysterious viruses of one sort or another. It seems if your immune system was tough enough to get you through childhood, you were destined for the long haul — as long a life, in fact, as any of us can hope for today.

Kudos to medical science. Its accomplishments over a very short span of time have been nothing short of phenomenal. They are as real as penicillin and by-pass surgery, and plummeting infant mortality rates throughout the world. Unfortunately, the real story often gets lost in the mix of mis-information. Contrary to the beliefs of the erroneous 55 year old woman above, it's not that old age is reaching to levels two and three times what it used to be, but that so many more of us today are actually getting to reach old age.

2

DETERMINING OUR AGE

"Not only are people living longer," Deepak Chopra, medical doctor and author of *Ageless Body, Timeless Mind*, says of our current burgeoning elderly population, "but they have more stamina, more quality of life, more mental alertness, more vitality than people at similar ages had a generation ago."

In researching the scientific studies he found that virtually all the biological markers of aging — blood pressure, bone density, fat content, cholesterol, muscle mass, sex hormones, sugar tolerance, vision, hearing, etc. — are actually reversible. At Tufts University they found that "if you took people between the ages of 84 and 96 and introduced them to a physical conditioning program — physical exercise, weight training, aerobic exercise, yoga, etc. — you could actually reverse all the bio-markers of aging."

Antioxidants, and a change in diet have also shown promise in the reversal process. And meditation. "If people have been practicing meditation consistently for five years or more, their biological age is about twelve years younger than the chronological age of their peers."

Chronological age. Just one of three ways we have of looking at how old we are. So if we don't like what the numbers say, maybe we should switch to another perspective. Chronological age is the one based on our date of birth; what the calendar says. Not much we can do about it, other than applying ink eradicator to our birth certificate. Next is our psychological age — how old we feel we are, or how young at heart we are, despite the number of candles on our fiftieth birthday cake.

Lastly, is our biological age, which is what all those biomarkers mentioned above are trying to determine. It's these signs of biological aging which Chopra and others claim can not only be slowed down, so that our body stays intact for a much longer period of time, but that many of the existent signs of deterioration can even be reversed.

3

PSYCHOLOGICAL OUTLOOK

Attitude is everything. Just ask any teenager. They don't walk down the street. They swagger. They strut. They seize possession of the space around them...well, at least the majority do. Their body is their calling card. It shouts loud and clear to the world who they are and how they want to be seen.

Our attitude toward aging — our dread or delight with the changing image in the mirror — is likewise shouted to the world as we strut or slouch through the joys of aging. "If you think that aging is synonymous with decay and decrepitude, then that's what'll happen," Chopra cautions. "On the other hand, if you think aging is glamorous, then you'll have a different expression of aging."

Now wouldn't that be a sight; middle-aged people actually embracing the glamour of aging. Much like children and adolescents have always done, itching at the bit to taste those 'older' years. What excitement and anticipation for the future. "I can't wait 'til I'm 18...when I get to 21!" Imagine the same anticipation about turning 45...64! So why do so many people see nothing but decay and gloom in the dawns yet to come?

We tend to glorify a ten to twelve year period in life, from early twenties to mid thirties according to Thomas Moore, and everything else is felt with a certain degree of discomfort. We leap from a couple of decades of wishing we were older, to endless decades of wishing we were younger, with only a brief golden age in the middle. But even that golden age, while we're living it, doesn't seem as great as it's later cracked up to be.

The problem once again comes down to attitude. Our cultural attitude. That it's bad to get old. That somehow we shouldn't age, although this is precisely what we do, indeed must do, from the very moment we are born. So we idolize the 'concept' of youth; that it's the only stage that counts, and the further we retreat from it, the rosier we paint how wonderful it was.

Of course this dread of putting on the years wasn't always so intense, nor in all cultures of the world; but then, the more life expectancy escalates, the more decades more of us have to complain about losing our so-called prime years. Still, I can't imagine people anywhere actually relishing the thought of losing their youthful vitality, trim figure, and effortlessly procured health. It's a universal hallmark of being young that we believe our youth will last forever. And thus we set ourselves up for the inevitable letdown, when we survive it.

So what do we survivors have to show for our years? Quite a lot, actually. It's called experience — the one thing that youth cannot procure, trade for, steal, or buy at any price.

In ancient times aging was seen as an achievement of some importance. It was the beginning of our personal age of wisdom. Our particular tribe bestowed upon us appropriate status, a status earned by the growing number of our decades of being buffeted by the rigors of life.

Nothing teaches like experience. Indeed, it's the only currency that can purchase wisdom.

4

ACTING YOUR AGE

Just adding years, however, is no guarantee that we'll have anything of value to contribute to our tribe or family. Of course it's easy to romanticize the myths surrounding our wisdom years, as though everyone is suddenly going to turn into this wise old sage, but as Moore says, "they're not going to." Like certain wines, some people just don't improve with age. Which is to say that experience can go a long way to helping us approach wisdom, but without a willingness to grow and learn, all we will actually achieve is old age.

In essence, age is a very fluid commodity. "You can have an 80 year old mentality when you're 20," Moore says of the age at which we are living. And vice versa. This is attitude writ large, the age at which we choose to live. For the most part, with certain physical limitations, "there's no reason why we can't do at 80 what we did at 40 or 20. There's no reason." Or as the old saying had it, people don't grow old; when they stop growing, they become old.

When Sam Keen was 62 he was feeling very old. After a lifetime spent in the pursuit of theological and philosophical truths, a degree from Harvard Divinity and a doctorate from Princeton, years as a consulting editor for Psychology Today and the author of a half dozen best selling books on spiritual issues and personal mythology, he felt that he had stopped growing. It was a time when he felt he was starting to close down, starting to think that he was getting old, that the grand old age of 62 was a time to start the preparations for old age.

Then one day on television he saw something about a group called the San Francisco School of Circus Arts, and he felt compelled to go down and check it out. One thing led to another, and before he knew it he was flying the trapeze. Five years later he opened his own trapeze school where he leads a program of helping abused women's groups, and kids who are trying to get off street drugs.

"My spirit wasn't ready to get old," he says now in his very active seventies. It didn't like the idea, so the trapeze became his way of reinventing himself, or uncovering an enthusiasm that he hadn't quite recognized through the years, and suddenly it infected his whole life. "So I now do things physically that I literally could not have done when I was 30, and I love it."

Jane Goodall, who was born in 1934, travels virtually non-stop for ten months of the year, in and out of airplanes and hotels and lecture halls, tirelessly and selflessly raising money for the protection of wildlife, and for the ecology and the environment in general. A grueling schedule that would exhaust most people at half her age. "I do not think about aging," she says of her current existence, which is a far cry from her leisurely years in the Gombe rain forest with chimpanzees. "I don't feel any older than I ever have...well, except as a baby of course."

For people like Goodall aging is something that occurs surreptitiously while they quietly get on with their life. And sometimes the more active stage just happens to come later than sooner. And with greater passion. When asked about it a number of years ago she said that she was doing at 66 what she could not have done at 36. "I mean I know I couldn't have kept up a schedule like this. There's no way."

Which is to say that the surest way to grow old fast is to sit around worrying about growing old. To avoid senility, the experts tell us, never stop growing: Activate our bodies, our full range of emotions, and keep challenging ourselves intellectually. As Chopra advises, have the willingness to step into the unknown and embrace uncertainty. Don't be afraid of appearing foolish in the eyes of the less daring. Or as TS Eliot said, "don't tell me about your old men being wise. Tell me about the folly of the old."

And so people railed at Sam Keen for his high wire act. Why didn't he act his age? Or why didn't he act as old as they acted at that age? And why was he making them feel uncomfortable? "Well I am acting my age," he would say in response. Whether 67 or 77 he was going to continue acting the way he felt like acting, not according to someone else's preconceived notions about age appropriate behavior.

Moore has an interesting perspective on this whole idea of psychological age and getting old. As an example he points to the life of the great English poet John Keats. Here's a man who died at 26. "Now what was his mid-life? And what was his old age?" And does any of it matter as we look at his insightful works and how they move us still to this day?

5

CONSCIOUS LIVING

A way to mold our psychological outlook is to be more conscious of the way we live on a daily basis. Such at least is the popular wisdom of our times. For some this means being intensely in the moment — trying to be conscious of every breath, of every movement of our eyes, every morsel we eat, the sound of children in the street, traffic passing by, and on and on. Kind of like marching to a mad martinet who intones, 'Imagine this as the last day of your life; what are you going to do?'

What most of us would do is go bonkers and do all kinds of absurd and inane things which we would have very little conscious recollection of come the end of the day. Variations on the same if it were 'knowingly' our last month or last year. There's nothing sane or healthy about such a preposterous and intense approach to life.

On the other hand, living consciously can simply mean being more aware of how much of the time we are *un*conscious. As Keen advises, "to catch yourself consciously acting unconsciously." As in running into some stranger at the supermarket and making a snappy or rude remark. To catch ourselves before we reply on automatic pilot, and choose consciously how we wish to respond to this minor altercation. Whether our choice then is to be rude or to be kind, at least it brought our awareness into the moment, we thought about it, and our choice was a conscious one. This is called living consciously.

In between all the billions of neural connections in our brain, as we saw earlier, is a synaptic gap. A chasm which must be leapt before a stimulus can result in a response. Stephen Covey, author of the remarkably influential *The 7 Habits of Highly Effective People,* described this gap as the metaphorical birthplace of our free will.

"Between stimulus and response is a space. In that space lies your power and freedom to choose your response. In those choices lies your happiness and your growth." As such, he concludes, "we're not (solely) a product of our genes, of our environment, of our upbringing, of the weather, of the circumstances, of our boss, of our spouse." We are in short the product of our responses, whether conscious or unconscious. Despite all the influences on us, moral codes and social responsibilities and family obligations, in the final analysis we have only ourselves to look to. Living consciously is very much a matter of pulling back that finger we accusingly point at others, and taking personal responsibility for who and what we are.

6

CONSCIOUS AGING

If conscious living means being less unconscious of our choices and taking greater responsibility for our responses, then conscious aging means taking this daily practice and applying it to our lifetime as a whole. That is, we become more aware of the fact that we're passing through various 'ages' or stages in our lives, yet in no way allow this recognition to determine how we will act or how we will envisage ourselves. We don't have to 'act our age' nor buy into the media's depiction of our age, no matter which age it may be. Especially not when that age is seen as a disease to be remedied.

Moore, while in his sixties, reported the experience of getting older as a great comfort, much the same feeling he found among his many friends of a like age. It seems that getting older has advantages which younger souls would envy if they ever paused long enough in their own anxiety to think about it. Age brings a certain comfort zone with it.

A feeling of gratitude arises, even, at being freed from worries about the future course of an uncharted life, about trying to become somebody of value, about career, and spouse and children yet to come. "The older we get the more comfortable we can be with who we are and what has developed," Moore says. We can just let things happen.

Novelist and acute social observer Erica Jong found a similar paradoxical joie de vivre after breaching that mid-life milestone known as the big five-oh. "I feel younger now than I did when I was writing *Fear of Flying*. Much younger." Not to mention feeling much more in control of her life now. But the control has little to do with what she sees in the mirror. Wrinkles and weathering have a way of making most of us wish we could turn back the clock at least in that regard, say to age thirty. "I wish I could. But I wouldn't give up what I know."

Women in particular, due to biological changes — menopause — soon come to note the surprising and refreshing benefits brought on by this new stage of life. "Once she is no longer confined to the culture's definition of woman as a primarily sexual object and breeder," Gail Sheehy writes in *The Silent Passage*, "a full unity of her feminine and masculine sides is possible. As she moves beyond gender definition, she gains new license to speak her mind and initiate action."

Sheehy points to new scientific findings that show that as women grow older they psychologically gain greater mastery over their abilities, and that this continues right on through their 60s and 70s, and perhaps beyond. Strangely we rarely hear in the media about these positive findings — only the aches and pains that lie in wait for us.

Still, as Joan Borysenko, medical researcher and pioneer in the mind/body field says, we shouldn't try to kid ourselves about it; that of course there are certain physical negatives to aging. But these are more than made up for by the gains. And in order to enjoy the gains it's important to have the right attitude. "When you're happy to be aging," the author of *Minding the Body, Mending the Mind* says, "when you recognize the gifts of aging, then your whole body is going to flourish."

The Secret of Living to 100

Conscious living and conscious aging kind of reminds me of the way Socrates thumbed his nose at the conventions of his time. When Socrates said that the unexamined life wasn't worth living he meant we should always question the 'common sense' assumptions of our society; not let ourselves be cajoled by the so-called experts into believing something simply because they say so. Nor into nodding agreement because the majority of people around us are doing so. Nor because it has always been accepted as 'common sense.'

Moore advises that the best way to keep our youthfulness, our vitality and passion for life is to disbelieve the society around us, question everything, much like we did in our youth. "I think it's awfully important to be a rebel to the society you're in, even if it's a good place."

What could be a more conscious way of aging — putting a giddy bounce into our step — than questioning at every turn what is meant by 'acting your age' at fifty, or sixty...or ninety, or one hundred?

Leonard Poon, of the Georgia Centenarian Study, upon being asked what if any traits did those over one hundred years old have in common, stated simply, "They want to have their way. They would not take your word for anything — they want to find out for themselves. And they're very protective of themselves." Talk about questioning everything — Socrates' true heirs.

7

MINDING THE BODY

Which brings us full circle to the psychological impact on the body physical. That is, not only can we feel and act almost any age we choose to; our physical body itself reacts in harmony to our psychological outlook. The much ballyhooed mind-body connection.

This connection is hardly mysterious to us. When two people fall in love we immediately see its dramatic effects. Even if they're in their eighties, the transformation is visible almost overnight. "They become real young again," O'Donohue recalls with the delight of a poet describing a first spring blossom. "And their eyes and their face and the texture of their skin takes on a new glow. It's a full chemical awakening in a way."

So this tremendous impact our emotions and thinking can have on our physical body is not some new revelation. But this type of impact is usually the result of love or grief or depression — things we don't normally program into our lives; they more or less just happen, the result of many intertwined factors.

Is it possible, though, to exercise a similar impact through our willful intentions?

Since attitude is so important, and since our perceptions, as we saw earlier, are so instrumental in creating our reality, then the answer should be a resounding yes. The only question is, to what extent?

For most people the only time they become acutely aware of their body, and thus their conscious influence on it, is when something goes wrong with it. They catch some passing bug, or break a bone, or become the never-ending battleground of a cancer or heart disease. At first they try to shoo it away by the magic of denial — 'It's not really broken, just a sprain.' 'It's indigestion, something I ate.' — then they rush off to the nearest hospital or drug store for lethal assistance.

Medicines are a wonder, a gift from thousands of years of work by midwives and shamans and tribal healers, and the last one hundred years of intensive medical research. Just witness what they've done for our average life span, or getting us back to work in three days instead of many weeks. But even the medical profession admits it doesn't know the real efficacy of most of its medications. A little matter called the placebo effect.

Take three hundred people diagnosed with the same stomach ailment. The first hundred you send home without treatment — presumably those without sufficient medical coverage (just kidding). The second hundred you give a month's supply of drug 'X', the latest and most effective combatant in this particular war zone. The final hundred get a placebo, an identical looking supply of drugs, except that these pills are filled with nothing but a harmless powdery sugar.

A month later all three hundred are re-examined. Roughly 75% of those on the 'X' drug have no further symptoms. Of those on the powdery sugar roughly 50% are symptom free. And perhaps 15% of the treatment-free are now cured; whatever it was simply went away on its own. So what caused the difference between the 50% and the 15%, since neither received any miracle drug?

The obvious answer is that those receiving the placebo actually believed they were taking a powerful drug that would cure them. Their belief convinced their body, and their body reacted accordingly, in effect curing itself. Attitude and expectations can indeed have profound effects on our body.

It's this very belief system which lies at the root of various shamanic and voodoo cures, (and curses). No surprise then that the spells work only on those who are card-carrying believers in the cult.

The Mind-Body Connection in Action

Both of the above, however, involve an outside party having to convince us, in order for us to convince our bodies, before we can mend ourselves. So what does it take for us to eliminate the middleman? Why can't we just swallow a piece of bread and say, 'Okay, stomach, this is drug 'X', a powerful ally to help us do battle. Now I want to see some improvement by the end of the day.'

This is the mind-body connection in its most straightforward format. If I feel miserable, depressed, worthless, it won't be long before my body exhibits this state in some physical disease. The same if I'm constantly stressed or overworked. Yet I am quite capable of changing my attitude, my expectations, my moods, and vanquishing the above diseases. The trickier part is to do battle with those particular ailments that weren't brought on by any attitude of mine.

Say, for sake of argument, I'm just one of the happiest people you'll ever meet. Skipping along through life, not an enemy, not a complaint, a loving caring family. And one day the doctor calls to tell me that if I don't come in for multiple bypass surgery, I'll never blow out another birthday candle. What did I do wrong?

Nothing, perhaps. My valve congestion certainly doesn't seem to be a result of my attitude or psychological outlook. But then there is that matter of diet; what I have eaten, and over-eaten. I am after all a member of the generation which bestowed upon an unsuspecting world the precious gift of fast food — hot, sweet, sticky sugar, and ever-so-irresistible fat. And unlike certain Presidential candidates, I have not been so virginly pure in my more than half a century that I did not sample the wicked charms of alcohol and smoke and certain drugs that are not likely to be found at the pharmacy.

But all of these can and have been mostly rectified. So how do I clear the congestion without submitting to the surgeon's scalpel?

Guided imagery is a mind-body technique which has gained a certain respect in healing circles, and is now being used in hospitals in several parts of the world. Yet no one can say exactly how it works, or when it will work. It's done by meditating on the disease we have and on our immune system, and if we're doing this in conjunction with drugs, then meditating as well on the medication as it courses through our body. The idea is that if in our mind's eye we can guide these microorganisms to do a thorough job, then we will have a much better chance of healing.

Of course this technique is used mainly as an adjunct to conventional therapy and, not having little shovels at its disposal, would be less likely to clear my hypothetically clogged valves all on its own. There are many, however, who beg to differ. They claim that no matter what the condition, from severest disease to common cold, if we have proper control of our mind we can then use it to alter our body in ways we can scarce believe. And it includes making us look decades younger — unless of course we're only a few decades old to begin with.

The logic is straightforward enough. If we can learn to drastically slow down our heart beat or alter our rate of metabolism simply by telling these normally autonomic systems to do so — and certain people can as has been shown in controlled experiments — then why shouldn't we be able to scare away unwanted viruses, and more rapidly heal open wounds, or iron out the wrinkles in our forehead.

If we do possess such ability — and there is no shortage of 'healers' whose claims go well beyond the modest examples above — it isn't exactly the easiest thing in the world to prove. Which doesn't mean that it doesn't exist, just that whenever it's put under scientific scrutiny it rarely performs up to expectations. But then again, that could simply be another case of the irony of paradoxical intent.

8

PRAYING TO CHANGE OUR LIFE

This attempt at mind over matter, certain psychologists have pointed out, is very similar to what people do when they pray.

Prayer, depending on our spiritual outlook, is either a direct solicitation of God to change something in our life; or is a means of contacting the unconscious part of our mind to work towards this same change. Either way we are in effect willing something to happen, whether it be to cure a deadly disease or to give us a fairer complexion.

Gregg Jacobs, assistant professor of psychiatry at Harvard Medical School, has published several studies on the way brain waves change during prayer and meditation, especially Theta waves which tend to put a stop to other brain activity. "Prayer is the modern brain's means by which we can connect to more powerful ancestral states of consciousness," he says of these states which are a natural part of normal brain activity.

In studies with Buddhists meditating and Franciscan nuns praying, Andrew Newberg, of the University of Pennsylvania, has discovered a small area at the back of the brain that somehow lets us know where our body ends and the rest of the world begins. Moreover, with intense prayer this can lead to a dissolving of the boundary between ourselves and the rest of existence — what the mystics have always called being one with God or one with the cosmos.

"It creates a blurring of the self-other relationship," Newberg says. "If they go far enough, they have a complete dissolving of the self, a sense of union, a sense of infinite spacelessness." Could this dissolving of the separation between self and others extend the boundaries of our mind-body connection?

In his book, *Healing Words: The Power of Prayer and the Practice of Medicine*, medical doctor Larry Dossey writes that he was amazed to find that there are literally hundreds of studies, from diverse cultures, which prove that this activity called prayer actually works. Not only does it work when we pray for ourselves — the obvious mind-body connection — but it even works when we pray for someone else.

"Remarkably the effects of prayer did not depend on whether the praying person was in the presence of the organism being prayed for," Dossey writes, "or whether he or she was far away." He says organism because apparently the studies were also performed on many non-human varieties of life, including bacteria and cancer cells, moth larvae, mice and new-born chickens. Not only did the effects of prayer register over great distances (shades of tapping into a universal unconscious), but they even worked when the people being prayed for didn't know they were being prayed for — thus eliminating the placebo effect. But then this should have been self evident from the experiments on the moth larvae and bacteria.

In his own practice Dossey has long used prayers for his patients as a kind of bonus on top of his medical expertise. But always with a clear eye on the paradox of intent. "Never once did I pray for specific outcomes — for cancers to go away, for heart attacks to be healed, for diabetes to vanish. 'May the best possible outcome prevail' was the strategy I preferred, not specifying what 'best' meant."

Does prayer work, then? It's hard to say. Certainly it seems to work for some people some of the time; but other times not at all. The same applies to the process of guided imagery, as well as to having a bright attitude and the most positive expectations. Whatever the catalyst is in giving the conscious mind authority over the body, we simply don't know what it is. It's unfortunately still an unsolved mystery. After all, if we managed to solve it there would be little further need of the medical profession, or for magical formulas or maps to the fountain of youth.

9

MIND OVER GUILT

No matter how much our conscious mind eventually learns to wield power over our body, it still will never control the grand sweep of our lives as a whole. That is, there is a real world out there and we are a part of it. Things happen all the time that are beyond our control, and always will be beyond our control, no matter how adept we get at directing our mind.

When Sam Keen speaks of creating our own lives and the world around us, and says that we can either do it well or poorly, consciously or unconsciously, he's talking about the same thing John O'Donohue referred to as our eyes of perception, the kind of eyes with which we look out at the world, and our chosen responses to what we see. Depending on the type of response, the world will react accordingly.

This doesn't mean we can stop an accident from happening, nor conversely, that if we happen to come down with some terminal disease, that it's our fault, that we caused it to happen — this all aside from the moralists who only too happily insist it's our punishment for something we did; and if we can't find anything appropriate to account for it in this lifetime, then it's a carryover punishment from some previous existence (talk about hedging their bets).

"You have to watch the judging mind," Ondrea Levine warns. The author, along with her husband Stephen Levine, of *Who Dies?*, is herself a two-time survivor of life-threatening cancers. "The mind will say, 'oh maybe I wasn't such a good person, or maybe if I was kinder I wouldn't have got this disease'." But when we look around at people we know well, we realize we're not the only ones who were *not deserving* of this suffering. "We've both known the kindest, most wonderful people that have had many diseases, so I don't believe it has anything to do with your not being a nice person."

"In my opinion, these beliefs — particularly the belief that you create your own reality — are level two beliefs," Ken Wilber writes in *Grace and Grit*, an intimate journal of his wife's losing battle against recurrent cancer. "They have all the hallmarks of the infantile and magical worldview ... I believe the hyperindividualistic culture in America, which reached its zenith in the 'me decade,' fostered regression to magical and narcissistic levels."

As If Disease Weren't Enough

What is most tragic is all those who, hearing of the wonders of the mind-body connection, how others have successfully employed prayer and guided meditation and powers of their mind to cure themselves, find that they are so lacking in being able to create any similar medical miracles, that they must be failures as people, or unworthy of God's grace. They fall into severe depression and feelings of profound guilt, not because they are dying of some horrid disease, but because they can't seem to make it stop. And there are only too many 'experts' eager to further convince them of their inadequacy. As if the disease itself weren't hell enough to endure.

Wilber is particularly angered by a national network of callous entrepreneurs whose leaders give seminars on how we can create our own reality, and teach workshops where we are informed unequivocally that cancer is the result of resentment, and poverty and oppression are states we brought upon ourselves.

Dangerous people. Dangerous agenda. When we're at our most vulnerable, circling birds of a predatory nature can be counted on to pay us a timely visit. Only problem is the world they 'choose' to erect around us is rarely one of compassion.

10

THE FOUNTAIN OF YOUTH

The Ancient Greeks were no less intrigued by the possibility of a longer life than we are today, especially understandable considering their average lifespan often dipped below twenty years. They were fond of the story of Eos and Tithonus. Tithonus was a handsome prince with whom the goddess Eos fell in love. But it was forbidden for one of her rank to marry a mere mortal, so she begged Zeus to make her young prince immortal. Zeus felt compassion for the goddess of dawn, and declared that her Tithonus would live eternally.

Sounds great at first, except that Eos forgot to ask that her lover also remain eternally young. Far from an eternity of bliss, the fate of Tithonus was to age forever. After many years of agonizing, and being thoroughly abandoned by his lover, he eventually shriveled up to something the size of a pea, totally unseen and ignored — yet as much as he wanted to, he could not die. A cautionary tale for anyone not considering the quality of those added years they so dearly crave.

Longer life is meaningless, even frightening, if we don't first find a way to solve the aches and pains that go hand in hand with getting older. And who says there is any reasonable hope of living beyond the apparent 120-year limit? All the hype about reaching 150 or even 200 years in the foreseeable future is just that. As far as the wonders of medical science go, significant strides have been made in helping more of us enjoy our lifetime in greater ease and comfort, but nothing at all in extending the limits of how long that can be. The fountain of youth it seems will not help us live longer, but it may help us live with a youthful spring in our step for a longer span in that life.

What everyone wants to know, of course, is can the fountain of youth be found in a pill? Can it be packaged and sold across the counter? A vitamin supplement, perhaps, or a magic bullet to mend our tired cells? "That is the Holy Grail," Robin Marantz Henig writes in *Scientific American: The Quest To Beat Aging*. "It has driven hucksters and con men for centuries, and it is the goal of many reputable researchers today."

Telomere Therapy, Antioxidants, Anti-aging Hormones and a host of drugs and creams are vigorously promoted as miracle antidotes to the unwanted signs of aging. And for the most part baby boomers are lining up to try them out. After all, this is the generation raised on drugs, from the polio Salk vaccine and miracle drugs of the 50s, through the street drug cultures of the 60s and 70s. When all else fails, the Beatles song assured, "I get by with a little help from my friends."

Few are waiting for final scientific imprimatur because the problem with aging is that it waits for no one.

Among the leading candidates for the fountain of youth:

Antioxidants (or Rust Protection). Inside the mitochondria of cells, normal metabolism produces unstable oxygen molecules known as free radicals. These molecules ricochet around the cells, damaging DNA and other structures. A kind of rusting away from within. The theory is that if antioxidants, like beta-carotene, can scoop up most of the free radicals before they do damage, then there would be far less incidents of cancer, heart disease and other age-related illnesses. The aging process itself would be slowed.

Unfortunately, as Henig points out, recent studies involving beta-carotene "have shown that this powerful antioxidant not only fails to slow aging or increase longevity but can even be bad for your health." As in those in a controlled study of smokers who regularly ingested beta-carotene, and ended up with a higher rate of lung cancer. Still there are other encouraging studies which indicate that antioxidants are helpful in battling certain kinds of cancer.

The fountain of youth, however, is not so cheaply purchased. "Everybody is talking about popping antioxidant vitamins," observes molecular biologist John Phillips of the University of Guelph. "The evidence is strong that taking moderate amounts of vitamin C and E is not harmful, but the evidence that it's actually useful for delaying aging is very thin." At the very least, nutritionists encourage, instead of supplements, try popping the real thing; like strawberries, blueberries, spinach, and red apples. If not a longer life then at least a tastier one.

Melatonin. This proven natural antidote to insomnia is now being touted as a major stress reducer, and as a primary anticancer agent.

It is also claimed to protect against Alzheimer's, schizophrenia, epilepsy, diabetes, cataracts, depression and sunburn, not to mention re-invigorating our sex life, and helping us to live twenty percent longer. Quite a leap for what was formerly just a sleeping pill. Once again, the test results are still not in on any and all of these abilities, although it does seem to lessen the side effects of everyday chemotherapy. So far the only down side is a groggy feeling from an overdose.

Anti-Aging Hormones. Human-Growth Hormone, DHEA, testosterone and estrogen have all been found to be at much lower levels in older people; in fact their production drops off dramatically as we age. So, the logic goes, if their levels are restored to what they were in youth, then the individual himself will be youthfully vibrant once again, and live considerably longer. As Henig states, this "newest and most scientific-sounding form of youth-restoring nostrums" has a slew of problems including increased risks of various cancers (breast, prostate), liver disorders, and masculinizing effects in women. "The jury is still out as to whether restoring hormones to a more youthful level bears any relation at all to making an older body look, feel or act like a younger one."

Telomere Therapy. Telomeres are DNA sequences that protect the tips of chromosomes the way a plastic cuff protects the ends of shoelaces. Each time a cell divides, the telomere gets shorter. After about 100 divisions the cell can no longer reproduce. The theory is to create virile rejuvenated cells by splicing new genetic material onto the ends of each chromosome. But is there any proof that bodily organs are weakening because of lost telomeres?

"It would be wonderful if there was such a simple molecular explanation of the aging process," says Robert Weinberg of the Massachusetts Institute of Technology's Whitehead Institute, "but biology doesn't necessarily oblige." Still, there may be some great hope for telomere therapy in the treatment of certain diseases, but the caution flags have to be heeded. What if the life of a cell could be extended indefinitely? "You have to confront the reality that you're creating a cell that is one step closer to cancer," Weinberg warns. "Cell mortality is an important impediment to cancer."

Stem Cells. The new kid on the block of longevity studies, stem cells may have a bright future in extending both the quality and quantity of life. Stem cells are at the root of all other types of cells; that is, they can turn themselves into whatever kind of cell needed — blood cell, nerve cell, muscle cell, etc. So whatever part of our body starts wearing away, these cells are enlisted to manufacture fresh new replacement cells. As we get older, however, the number of wearing out cells rapidly begin to outnumber the ability of the stem cells to replace them. And so we start the downward decline of moving slower, thinking slower, and generally not being able to perform as young as we like to think we are.

What we need is a tune-up. Such is the belief of researchers who say that with a regular dose of fresh stem cells, we could all live long and prosper in health. The major source of these stem cells, however, is aborted embryos (naturally or otherwise induced), and this raises major ethical concerns which are likely to create major legislative strife. More than this, there are enormous chasms between the theory, as attractive as it may sound, and its practice. We are dealing here with therapies that if they prove to be viable at all, lie far off in our distant future — certainly in the sense of being a youth-inducing elixir. On the positive side, it may be possible in the next decade or so to use stem cells to grow replacement organs for transplant — our very own private organ bank. Not quite the fountain of youth, but it can seem like one if we're waiting in line for years for a new liver.

Disease as a Healthy Business

None of which has anything to do with the current popularly held wisdom that 'aging is a disease.' Lili returned recently from an anti-aging/health convention in Chicago whose theme was that aging was a disease, and that the various health-related industries in attendance had just the pills and products to cure it.

I sifted through a mound of their magazines, flyers, and advertisements, each declaring in its own way that it had the secret to stop the aging process, to bestow eternal youth in an ever expanding life. Rejuvenating sprays, healing lasers, ancient 'secret' formulas — complete with scientific looking diagrams, medical sounding names, and the assurances of friendly looking 'eminent' physicians. There were so many 'medical wonders' afoot that, if they really performed as they claimed they did, it's a wonder anyone was still in business.

Aging, quite simply, is not a disease. Similarly, the end of life is a part of life, not a defeat. Aging is the very nature of life, the same life these experts claim they are trying to prolong. Aging is maturing. Aging is opening up to the possibilities of wisdom. Aging is the healthiest thing we can do; how in the world can they construe it as a disease?

The medical industry has much to answer to; but then, it has a long history in this area. For every genuine cure of a genuine ailment, there are at least as many bogus solutions, often to even non-existent problems. And we don't have to go back to the days of bloodletting or drilling holes in our skull for the relief of some malevolent pressure. Not long ago the medical profession made an illness out of PMS — creating a burgeoning cornucopia of on-going cures — and before that a similar fate befell menopause. And the beat goes on. As Anita Roddick (*Business as Unusual*) says, they've gone and constructed two more "extraordinary phony medical conditions. One is cellulite. The other is aging — both of which have enormous potential in terms of sales."

It is interesting that the most prominent line of the Hippocratic oath — from the teachings of Hippocrates, the 'father of modern medicine,' nearly two and a half thousand years ago — is "and never do harm to anyone".

Throughout the world today, in order for a man or woman to become a medical doctor, they must swear by this oath. It's unfortunate, then, that the medical profession itself doesn't have to live by a similar code of ethics as it elaborates and pontificates on the nature of diseases which do not in fact exist. How much harm do they do to millions of people who desperately try in vain to cure a situation which is simply the natural progression of a healthy life?

Tonics and Potions

Health food stores and pharmaceutical giants alike will continue to do a thriving business. According to *Scientific American*'s Henig, "New variations on old-fashioned snake oil — most of them dressed up in long scientific names ending in 'ine' and 'oid' — continue to gush through the pipeline. And, of course, they will keep on coming as long as people continue to look for the latest shortcut to the ever elusive fountain of youth."

Tonics and potions have long been a mainstay for treating those in need of a little pick-me-up along life's journey. Sometimes, though, the old ways are more ingenious and considerably less masked in technical jargon than our current variety.

Personally, I prefer the Ancient Greek recommendation that to regain their youthful vigor, older men should practice *gerokomy* — the time-honored therapy of sleeping with young virgins. I'm sure, with today's serious thrust to gender equality, the same could be arranged for older women. The only problem seems to be where to find a never-ending supply of virgins. (But then someone is bound to invent a potion to rectify the situation — perhaps a morning-after pill to restore, if not the flower, then at least the bloom of innocence.)

11

THE LAND OF MAKE-BELIEVE

When all else fails in trying to maintain a youthful look, we can always pretend. That is what children do, isn't it — pretend? They dress up in mom's and dad's clothes to look older; we in turn can squeeze into some version of the hip clothes that are all the rage with twenty and thirty-somethings. And get a sportier car. Hang out at singles bars.

It's amazing really the steps people will go to, especially during the so-called mid-life crisis, to convince themselves — though rarely do they succeed in convincing others — that they are really decades younger than they actually are. Face-lifts and tummy tucks, hair removal from unwanted places, wigs and toupees added where desired. Wardrobe makeovers. Painful medical injections.

For the most part we're not kidding anyone with our freshly folded and stapled new look, except perhaps ourselves. Especially if we have suffered great pain and anguish in the process; it must have been worth it, right?

Many of the women authorities in this area have taken an admirably compassionate approach; they may not condone the idea of resorting to the knife, but at the same time they understand that for some, their self-esteem is hanging in the balance. As Joan Borysenko says, "My own sense is, if there is something in your face or body that creates such grief for you, that you close down around it, that you lose your sense of being connected and related to the rest of life, so go fix it."

Anita Roddick's take on cosmetic surgery is more aesthetic than critical. "I'm not against it. If anybody feels that she wants to ...she's got my vote. I just think it looks bloody boring, because everybody looks as though they extruded out of this conveyor belt of the same look."

Perhaps what we need to see more of, and in a stronger public light, is famous women standing proudly in the face they have sculpted so painstakingly through the decades of their careers. Marilyn Monroe is quoted as having declared, not long before she died, that "I want to grow old without facelifts. They take the life out of a face, the character. I want to have the courage to be loyal to the face I've made."

Injections are a lot less drastic than surgery. Some of them even work. Anyone in need of puffy lips, or a wrinkle-free forehead? For a mere few hundred dollars we can have one injection of Botox. It's only a temporary measure, but Botox is said to be very effective in masking wrinkles — if we don't mind inserting botulism toxin under our skin.

"It's relatively simple from a consumer point of view," says dermatologist Alastair Carruthers, who along with his wife Jean Carruthers, both medical doctors, helped pioneer Botox. "You sit there and get a few needle pricks. There is no down time. You're back to work. The side effects are zero and it works with a capital W."

Vanishing Cream Miracles

Cosmetics, on the other hand, are a considerably less painful way to fake it. But we needn't get our hopes up. Just because a cream is touted by a ravishing movie star and costs two hundred dollars instead of a similar sized jar at five dollars, doesn't mean it's going to take away our years of wrinkling. The advertising industry may be exceedingly clever in what it does, but what it does has nothing to do with creating miracles.

"Incredible strategy to take the money from you," Roddick says of a world that is near and dear to her heart. As the founder of The Body Shop, she knows more than a thing or two about what a cream can and cannot do. "There is not one thing a cosmetic can do...I mean not beyond cleaning, polishing and protecting the skin and hair. End of story."

And yet, despite her endlessly preaching this reality at every chance she gets, she is stymied at people's unwillingness to accept what should be obvious to all. They can't wait to plunk down their money and try out the latest, and fully guaranteed, products that have as much chance of success as their moisturizing pads have of turning into gold. Nor is this limited to the area of anti-wrinkling creams. "There's no lotion or water and oil emulsion that you will put on your breasts and 'boosh,' they grow; or put on your thighs and 'woosh,' they diminish. It's a big lie."

Hope burns eternal, but the fountain of youth is still not to be found across the counter. However, a five-dollar container of moisturizing cream can genuinely soften up our tired, dry skin. Feels great too.

12

A PASSION FOR LIFE

A nunnery may be a strange place to go in search of the fountain of youth, but we are indeed thirsty, and tired of coming up dry. In *The Journal of Personality and Social Psychology* there is a report on an ongoing study of some six hundred and seventy nuns located in six different convents, from Minnesota to Connecticut. The main probe was to determine if there were signs in early life that pointed to dementia and Alzheimer's in old age. The study was made possible by the simple fact that all nuns had written personal essays on themselves upon entering the convent. Some six decades later these could now be compared with their current mental condition.

Not surprisingly, those with better linguistic and mental development — as seen in the sentences and complexity of ideas in their essays — were much less likely to develop mentally diminishing diseases in later life. What was not expected in *The Nun's Study* was finding that those with a positive emotional attitude to life, even at this early stage, lived significantly longer than their peers. As much as ten years longer.

In somewhat related studies, it has been shown that people rated as optimists were far more likely to be alive thirty years later than their pessimist peers. I guess in a way this lends credence to those who don't think brightly of the future. For them at least there isn't likely to be much of one.

On a more entertaining note, in the *Annals of Internal Medicine*, researcher Don Redelmeier reports that those who have received Hollywood's highest honor, the Oscar, live on average 3.9 years longer than actors who have not, including those who were nominated, but lost. This doesn't sound so astonishing until we consider that if all forms of cancer were eradicated right now, it would only add 3.5 years to our life span.

Redelmeier isn't offering any definitive answers to explain the phenomenon (only that winners might be better taken care of by others with a vested interest), but whatever it is must pack a whale of a wallop. Katharine Hepburn received four of these longevity doses (a record), and was still a voice to be reckoned with when she died in her 97th year. (Then again, Bob Hope, who died soon after his 100th birthday, toiled in over 60 films yet won zero Oscars, though he did receive four honorary Oscars for his humanitarian efforts. To offset these negatives he clothed his long life in self-deprecating humor: "I don't feel old. I don't generally feel anything until noon, then it's time for my nap.")

Roberto Begnini is another happy multiple recipient. Who can forget his exuberance upon winning two Academy Awards for *La Vita e Bella* (*Life is Beautiful*); his jumping up on the backs of chairs, dancing and laughing and singing for joy. What an exaltation! Pure unbridled happiness. The sheer thrill of being alive.

Recipe for the Fountain of Youth

But then folk wisdom has always held to the belief that 'laughter is the best medicine.' Well, it may not be able to compete with penicillin when dying of pneumonia, but it's one of the easiest prescriptions to fill and its benefits are immediately felt. I know from my own experience, when I had badly bruised ribs from a fall, my young children put some slapstick comedy videos on so they could keep me company in bed. Every time I laughed the pain shot across my chest. Yet we played the tapes over and over, as they laughed harder on seeing me laugh, as I laughed in unison with them. The cascading laughter made both time and pain disappear. Needless to say, I wasn't long confined to bed.

Perhaps the true ingredients of this magical fountain have been staring us in the face all along. We've seen the power of attitude and expectations, and how our perceptions shape so much of what our lives become.

The Fountain of Youth, like the heroic journey, is but a metaphor for what is to be found in the depths. And like the hero who has found some profound truth that he will share with the world, this life-giving spring is anchored in the finest qualities that set us apart as humans.

So, more than drugs and cosmetics, more than facelifts and injections, more than cell therapies and wonder diets, in the end it is our psychological age that proclaims us as biologically fit and appealing. Joy and laughter. A positive outlook. Meditation and relaxation in lieu of anxiety and stress. Soul food to feed our need for beauty. And art, to see eternity in the everyday. The simple ingredients to a cocktail called The Fountain of Youth.

In sum, deep inside we crave adventure, we crave new experiences. And we need to stop perceiving our every act and mishap with such grave seriousness.

Bernie Siegel (*How to Live Between Office Visits*) is a medical doctor who has spent much of his life working with dying cancer patients; he has written in many popular books about the wisdom these lives have instilled in him. He's what I would call an old-fashioned cracker barrel philosopher, a humorous one at that. He's all in favor of people taking care of their physical health, naturally enough, but not to the detriment of their soul.

"It doesn't mean you can't go out and have a steak, and lobster and an ice cream cone," he says of the strict seriousness with which most people envision a healthy diet. "Don't die without experiencing life. Don't do things to avoid dying. Don't love, meditate, exercise, eat vegetables to avoid dying. You *will* die, and you will be in group therapy in heaven — full of resentment. But do things to improve the quality of your life. And that's why we have a problem. That 80 % of people aren't thrilled with living."

The Magic Elixir

The thrill is gone — for those who have stopped growing. Vitality has deserted their once youthful outlook. Time to belly up to the fountain of youth and drink freely from that spring of life. As Ernest Hemingway noted, "It is more important to *live* than to outlive."

Hippocrates, that esteemed patriarch of the medical world, didn't head off in some mad search for a potion to bestow longer and healthier lives.

Around the same time that Socrates was inspiring Plato and others to live a meaningful life, Hippocrates came to the conclusion that the best way to keep sickness at bay is to practice moderation in all things — drink, food, sex, physical exertion. That is, we can enjoy Siegel's lobster and ice cream, and a bottle of wine to wash it all down; we just have to remember to tip the scale back on the other side. If we practice harmonious balance, Hippocrates assured, we will have our youthful long life, "a sound mind in a sound body."

Harmony. The balance of Yin and Yang in all aspects of our being. Or seen from another perspective, we can't experience pleasure if we don't know what pain is. We can't enjoy success if we've never tasted failure. We can't possibly let go with the exuberance of a Roberto Begnini if we've never cried aloud in anguish.

"Today it's common for people to say, oh go ahead, get on with life," Moore says in reaction to those who advise others to get over having recently lost a husband or wife, to get right back out there and move on, to lock up their true feelings, denying their very existence. When the most important thing to do is to go through it, feel the loss, live it. "Don't just find ways to brush it off. Let it come home. Speak for it. And speak of it."

The young Paul McCartney in the mid 60s had a similar take on the importance of honestly feeling whatever it is you are living at the moment, and not standing aside from it, as though it were happening to someone else. In *Hey Jude,* his sage advice to John Lennon's son, Julian, he wrote, "For well you know that it's a fool who plays it cool, by making his world a little colder."

In the end, the fountain of youth is *living* life, feeling life, having a passion for life. We wear down and rust not because the parts are no longer any good, but because we have ceased to employ them. The magic elixir, the secret ingredient in the fountain of youth, is our passion.

PART 3

REINVENTING
OUR FUTURE

The future we create:

- *Creating a more ingenious life by learning to treat time not as our foe but as a doorway to the eternal moment, where we arrest time, are transformed and enchanted by the creative impulse, and time-travel into ever-widening dimensions of our being.*

- *What it will take to evolve to a Type I global civilization, where we replace our Stone Age 'us and them' mentality with an interconnected web of compassion, and as a people united launch into a Star Trek future of discovery and awe.*

In searching for truth we are in fact searching for freedom from uncertainty. We all long to be free. We long to see with new sight.

IX

LIVING IN ETERNITY
LIVING IN TIME

We live in a time machine. Whatever we call God does not.

What is meant by time and by eternity? The ways in which we time-travel and escape our time-bound reality. Getting in touch with the eternal moment.

The trick to stopping time: ingesting art, being 'here now.' Arresting art, spine-tingling music, meditation, dancing, and chanting. Time-traveling right outside of time.

In learning to stop time, we discover how much more of it we have:

- Stephen Hawking
- Einstein
- Paul Davies
- Meister Eckhart
- John Gribbin
- Heraclitus
- Stephan Rechtschaffen

1

THE POWER OF STOPPING TIME

"He who cannot draw on three thousand years
is living from hand to mouth."

— Goethe

Time travel! Now there's something to get excited about. When I was a little kid I had fantasies of traveling through time as if it were no more difficult than crossing the street or changing my jacket. In an instant zipping back to some historic time and place, experiencing the sights and sounds and smells of what life was really like then; say, in ancient Rome burning under the emperor Nero, or in Galilee alongside a certain itinerant preacher, or heroically fighting alongside the Knights of the Roundtable, or watching as ancient Egyptians put the finishing touches on the Great Pyramid.

There was, of course, always that internal struggle about whether I would reveal myself to locals of the era, and perhaps show off my superior knowledge of the mysteries of the universe and some of the wonders yet to come. But then that would be meddling, and meddling could cause problems. Problems like the major time-travel conundrum: If I go back in time and kill my infant grandfather (accidentally or otherwise) where does that leave me? And who is it then who has traveled back in time to do this dastardly deed?

Which is why travel to the future always seemed a lot less messy. There I would learn of great marvels and see the wondrous 'progress' our species had fashioned for the world and all its inhabitants. I would return to the present with a modest knowledge of things to come, just enough to tempt the imaginations and envy of my friends, and keep me enthralled until my next voyage beyond — never for a moment thinking that now in the present, I was about to inadvertently toy with the careers of grandfathers-of-the-future in their infancy.

Traveling Right Out of Time

So where exactly is time? Where is eternity? How do we get from one to the other? What are the ins and outs of yesterday, today and tomorrow? And why this fascination with time travel? Could it be an unconscious desire to taste the pleasures of that other side of the coin — eternity?

Eternity, it is said, is where we step outside of time. What some call God's time. Einstein's Theory of Relativity tells us that the dimension of time and the dimensions of space are bound together as one. That is, when the space part of the universe and its three dimensions were created, so was time. Outside of the universe, and before it was created, there is no time. This is what we call eternity.

It's rather ironic that in an everyday sort of way we tend to think of eternity as a very long, or limitless span of time. When in fact, it is no time at all.

Plato aptly called time the moving image of eternity, and O'Donohue deliciously quipped that time is eternity "living dangerously."

Stephen Hawking in *A Brief History of Time*, states that the whole concept of time simply has no meaning before the beginning of the universe. Nor is this some new idea born of Einstein's theory of relativity. "This was first pointed out by St. Augustine (354-430). When asked: What did God do before he created the universe? Augustine didn't reply: He was preparing Hell for people who ask such questions. Instead, he said that time was a property of the universe that God created, and that time did not exist before the beginning of the universe."

It's senseless then to talk about what happened before the universe was created, or what God did with Himself then. Just as it is senseless to speak of being bored in eternity when we cash in our current existence for one of reclining on clouds and playing harps. Like the early European cartographers who wrote "Terra Incognita" on the area west of the Atlantic Ocean, we can only say of eternity, with any certainty, that it is something outside of our comprehension.

The ultimate form of time travel is not in space or in time, but right out of time.

I think the simplest and least baffling way to look at eternity is as one very fast instant — a flash, a nanosecond, the shortest span imaginable. In that briefest of instants, all of time, from the Big

Bang to the end of the universe, is all seen 'at once.' All that we ever did or said, alongside the life of every dinosaur, and the birth of every billion-starred galaxy, are all seen as one simple snapshot of experience. A gestalt all happening at once.

It's mind-boggling, especially when we realize that this very brief instant is only a part of our time-bound description. In reality there is no beginning to this 'instant,' and there is no end. Time, as Hawking wrote, "had a beginning at the big bang." Eternity had no beginning. It is 'timeless.'

2

AT THE SPEED OF LIGHT

This is explained in part by Einstein's theory. A photon of light travels, naturally enough, at the speed of light. Yet, *at* the speed of light, time stands still. "This means that for a photon time has no meaning," explains cosmologist John Gribbin in *In Search of Schrodinger's Cat.* "A photon that leaves a distant star and arrives at the earth may spend thousands of years on the journey, measured by clocks on earth, but takes no time at all as far as the photon is concerned." Each near miss it had across those billions of light-years of space all happened at the exact same instant at which it struck the retina at the back of my eye.

"The mystics and popularizers," Gribbin says, "who seek to equate Eastern philosophy with modern physics seemed to have missed this point...it tells us that everything in the universe, past, present, and future, is connected to everything else, by a web of electromagnetic radiation that *sees* everything at once."

But how is one to take in such a massive overload of information? Psychologist James Hillman suggests in *The Soul's Code* that God invented time so that everything wouldn't all happen at once for us, but would slow down, events unfolding one after the other, convincing us that the one causes the next.

Interesting Questions about God

Which raises some very interesting questions about God. For instance, if time is part of the physical universe and not part of eternity, does God experience the passage of time? And if not, then how does God interact with us? ...as in, answering prayers, handing out commandments, causing floods? Or is it through us that God experiences the world? Which would make each and every one of our lives extremely more important than we could imagine.

That is, do we choose to see the world — and after all, this is precisely what any religion has to offer us: a choice of perception — as a place where God interacts in this space/time along with us, making demands, listening to our supplications, altering the course of history? Or do we prefer to see God as the creator of our universe, outside of it, experiencing it through the grace of our every breath?

The word 'eternal' has two quite different meanings, theoretical physicist Paul Davies explains in *God and the New Physics*. "In the **simpler version**, eternal means everlasting, or existing without beginning or end for an infinite duration." In this sense eternity is a form of time, an endless form, which can be altered in many ways, including by humans.

"A God who is in time is, therefore, in some sense caught up in the operation of the physical universe." Which would seem to indicate that when time comes to and end, so would this God. Which would also mean that he is not the creator of the universe if he did not create time and subsequently not omnipotent if he answers to the physics of time.

Which leaves us with that **other meaning** of eternal — that is, 'timeless.' "St. Anselm expresses the idea as follows: 'You (God) exist neither yesterday, today, nor tomorrow, but you exist directly right outside time'."

If God is timeless, there is a sense then that God cannot be said to think, because it takes time to think. So how is it possible for God to acquire knowledge? "If God knows, for example, the position of every atom today, then that knowledge will change by tomorrow", Davies argues. "To know timelessly must therefore involve his knowing all events throughout time."

To get my mind around this time/eternity conundrum, I sometimes stop and think about what will happen when I finally leave time altogether. Die, in other words. My father died recently. His father died some 30 years before him. And one day I will die. Yet when I awake in eternity, I will find that we all three have arrived at the same instant. How else could it be, if there is no passage of time in eternity! All at the same instant. Which makes it rather senseless for loved ones to wish to die 'so they can go and join him right away.' Might as well go and live on as long as we can. He still won't beat us to the pearly gates.

The Experience of Eternity

John O'Donohue looks to the mystic Meister Eckhart to shine some light on the subject. He says Eckhart was once asked where the soul went when a person died. He said, "no place. Where else would the soul be going? Where else is the eternal world? It can be nowhere other than here." It's only because we are bound by our space/time way of thinking that we have spatialized eternity, locating it 'up there someplace' as though it were part of some distant galaxy. But it's right here, wrapped in some unknown embrace with our existence.

In the eternal world all is sandwiched together, with no space between; there is no distance. In eternal time there is no today, yesterday, or tomorrow. In eternal time all is now.

Perhaps Joseph Campbell in *The Hero With a Thousand Faces*, put it most poetically when he described the time/eternity duality as two aspects of the same experience-whole, as two planes or sides of the same nondual entity. Echoing the ancient sages of India he called it *the jewel of eternity in the lotus of birth and death. Om mani padme hum.*

And so somewhere buried within my time-bound day-to-day existence lays the eternal. But how to experience it? Daily? As Campbell said, if we don't get it here, we won't get it anywhere, because it's the experience of eternity in the 'now' that is the function of life.

3

WARP SPEEDS

Still, the time machine beckons. Get me the right Delorean and I'll head off *Back to the Future*, forwards and back, in a flash. Or that wobbly wheel-less vehicle in *The Time Machine*, which though immobile sailed through hundreds of thousands of years of change. Or any Time-Warp, Time-Tunnel, Worm-Hole, Black Hole which science fiction and science fact have conjured up to get me safely from one point to another, beyond the restraints of time.

Yet the only reliable time machine we can point to is the massive size of space itself. If we want to see how things were hundreds and thousands of years ago all we have to do is look up at the night sky; the light from most of those stars has taken that long to reach us, so what we are seeing is how they looked then, not now. With a large enough telescope we can peer back in time millions, even billions of years. In fact, we don't even know if many of these stars and galaxies even exist any more, perhaps having blown themselves up long ago, their light living on like some ghostly apparition. Of course knowing what these tiny specks of light looked like long ago isn't exactly what we had in mind while eyeing that nuclear-boosted Delorean.

Black Hole Adventures

As Paul Davies warns, though, there isn't much hope for the astronaut who aims his spaceship at a black hole expecting to tunnel through time. "At the instant he enters the black hole, all of eternity will have passed outside according to his relative determination of 'now.' Once inside the hole, he will be imprisoned in a timewarp, unable to return to the outside universe again, because the outside universe *will have already happened* (italics added)" So to emerge from the hole he would somehow have to have come out of it before he went in. Such terminally Alice-in-Wonderland enigmas similarly result if we try squeezing through a cosmic 'wormhole.'

So unless any of us have already come out of a black hole — in which case, what are we waiting for to let the rest of the world know about it? — there is virtually no hope of our pulling off the feat in the future, unless of course we find ourselves emerging from a black hole at some point prior to our departure. It all gets rather bizarrely complex and twisted in this never-never land of conjecture without even a modicum of historical experience. The best we can really do for the moment, I'm afraid, is the Hubble Telescope. That, and science fiction.

All space travel stories in science fiction, including the Warp Speeds of *Star Trek* and the Long Ago In A Galaxy Far, Far Away of *Star Wars*, are ways in which we escape our time limitations, if only mentally/emotionally. Yet from such imaginings spring wondrous new realities.

HG Wells, who wrote *The Time Machine* between 1886 and 1895, described right on page two how "any real body must have extension in four directions: it must have Length, Breadth, Thickness, and — Duration...

There are really four dimensions, three which we call the three planes of Space, and a fourth, Time..." Not a particularly astonishing statement, until we realize that Einstein did not publish his Relativity Theory until 1905, and the description of a space/time continuum wasn't added until 1908! HG Wells hurled his nameless hero through space and time based on a theory which itself still lay in the future.

So...while waiting for the Enterprise to dock at the nearest space station and take us to frontiers where no one has gone before, we might best use our 'time' by practicing ways to escape time's constraints altogether- by heading off into eternity. At least in brief spurts here and there.

4

ETERNITY NOW

Meister Eckhart found a place in the soul that is eternal. Time, he said, makes us old, but the soul harbors a place that time cannot touch. In *Eternal Echoes* John O'Donohue adds that through the soul we discover a way of inhabiting the eternal side of our life. The soul it seems lives mainly in eternal time. Or at least craves to.

In fact the soul needs eternity all the time. Not just the concept of eternity, according to Thomas Moore, but it needs the actual experience of eternity everyday. Some experience, that is, that feels like it's outside of time.

There are many moments in the day when time can be stopped to let the eternal in – awe-inspiring vistas of mountains or lakes or sunsets or blossoms. Sculptures and paintings and architecture can stop time, as can a beautiful dress or a smile or a newborn tasting its first experience of life. Just a few of the ways the soul can dine on the eternity that it needs, and it needs it every day.

Needing it every day means having to nourish it daily; finding a way of providing it with 'soul food.' Something to do with being here fully in the present moment. We hear a lot of talk about parachuting into that mysterious space known as the 'present moment.' But what exactly is this moment, and how can we live there for any length of time?

Zen Buddhism says there is only now — all else is illusion. But then it goes on to add that even that is an illusion. Yogic meditation seeks to quiet the turbulence in the mind so that we may be more fully in the present. In fact, the purpose of all meditation is not to help us relax or fall asleep, as some believe, but to bring us fully into the moment so that we are acutely aware of just this 'now.' To do this we must silence the internal dialogue, the reflections and memories of what has gone on in the past and the anxieties about the future, the monkey chatter that incessantly clutters our mind and distracts us from what is really happening around us at this very second. That great feeling of relaxation and calm is but a byproduct of this process. The truth is that it feels great to be fully in the moment.

Timeshifting

Blocking out that internal noise is the methodology of all forms of meditation, of monks singing Gregorian Chant, of Whirling Dervishes dancing, of repeating a mantra or OHM, of being entranced by a particular vista, of concentrating on the ebb and flow of our breath, or as the old song would have it, "gaze at the moon till I lose my senses." Nor is this restricted to any particular setting or position. Great athletes so successfully enter the moment that they are one with the ball as it flies to its target. Great dancers seemingly dance out of their skin. Others need merely walk, one step, one step, one step.

The great basketball player Bill Russell wrote of "those moments in a game when teammates and opponents are playing to the maximum of their ability," when they are, as Stephan Rechtschaffen called it in *Timeshifting*, "entrained not only with each other, but with the game itself." Where winning or losing is no longer the concern, but the sublime "*act* of basketball, players united in sport on the highest level" Or for those of us not so athletically gifted, the *act of living* elevated so far above our usual petty concerns that we dance out of our egocentric skins.

Football quarterback, Joe Montana's abilities are similarly the subject of an entire chapter in Timothy Ferris' *The Mind's Sky: Human Intelligence in a Cosmic Context*. Being a scientist, Ferris talks of the quarterback's ability as the programming of his premotor cortex. "To introduce conscious decision-making into the process would usually wreck his timing. As Montana remarked, 'If I ever stopped to think about what happens, what really makes things tick, after the ball hits my hands, it might screw up the whole process'." All reflection and anticipation have been abolished. He just is.

Or as Nijinsky, the greatest dancer of the twentieth century explained it, when he was in the middle of his ballet it was as though he was outside of himself, watching from the audience.

Once in this magical moment, the challenge is to expand it to suit our needs, what Rechtschaffen calls 'timeshifting.' That is, a moment isn't a specific amount of time, such as a second, a microsecond, a minute, an hour. It is however long we can make it be. In a sense that is why a particularly enjoyable hour can seem like just five minutes. A painful five can seem like hours. Expanding the moment not only pushes apart the past and the future, but introduces us to the eternal moment.

What is the link between the slowing down of time in the mystic/philosophic sense, and the slowing down of time in the relativity/quantum universe? In each we live longer. In each, everyone else appears to be moving too fast, not taking enough time to appreciate what is around them. And in each, time dilation is not some kind of delusion caused by how we choose to see things. It is very real; in fact, fundamental to the nature of the universe

5

EXPANDING TIME

Time, in essence, is very malleable. It is what we perceive it to be, and what we choose to make of it. As Stephan says, a day holds both twenty-four hours and an infinity of time. Yet the modern world we live in has chosen to see it in but one way, "as so many ticks on a clock," worth 'x' number of dollars per hour. The experience of life is lost in the rush.

We miss out on some of the greatest moments of our lives simply because we are in a rush to be elsewhere. Being here and now has become a rarity for our kind.

Many people live their lives haunted by the past; forever retracing in their mind the things they haven't done but believe they should've done. They are prisoners of their regrets. While others are haunted by the future, anxiously filling their present moments with possibilities and probabilities, most of which will never come about. To paraphrase the elder statesman Winston Churchill, his only regret in life was all the time he wasted worrying about things that never happened.

No wonder we have no time left for the moment. And all these gadgets — computers, toasters, cell phones, indoor plumbing, cars and jets — that, ironically, were supposed to free up tons of 'time' for our enjoyment, have left us anywhere but in the present, fretting about ways to pay for them, and how to acquire more of the same.

We try to live efficient, complete, and productive lives, all the while struggling against the natural rhythms of time, and the natural rhythms of the different stages in our life. Both Goethe and George Bernard Shaw complained that youth is wasted on the young, going in any and all directions, unsure of their way. How apt a description of our culture as we begin a new century lost in the mysteries of time.

We are, in short, 'stressed out' over time. We have inadvertently entered into a race against the very machines — Internet, fax, E-mail, etc. — which we invented to take away some of the pressures imposed by modern living. We can't win in this insane contest. We can't even keep up. We are stretched beyond our limits, trying to jam more hours into the workweek, more hours into the day. Where oh where is the time for us? For us to be in the present moment, for us to enjoy the soul-food delights of eternity?

Nowhere. This is what we call 'stress.' The number one serial killer, bar none, of our times.

As medical doctor Rechtschaffen explains, there are quite distinct physiological and psychological effects brought on by prolonged stress. "In the early stages, stress weakens our adrenal glands, stomach lining, and immune system. Unrelieved, it eventually leads to the breakdown of vital body systems, causing heart attacks, strokes, degenerative diseases, and even cancer."

All this because we don't know how to deal with time.

One of Life's Greatest Mysteries

Time is one of the greatest mysteries of life; everything that happens to us, and everything that we say and do and think can only happen through time. When it passes, which it does with every heartbeat, it takes everything away with it. In his Irish lyrical manner, O'Donohue calls this transience the force of time that makes a ghost of every experience.

"There was never a dawn, regardless of how beautiful or promising, that did not grow into noontime." And there never was a noon that did not slip into afternoon, never an afternoon that did not fall into evening, and never a day that did not pass into the graveyard of night.

The only ground on which we have to stand is the present moment.

We yearn for our daily moments of awe, what the mystics in their ecstatic visions call the eternal presence (present?). For most of us this takes training. Ecstasy does not just drop from the heavens; eternity does not just open up before us. We have to unlearn our 'busyness' and train ourselves to do more than just stop and smell the roses, but to allow that moment to become one of the most significant in our day. Then, strangely enough, we begin to perceive a whole different world before us.

When we learn to shift time, we discover the joys of settling into the moment. Relationships become fuller, work less a chore and more an accomplishment, and stress and anxiety become easier to let slip from our grasp. Shifting time is not a panacea, but a welcome break from the hectic pace of modern life. Something we've all likely experienced from time to time. We slip into the flow. We're relaxed, at peace with ourselves and with the world, in quiet harmony with the pulse of the universe.

6

DANCING TO THE BEAT

One way to accomplish this is by a system called 'Entrainment' — a way of making rhythms fall into synchronization with each other. Much like light waves becoming stronger when the crests of the waves fall in line with each other, and when they do the opposite, they cancel each other out. He calls rhythmic entrainment one of the great organizing principles of the world, as inescapable as gravity.

Music is a great entrainer. It can put us 'in the mood' in a flash. Whether it be romantic, or patriotic, or nostalgic, music can entrance us like nothing else can. Just ask any successful dictator, or Golden Oldie radio station manager. It has served as the attention-getting device of choice in all major religions, whether it emanates from the tinkle of a bell or the voices of a hundred chanting monks.

Ceremonies and religious rituals, since long before history was written, have incorporated drumbeats and repetitious chants to bring members into a slower rhythm, to a place where they can taste the deeper spiritual nature of their existence. Drumming, in fact, can induce an entire community to slip into a shared rhythm, a sacred rhythm that opens the participants up to some 'other world.'

Not just drumming and chanting, but rhythmic bowing, and dancing, and the endless repetition of a sound such as 'ohm.'

Rock 'n Roll Entrainment

Music, unfortunately not only works for slowing down our world so we may experience the eternal in the present moment, but works equally as well for speeding it up. It's difficult to say which came first, the fast fry chicken or the two-minute egg, but our music had little choice but to speed up; society was telling it to. Popular music in this past century was entrained by the rapid changes of our world, and the world was entrained to the beats of jazz and big band and rock & roll.

Something to think about the next time we select a radio station or CD to unwind to. If we think gansta rap will have no different effect on our mood than the Beatles, or that Beethoven's Fifth will have no different effect than Rachmaninov, then we're obviously not 'feeling' what we're hearing.

Our current world for the most part acts like there is no such speed called stillness, no gear but overdrive. Which is why it takes such a concerted effort to slow down. Our choice of music may be our most important choice of the day, our passage to the eternal moment.

As philosopher Blaise Pascal pointed out more than three hundred years ago, "All human evil comes from this, man's inability to sit still in a room."

Stephan tells the story of a time when he was on vacation in the Caribbean, and he took a drive up to the top of this mountain which a friend had recommended, to see the view. He was standing beside his rented car, entranced by this truly magnificent vista, when along came a couple in another car. The man jumped out, said something to the effect of 'wow, what a great view,' snapped a picture, and drove off, all in a blur of thirty seconds. The utter enchantment of the moment lost in a mad dash for instant gratification, for the knowledge that he had 'been there, done that' and had the photo to prove it. Now on to the next wonder of nature.

I suppose we have all fallen prey, on occasion, to this rush to see and do so much that we are not really present for anything at all. This can be especially true for itinerary-heavy tours of foreign places, ending back home with as sparse a memory of the sights as those held by the blurred and unenlightening snapshots. And that's a great shame. Just one of these missed eternal moments may have immeasurably opened our doors of perception in ways we can scarce imagine.

POOLS OF SACREDNESS

What I'm referring to are those so-called 'magical places' that sprout up here and there in various parts of the world. Sometimes they are to be found untouched in nature, often with ancient legends attesting to their otherworldly presence. Other times they are the site of almost continuous temples and shrines, each built on top of the ruins of the other, on down through the historical record as civilizations have come and gone.

One of these is to be found at Urfa, the legendary birthplace of Abraham. Today the waters are held holy by the Muslims who control the sight; but long before, these waters were sacred to Christians, before them to ancient Greeks, before them to Mesopotamians, and so on back through time.

As archaeologist and author John Romer explains in *Testament*, "what you've got here is this 'pool of sacredness,' and the religions that have come and gone through the ages are sort of decoration for something much deeper." A deep feeling of sacredness becomes associated with a particular spot, which in turn the cultures that come and go over the ages exploit for their specific brand of theological expression. The beliefs within the culture wed the sacredness within the spot.

What we're talking about here I believe is this arresting of time, this stopping the moment, this experience of the eternal, which some places on

the planet just seem to encourage. I know; in many of these special places I have temporarily simply left time, at least as we usually experience it. And there is no way I can predict where or when it will happen. Sometimes I will just turn a corner in a dusty little hamlet, and time will come to a halt, for how long I cannot say. At other times I will be stumbling amidst the fallen pillars of some old ruins, and I will be swept away. What I do know is that it usually happens when I have left my camera in a bag somewhere. And I do have to make a conscious effort to shut out all the distractions around me. A state of quiet walking meditation.

These 'pools of sacredness' are not the only places where the eternal opens up to our awareness, or more correctly our awareness opens up to the eternal. But they do serve as great eye-openers for what is possible in the day-to-day.

Then again, so are those wondrous occasions when we simply 'lose track of time,' times when something hits us with such incredible impact, be it good or bad, that we are yanked abruptly and totally into the moment.

8

ARRESTING TIME

Great art is the great stopper of time. Great art transcends time, and it will transcend those of us who are caught in its spell.

Art reveals to us what is already there in the ordinary, yes, but without art, as Moore writes in *Care of the Soul*, we live under the illusion that there is only time, and not eternity. Art expresses what the soul needs for sustenance. It lays claim to the eternal masquerading as the everyday, and offers up its treasures for our delight — the whole world in a grain of sand.

Countless times have I stood in an art gallery or museum, immobile, totally transfixed by some incredible painting or sculpture or ancient artifact. It's as though I'm somehow both outside the painting looking in, and simultaneously inside the painting, a ,part of its life, perceptions, and reality. The artist has captured something about the essence of the moment he is portraying that is time-bound, yet eternal, as it resonates through time to the soul of my being. There's no secret to what rates as great art to my tastes and opinion: either a work stops time and invites me into the eternal moment, or it's just wall decoration.

Great music, played and perceived on the highest levels, can attain the same heights, the same epiphanies. It sends shivers down my spine as it rivets me to a comprehension buried deep within, wrenching me clear away from all other considerations. As British music psychologist John Sloboda says, it can "arouse an emotional response of intensity rarely experienced in everyday life."

Music is allied with the opposite side of the brain (the right) from where language is centered (the left). Song and music, in fact, are believed by some experts today to have pre-dated language. Darwin even theorized that people sang before they talked. Thus this tremendous innate ability to respond to certain deeply felt chords, to take us right beyond our language-controlled existence.

It could be a Beatles' tune, an operatic aria, a blues riff; it won't happen every time we hear it, but when our attention and the mood is just right, and when the playing is of the highest order, then our whole being will shudder in ecstasy as it is blown clear out of time.

"At the moment music moves you, it's as if you're in a flow channel," University of Guelph music professor David Elliott points out, "where you lose track of time, where everything else becomes unimportant." As songstress Jane Siberry put it, "music can change our psychological and spiritual state as immediately and as powerfully as any drug."

The eternal, we remind ourselves, is nowhere to be found in our ruminations about the past or our fantasies about the tomorrows yet to come. The eternal resides solely in the present moment.

The Buddha taught that life, all life, can only be lived in the present, and that missing the present means missing life itself. Rechtschaffen tells of his early days wandering around India, practicing what he thought was good for his spiritual development, when he came across a monk who was rather amused by him. "He told me to forget (my Zenism meditation) ...just settle into a fuller experience of the present. There were no other states of consciousness to attain, nothing else I needed to be doing. The answer was simply to pry open the door to a fully conscious experience of now."

Sacred Time

That is, to use some method to separate what is often called 'sacred time' from the ordinary everyday variety. For this people have since earliest records used various sorts of rituals — incense, icons, chants, song, dance, bowing — shifting attention from the time-bound to the eternal. Ritual however is not the exclusive province of organized religion. In fact we all use rituals daily whether we recognize them as such or not — how we prepare ourselves for facing the day, for the office, for meals, for being a parent, for driving the car, for going on vacation, for being a lover.

The great religions of the world have incorporated these particular methods for no other reason than that they work. They are successful in slowing down the world for us so that our attention is more and more focused on the present moment. The only magic involved is in the attention itself.

In Stephan's words, "there is nothing mystical about being truly present, and yet it is what mysticism is all about."

In our normal state the majority of us see only with our time-bound perception. Consequently we forego the pleasure of experiencing those mystifying glimpses of the eternal which inhabit even the most ordinary moments, those same fragments of eternity on which inspired artists dine all the time. With just a minimal effort we too could begin to partake of this feast and make it a part of our daily existence. That is, by awakening the artist that is hidden within each of us. The eternal in our present moment. The jewel of eternity in the lotus of birth and death: om mani padme hum.

If we are to take another step in this pursuit of truth, we shouldn't be afraid to step outside the constraints of time into the eternal moment, and there dine on the creative impulse as often as the hunger arises.

X

THE AGE
OF
ENLIGHTENMENT
II

Compassion will change our world. Nothing else can, for the better.

The wisdom imparted by the tale of The Fisher King, of the devastation wrought on our world by a simple lack of compassion.

The 'us and them' thinking of our Stone Age ancestors has become our 'justified' wars and acts of terror; yet we all share the same grandmother.

What it will take to evolve to a Type I global civilization. Dreaming of a Star Trek federation of planets. Learning to laugh at our illusions. What's to be done to create a better world?

The wisdom we weave:

- The Dalai Lama
- Joseph Campbell
- Carl Sagan
- Michio Kaku
- Edward Wilson
- Thomas Moore
- Teresa of Avila
- Einstein
- Steve Allen
- Sam Keen
- Alain de Botton

1

THE POWER OF COMPASSION

Now when Perceval comes to the grail castle, he meets the Grail King, who is brought in on a litter, wounded, kept alive simply by the presence of the Grail. Perceval's compassion moves him to ask, "What ails you, Uncle?"

... (this expression) of compassion, the natural opening of the human heart to another human being. That's the Grail.

— Joseph Campbell *The Power of Myth*

The Fisher King was the appointed guardian of the Holy Grail — the hallowed cup which legend says Jesus drank from at the last supper, and which even caught his blood as it ran from his body on the cross. But the Fisher King had been gravely wounded in the thigh or groin area, and was unable to get up from his sick bed. For years he lay in anguish, his open wound festering, incapable of healing. His illness gradually overtook his kingdom, where everything lay parched and brown and dying.

The Knights of the Round Table were sent off in all directions to locate this mysterious castle and its treasured relic, but none could find it, until Perceval came along. The simple knight Perceval (piercer of the veil, in French) or Parsifal (fool or dunce, in German) as he was also known, was able to see, perhaps because of his lack of sophistication, what no one else could see. He stumbled upon the Fisher King's castle. A great banquet was held in his honor; a procession passed before his eyes with the king carried on his sick bed, trays and trays of food and drink, and the Holy Grail. Amazed at all he saw he ached to ask about so much, especially the grail, and what had happened to the king. But being mindful of his knightly training he chose not to speak out of turn, and thus failed to express his true feelings.

When he awoke in the morning everyone had gone. He went in frantic search of them, and when he stumbled across the bridge to the mainland, the kingdom itself seemingly vanished. Years and years passed as Perceval searched desperately to find the grail king; he was heartbroken, devastated that he had not done what he knew he should have done. At long last the mist suddenly evaporated before his eyes, and there stood the castle again. This time he did not stand on ceremony. He went straight up to the Fisher King and on bended knee grasped his hand and asked, *"What ails you, Uncle?"* He didn't ask for the Holy Grail; he didn't ask where they had disappeared to all these years. His only concern was for the frail king and his suffering. The true expression of compassion.

Just then the Fisher King arose from his bed and for the first time in what seemed forever, he smiled. His wound was healed, completely, his strength restored. The gloomy castle was filled anew with light and laughter. The parched land and rotted trees throughout the kingdom began at once to turn lush and green with life. The sound of singing birds echoed throughout this former barren wasteland. *For lack of a little compassion* so much life and happiness had vanished from the world.

The wound inflicted was by a world which no longer cared, a world which had lost its spiritual rudder, a world which little practiced the teachings of its sage founders, a world as inauthentic as the parched landscape of the Grail Kingdom. Because the King was wounded by this uncaring world, only a representative of this outside world — outside the realm of his kingdom — could heal the wound which so badly disabled him. Perceval the knight, as innocent representative of this world, began anew the healing process, by expressing his true compassion.

The Great Myth of the Western World, or so it is often romantically called. There are many versions and even more interpretations, including a modern updating in a Hollywood movie called *The Fisher King*, wherein the King's (Robin Williams) unfathomable wound is eventually healed by the ever-growing compassion welling in Perceval (Jeff Bridges). As in the original Grail story, the healer and his world are as much healed by the healing, as the healer has wrought.

The theme of the Grail romance, as Campbell says of this seminal medieval myth, is that the entire territory of one's existence has been laid to waste. This wasteland is a place where "everybody is living an inauthentic life, doing as other people do," meekly doing as they are told, lacking the courage to live their own life on their own terms. That's the essence of the wasteland, and what T.S. Eliot meant by his poem *The Waste Land*.

The Grail and Our Modern World

So how can we unveil this mysterious Holy Grail? According to Campbell, the vanishing Grail Kingdom is right here, inside us. This "natural opening of the human heart to another human being." That's the Grail. Yet it might as well be in another galaxy. We rush off on our intense spiritual Quests in search of some mythical cup that will bestow the healing magic of eternal life on all those who drink from it. To heal our world. To heal ourselves. Yet, like the Fisher King, our 'natural opening' has been wounded; it has shut down, just like the world around it.

This cultural story seems hardly less applicable today than it was in the time of those quest-happy knights. By keeping a tight leash on our compassion, as has been the fashion for many centuries now, are we not as responsible for the ills of the world as Perceval was for the King's suffering those additional years?

In a wasteland the surface doesn't represent what it's supposed to represent; as with the people in it. Campbell tells of once overhearing a family argument in a restaurant where the father insisted his son take the university courses he wanted him to, and the mother saying to leave the boy alone, to let him take what *he* wanted to. The father howled incredulously, "I've never done a thing I wanted to in all my life." Life in the Wasteland.

So too with the European consciousness which has pervaded our Western world. In its drive to name and categorize everything, it managed to successfully separate spirit from matter, thus displacing our heritage as spiritual beings. "That is to say, nature intends the Grail," Campbell says of this part of our being that has for all too long been relegated to the periphery, as though it were some esoteric indulgence.

Poetically he calls our spiritual life the flowering and bouquet, the perfume and fulfillment of a life, not some imposed supernatural quality.

We're so conditioned to hearing that spiritual concerns have no place in a secular world that we have to step back and refocus to even conceive of the 'secular life' as being infused with spirit. Spirituality is not some added on feature; it's an authentic expression of our human nature, as much our birthright as are our eyes and appetites and libido. And one of its most cherished forms of expression, as the Grail legend demonstrates, is compassion.

Compassion quite simply means 'with suffering.' A type of love where we are willing, if need be, to undergo suffering in place of another; at the very least to desire to alleviate their suffering, to feel suffering along with them. It goes far beyond mere tolerance. A world where all peoples learn to tolerate all others is a world sitting on a powder keg. Like tolerating a certain obnoxious relative at a family gathering, one wrong gesture, one word said inappropriately, and fireworks explode all around. Tolerance is at the root of compassion, but on its own it lacks benevolence — this positive caring for the welfare and well being of another.

In Corinthians St. Paul called it *caritas*, or a special sort of love: "Though I have the power of prophecy, to penetrate all mysteries and knowledge, and though I have all the faith necessary to move mountains — if I am without *caritas*, I am nothing." In Buddhist tradition the highest form of compassion is practiced by those who, although they have earned their entry into the bliss of Nirvana, choose to remain behind to help those who are still on the path.

The Grail — as symbol for living an authentic life, a life lived not only on our own terms and impetus but informed by the conditions and sufferings of others — is the fount of compassion. Any life ignoring these sufferings and ecstasies is inauthentic, because it ignores our ultimate connectedness to all others.

So the wisdom of the ages informs us that we need to grow in this area, constantly. But then developing our capacity for compassion isn't exactly difficult. Just look around for some juicy, irritating, unbending enemy.

2

THE ENEMY 'I'

"Anger and hatred are the greatest obstacles to love and compassion," the Dalai Lama warned in 1986 at a conference in India, as reported in China Galland's *Longing for Darkness*. "Tolerance is the key to compassion, and for this we need enemies to give us the opportunity to practice tolerance. Enemies are very important, they give you the opportunity to develop and grow."

And so, are we to get down on our hands and knees and give thanks for September 11, 2001? This unbelievable opportunity to develop and grow! In an instant our illusions shattered. We cannot make light of these traumatic moments in our common experience. It's not that, oh my God, we have enemies out there who really hate us. It's, oh my God, we *are* the enemy, at least to those who hate us, if not as well to ourselves. Did we not notice that *we* lacked compassion, that *they* lacked compassion? Were we not aware before this date that we were already, like the Fisher King, crucially wounded, already living inauthentic, unreal lives, unable to rise up and rejuvenate our wasteland?

In ancient times, when our whole world was our tribe, compassion was easy. Compassion held us together. We knew everyone, and everyone counted. But as our tribe shrunk to a smaller and smaller portion of our greater daily experience, compassion became less and less of a personal practice. Eventually it became barely perceptible even within our own tribe. Compassion, it may even be said, was a hallmark of the ancient matriarchy, its disappearance a derivation of all the overkill and butchery that has so marked our species in recent history. To in some way 'put the world right,' to re-infuse it with this life-affirming quality, perhaps what we need is to alter our perception — to see for a change the entire planet as but one big boisterous tribe.

Us and *Them* have always been the favorite words of those who would lead us in hating and killing and raping and denigrating. How else to stir up our righteous passions about how great we are and how evil are the others. The absolute antithesis of compassion.

The problem is that compassion can only really take hold on the 'us' side of 'us and them'; enemies do not have compassion for one another – if they did, how could they keep on butchering each other's children and loved ones? So in order for compassion to spread throughout the world, we have to replace our tribal perception of 'us and them' with the far more inclusive perception of the whole world as being 'us'!

Shortly after 9/11, while forming some of the ideas for these pages, I spent three weeks living in Jerusalem — bombs, bullets and sirens exploding in all directions (longing for peace in the 'city of peace'). Every day there was another 'homicidal-suicide bomber' pulling the switch. There was nowhere we could go to feel safe, to take our family, to breathe in a sane world. The supermarket, Mea Shearim, a cafe, Ben Yehuda mall, a bus, a pizzeria, outside a synagogue. Lili and I were out and about every day, passing through all of these places; and all of these places, within a day or two before or after (sometimes hours), were the sights of dozens of men, children, women, innocents, being blown to bits as they went about their daily business.

I had to keep telling myself that this was the new millennium; that the world had turned a page on the war-drenched twentieth century and ushered in the Global Village with a promise of cooperation and agreed upon peaceful solutions. Apparently not everyone was reading the same book. Lili and I had come to Jerusalem to welcome to the world our daughter's new daughter. She and her husband had moved here from Cleveland so he could complete his graduate studies in Judaism and become a Lubavicher Rabbi. So daily I strolled my grandson, a toddler, through the crowded streets and quiet, mostly abandoned parks with their carefully tended peace gardens, surreal, as though transplanted from some Eden.

Not far away, in the villages and refugee camps of the bombers, massive tanks rumbled, cannons and machine guns and bombs exploded, the lives of the innocent and not so innocent extinguished in tandem. I met with individuals from many sides in this convoluted maze that has been woven over the past century, and the only thing they all have in common is a sense of utter dread and sadness. As Lili remarked at one point, there's no smiles, there's no laughter, there's no happy music. Every radio is tuned to non-stop news, and the news of course brings but more tears and wails and anguished grief. Tribal compassion is here alive and well, but, as is the norm, strictly in an us-and-them sense.

And I so longed to smile and laugh again.

Longing for Peace with the Enemy Us

As Sandro Contenta, a Middle East correspondent wrote at the time of yet another attack and counter attack, "Both sides grieved, as they have for the past 18 months, yet both seemed oblivious to the other's pain." Of course this doesn't apply to everyone; there are countless unsung heroes who are tirelessly reaching out with heartfelt concern to the 'enemy.' But as tribe-to-tribe, compassion is kept on a tight leash, not passing through the myriad security checks. How else could the killings continue?

This is not some insane plea for everyone to show compassion for those who are about to incinerate them and their children. Compassion will not stop such murderous intent. What should be obvious, however, is that if this care and consideration had been shown in the first place, this murderous intent would never have developed, at least not as one tribe to another. And this applies to every part of the world, not just the Middle East. Every group has its quota of vicious fanatics who would take great joy in silencing the Mother Teresas, Mahatma Gandhis, and Dalai Lamas of this world. But to allow this extremely small minority to speak for everyone else — and it is no idle assumption that the vast majority of people are decent, caring, and in favor of a fair shake for the other guy — is to play an insane game that may in the not too distant future incinerate every last one of us.

My mother was born 'on the wrong side of the tracks,' as far as religion goes, in Northern Ireland during the Irish war for independence; her family was soon forced to flea with her for their lives to a safe haven across the Atlantic. I just happened to be passing through Belfast in '69 when a new round of violence broke out between Protestant and Catholic neighbors; I was grabbed off the sidewalk by a group of young toughs who were about to beat the living daylights out of me, until they heard my 'foreign' accent and let me go on my way. More than thirty years later righteous murders continued to ravage the lives of these young toughs' own grown children.

During a State of the World Forum in San Francisco in the late '90s, I was sitting during a luncheon beside an eloquent Pakistani diplomat. He lectured me and the rest of the table on how peace was so easily attainable if people would only learn to be tolerant and understanding of the other side; that the ethnic cleansing in Serbia and Bosnia would cease, that Arabs would learn to live side by side with Israelis, that Protestants and Catholics could again walk safely in the streets of Northern Ireland. I verbally applauded his erudite take on these situations and added that it would also be great if India and Pakistan could similarly stop their incessant saber rattling with nuclear weapons and learn to live as friendly neighbors. He stopped silent for several moments in pained anguish, then in a loud voice, as though to insure that all could visually hear his blindness, said, "No, no, we could never make peace with India. They are all liars."

Similar mistrust and programmed stereotyping offers justifications for Hutus to slaughter Tutsis in Rwanda, Chinese to dismantle Tibetan culture, Islamic Jihad to attack the overwhelming forces of Western Culture, and on and on throughout the world's interminable struggles. Each is absolutely certain that they are right, even to convincing themselves that they are doing the will of God, and they are doing the world a favor in attempting to rid it of the other.

"Instead of clearing his own heart the zealot tries to clear the world," Joseph Campbell says of this narrow-minded take on reality. Consequently, whatever we consider to be the laws that God has lain down apply only to our group, however we may wish to define it, and in turn we are free to hurl abuse and even attack with massive weapons of destruction those "uncircumcised, barbarian, heathen, 'native', or alien people" who happen to be on the 'them' side of us and them. And feel righteously proud of ridding the world of them.

The trouble is we can no longer afford to play this millennia-old game. The 'selfish gene,' programmed deep within each one of us for the survival of our particular genes and those of our kin, needs now to be brought to the fore in aid of a broader tribe.

So let's get very real and down to earth on this crucial point. It's not some pious peace initiative that will make the world's combatants bury the hatchet and turn their swords, scimitars, and cruise missiles into plowshares; not out of some goody-goody sense of brotherly love that we will call off the dogs of hate and xenophobia — but for selfish reasons, for our own personal self preservation. And ironically, it's in the Global Village, interconnected and inter-affected as it is, that our selfish needs can best be gratified by cooperating with others – indeed, the greater the circle, the greater the results.

Ideally what would happen next is we would gradually warm to the idea of a refurbished Age of Enlightenment, giving birth to a planetary society of unbridled creativity and cooperation. Of course, given this past century of ethno-violence and mass slaughter, we are more likely to laugh mockingly at such naïve pie-in-the-sky musings. Yet, surprisingly, we can with a certain degree of confidence predict a significant shift in our global heart because we humans are by nature an altruistic species, and as Sagan and Druyan wrote, altruism is very close to love.

Indeed, the human race is on the brink of an enormous leap forward, if only we can hang on just a little bit longer and not annihilate ourselves first.

3

A TYPE I CIVILIZATION

In *Hyperspace: A Scientific Odyssey Through Parallel Universes, Time Warps, and the 10th Dimension* Michio Kaku writes that it's highly likely intelligent civilizations have been springing into being throughout our galaxy on a regular basis, "but that few of them negotiated the uranium barrier, especially if their technology outpaced their social development." By the *uranium barrier* he means nuclear war, getting past the temptation of pushing a few buttons to watch the fireworks fly as mushroom clouds sprout throughout the globe — still very much a possibility for our species at the dawn of this new century.

Successful intelligent life forms, since we haven't actually met any, can only be categorized theoretically, but at least it gives us some idea of what may lie ahead. Kaku uses a system first developed by Russian astronomer Nikolai Kardashev to rate the types of civilizations we may come across in deepest, darkest space. It's based simply on their ability to harness nature's energy sources.

A Type I civilization has complete control of all energy resources on its planet; it can "control the weather, prevent earthquakes, mine deep in the earth's crust, and harvest the oceans." Here we don't just predict the weather with unfailing accuracy, but we direct the storms and the calms to suit our purposes, as we do with volcanoes and tides and currents. Needless to say the concerns of the entire globe would have to be considered in each such prescription.

Much further along in advancement, perhaps by a thousand years, a Type II civilization is one that has managed to control the power of the sun itself, and all its attendant satellites. And a way off in the dawn of a few more millennia of our descendants may lie the birth of a Type III civilization, one that amazingly controls the power of the entire galaxy. Minding, of course, that it's a fool's game trying to put a timeline on future developments; we've already seen how vast is the capacity of our present brains, and what incredible leaps and bounds our knowledge has taken in recent decades. The future may be a lot closer than we dare imagine.

Meanwhile, by contrast, the world we presently live in is classed a Type 0 civilization, "just beginning to tap planetary resources, but does not have the technology and resources to control them." As a civilization we are "like a newborn infant."

Blowing Ourselves Back to the Stone Age

Some scientists speculate there have been perhaps thousands of planets in our immediate galactic neighborhood that have reached our Type 0 level. The reason we haven't heard from any of them as yet, despite our constant scanning the stars for signals, is the uranium barrier (Stephen Hawking refers to this scenario as a sick joke). Using our own recent history as a guide, it is only little over half a century since we've been capable of sending signals out to potential listening ears in outer space, yet for most of that short time we have also been quite capable of using the nuclear option and blowing our civilization back to the Stone Age.

Considering the billions of years in which it is possible that other planets in our galaxy may have reached this particular point — and in a mere handful of decades annihilated themselves (as we still could) — what is the probability that this tiny infinitesimal sliver of time would just happen to coincide with our own few decades of listening for an intelligible word?

It seems we're just too smart for our own good. That while our intelligence leaps and bounds forward exponentially — amassing in Kaku's estimation more knowledge since World War II than all the knowledge amassed in our 2-million year evolution on this planet — our emotional ties and reactions, whether religious or cultural or bound to some tormented piece of land, are still wrapped up back there in tribal and Stone Age allegiances.

In short, our emotional development has not kept pace by half with our great evolutionary leaps of the past few millennia. All those essential emotional qualities which were more or less denigrated under the rise of patriarchy have once again to be brought to the fore and redeveloped, or we'll never become a planetary society capable of reaching to the stars. Increasing our intellectual abilities on their own will not do the trick.

In *The Future of life* Edward Wilson offers that the human brain apparently evolved to protect a narrow band of interests, as in what is best for my tribe and my hunting grounds and my children and grandchildren. Such an outlook was a sound survival technique in a Darwinian sense, good 'common sense' at that time. Yet, for the most part our six and a half billion fellow humans (including whatever tribe we subscribe to) still think and react in this antiquated fashion today.

Stone Age Thinking in the 21st Century

And why do we tend to think in this shortsighted way? The reason is simple, Wilson says, "it is a hardwired part of our Paleolithic heritage." For most of antiquity those who worked for the short-term benefits of their small group ended up prospering more and leaving more descendents, even when the long-term effects meant the disintegration of their people or empire. They wouldn't or couldn't see down the road far enough to 'do the right thing' for their distant offspring. Nor has this changed much.

Wilson's *The Future of Life* is about our delicate environment and how, like the uranium barrier, if we don't pay serious attention to it right away, it too could lead to our downfall. But the abuse of our habitat isn't a sexy topic, not yet compelling enough to drag us away from our overriding obsessions with reality TV, sports, and accumulating personal fortunes.

Despite there being more people born during the 20th century than in all of recorded human history put together (though some say this is a bit of an exaggeration), we continue to act as though the earth were of infinite size, and its fresh water, fossil fuels, and food supplies a cornucopia that can never be depleted. This as we uncomfortably enshroud ourselves in our own unre-cycleable refuse.

Short term versus long-term thinking, the concerns of my tribe versus the concerns of the global tribe. It's certainly not difficult to select values that will help our community or nation in the short term, Wilson writes. Nor for that matter is it difficult to select the right values for the whole planet, and even into the distant future. Except that those emotional ties to Stone Age clans continue to overwhelm our better judgment. But we have no choice in this matter if we expect to go on. We have to override these innate feelings because the only way to get an ecological ethic to work is for it to apply to all of humanity in all parts of the globe. Otherwise we cannot escape from the tragic predicament we now find ourselves in.

We've wedged our way into this bottleneck by using outdated thinking to tackle very modern problems. Kaku writes, "As long as pollution is produced by individual nation-states, while the measures necessary to correct this are planetary, there will be a fatal mismatch that invites disaster."

The same is true for the way we govern ourselves. We still labor under the illusion that nations run this world, and democracy sets us free; where in fact, multi-national corporations hold tremendous sway in running the world and its flow of wealth, yet we have virtually no say in what they do for, or with, our planet and its resources. As the popular documentary *The Corporation* cleverly reasons, if corporations are legally classified as persons, which they are, then their social behavior classifies them as psychopaths – self-interested, irresponsible, lacking empathy and remorse, and relating to others only superficially, via public relations spin.

Most important is the flow of wealth. Throughout history the well-to-do have always had a lot more in terms of real power and possessions than the rest of society, regardless of the political system involved. This is not likely to change soon, but there are extremes to be avoided. When the gap between the haves and the have-nots reaches the point where a few percent of the citizens control some 90% of the wealth of a nation, while the other hundreds of millions are left to fight over what's left, the social fabric has no choice but to rip apart, spilling out into the streets in anarchy, senseless violence, and social dissolution. Yet, despite history in every part of the world repeating this horrendous tale of the end result of unconscionable disparity, we continue to deceive ourselves by blindly prying the gap farther and farther apart. The same holds true for the growing economic gap between nations.

A Special Tenacity and Unselfishness

This all having been said, I don't actually believe we will blow ourselves up, or destroy our intricately interwoven societies, not now or in the foreseeable future. There is something extraordinarily redeeming about our species, some overwhelming will-to-live no-matter-what that has pulled us through the worst of plagues and disasters and mass slaughters, which will continue to guide us safely through the toughest of times. And if we on this planet can manage to do it, then why not those on other worlds? It takes a special tenacity and unselfish giving to get to where we stand today that makes it highly unlikely that we'll simply fade away as yet another failed experiment in intelligent life forms.

So we move on to our next big leap — establishing a planetary-wide civilization. To become a Type I civilization first we need "a cohesive social unit that is the entire planet's population. A Type I civilization by its very nature," Kaku says, "must be a planetary civilization. It cannot function on a smaller scale."

To reach this level we need to totally revamp the kind of thinking that has guided us since the end of the Stone Age. It will hardly be easy. As Heinz Pagels wrote in *The Cosmic Code*, "It will try our deepest resources of *reason and compassion*."(Italics added) But reason and compassion are not foreign concepts to us. And the brass ring of a Type I civilization is certainly worth the effort. Then, with some justification, we can dream of joining those futuristic science fiction worlds which so enthrall our imaginations — like that prime example of a Type II civilization, *Star Trek,* and its Federation of Planets.

Our Biological Eve

Perceptions and illusions. On the one hand we claim we want to see this greater world of enhanced health and prosperity and possibilities for everyone, while on the other what we *expect* to see is the same old greed and violence and selfishness for which our kind has become famous. And so by falling back on these tired old perceptions, this is precisely what we help bring about.

From his monastery deep in the forest Buddhist monk Punnadhammo Bhikkhu stays in constant touch with his connections to all life. "When the world is divided into 'us and them' we don't see others as beings in their own right," he writes on the Internet. "This division is spiritual poison. Buddhism teaches that it is also essentially false. There is no real division between beings. All, without exception, share the same intrinsic nature."

Molecular anthropologists tell us they can now trace every single person on earth back to a single 'Eve' who lived in East Africa about 150,000 years ago (one source claims a more precise 171,500 years ago for the birth of this Eve). Not that she was Eve in the Biblical sense, as the first woman; there were plenty of other women and groups of people at the time (some 10,000, and many before). Just that each and every one of the over six billion of us on the planet today can genetically trace our roots back to this one woman, something that cannot be said of any of the others. For the next 70,000 years or so her lineage grew and spread all over Africa. Finally, around 80,000 years ago (some say a more recent 52,000 years back), wave after wave of her descendants broke out of Africa, likely through the Saudi peninsula, and by first hugging the coastlines before heading inland, eventually settled in every sort of climate, in every livable part of the earth.

This is very recent information made possible by DNA analysis, in particular the information found in the mitochondrial DNA, which is passed on only by the female side. And it's amazingly precise, like a road map of some bizarre trip taken by our ancestors as they meandered around the world. From our ancestral Eve we spread out of Africa populating every part of the world, along the way developing progressively stronger tribal ties to our little groups to help us survive in perilous circumstances. These primitive tribal ties persist today in the form of colors, creeds, 'races,' cultures, languages, and ties to ancestral lands.

But now there is no space left into which to expand, at least not on this planet. So here we are at the beginning of the 21st century, our numbers bulging, swelling by the hour, doubling every forty years, and our entrenched tribal allegiances far from being of survival value, are our most serious threat to continuing on as a species. It's time now to take a look again at our family album, to recognize our ancestral Eve as the *Grandmother of us all,* and we her one family of descendants.

One could even say it's propitious that the most powerful nation-state in the world today with the most pervasive media, is, along with a few other Western states, a land of immigrants — an incoming of peoples and cultures and ethnic origins from every part of the earth, coming together to see itself as *one people united.*

4

FUNDAMENTALLY SO

In the early 1990s certain cultural commentators predicted that the number one global problem of the new century would be religious fundamentalism. Not that the beliefs of fundamentalists of whatever religion are a problem in themselves, but that these adherents tend to be so certain that their beliefs and theirs alone are the right ones — God's definitive instructions to mankind, as it were — that all others must obviously be wrong. At the very least, those others have taken an unholy diversion from the one true path. Having narrowed their perception to this tunnel vision of reality, how in the world can they then open up to their fellow humans who don't share their vision? How can they see them as equals 'in the eyes of God'? How can they help bring about this greater global civilization of the future — a generation or two down the road?

"Almost all groups agree in holding other groups to be inferior to themselves," the great American historian Will Durant wrote in the mid-1930s of this species-wide propensity. "The American Indians looked upon themselves as the chosen people, specifically created by the Great Spirit as an uplifting example for mankind. One Indian tribe called itself 'The Only Men'; another called itself 'Men of Men'; the Caribs said, 'We alone are people.' The Eskimos believed that the Europeans had come to Greenland to learn manners and virtues."

As such, much like our attitude towards dogs and cats and other friendly species, these tribes didn't hold outsiders to the same high moral standards as they did their fellow tribesmen; but then neither were these outsiders protected by its code of restraints. "Commandments and tabus applied only to the people of his tribe; with others, except when they were his guests, he might go as far as he dared."

Well, as an avid traveler, at least that's one double standard I'm glad has changed in recent history. The turn-around began with a little document called the passport; with it the bearer who was granted entry into a foreign land and culture was assured safe passage, at the very least to be subjected to no harsher laws than the locals. And so today the world is open wide for all to travel without legal impediment. However, this does not guarantee that we'll be considered moral or spiritual equals by those whom we visit outside of our cultural circle. Tribal brainwashing, ours and theirs, still informs each of us that we are somehow intrinsically superior.

Seeing Others As We Never See Ourselves

"Ethnocentrism is the belief that our group (whichever it happens to be) is at the focus of everything good and true, the center of the social universe," Carl Sagan and Ann Druyan wrote about this common inborn myopic view of the world. "*We* do things the way they were meant to be done. Xenophobia is the fear and hatred of strangers. *Their* behavior is wrongheaded or weird or abominable. They don't have the same respect for life that we do." (How often have I heard this canard thrown about in heated debate?) "And anyway they're out to get us. 'Us against them,' again." This kind of behavior, they remind us, just in case we think it's a sign of our highly evolved human status, is extremely common among pea-brained birds and our fellow mammals.

Albert Einstein described this experiencing of ourselves as separate from others as a kind of optical delusion of consciousness; we should instead "widen our circles of compassion to embrace all living creatures and the whole of nature and its beauty."

So how do we as a tribe, as a tribe of tribes, wriggle out of this straightjacket, this bottleneck which will not allow us to grow or expand any further? A life built on lies and hypocrisy, misconceptions and lockstep thinking, is not a life we can call our own. It diminishes us, making us small in our own eyes as well as in the eyes of the universe.

Some claim to have come around to this broader universal acceptance of human kind in all its forms, though unfortunately, as any major crisis tends to reveal, it's often more in words than in actual practice. But there are some. However, it's microscopically rare to find an actual world *religious leader* who places humanity first, ahead of all other tribal, cultural, and religious considerations.

"When I was younger and living in Tibet, I believed in my heart that Buddhism was the best way," the Dalai Lama writes in *Ethics for the New Millennium*, a sentiment echoed by many a true believer wrapped in a fervor for his faith. "I told myself it would be marvelous if everyone converted. Yet this was due to Ignorance."

This humble admission of ignorance comes as a result of his many years of roaming the earth, encountering every religious practice and belief system, and realizing that there is no single religion that satisfies all of humanity. What's more, he's come to the conclusion that humans can live quite well without appealing to religious faith. These may sound, he admits, like strange statements coming from a world religious figure, but there is a bigger picture to which he feels called to answer.

"I am, however, Tibetan before I am Dalai Lama, and I am human before I am Tibetan." So while his responsibility as Dalai Lama is to the Tibetan community, and as a monk his responsibility is to further harmony with other religions, "as a human being I have a much larger responsibility toward the whole human family — which indeed we all have."

The Spiritual Path

The Dalai Lama makes a distinction between religion and spirituality similar to what we said earlier when pointing out that this journey was a spiritual quest, and not a religious one. That religion is concerned with a particular faith tradition, with its dogmas, rituals, prayers and claims to salvation, and a concept of heaven or nirvana. By contrast, he says, spirituality is concerned with qualities like love, forgiveness, contentment, patience, a sense of responsibility, and compassion, qualities that bring happiness not only to oneself but to others.

He further says that anyone should be able to develop all these qualities without having to turn to any particular religion or metaphysical system. Which is why he has even stated, "Religion is something we can perhaps do without. What we cannot do without are these basic spiritual qualities."

Profound thoughts to keep in mind the next time we hear some politician or public figure confuse the separation of church and state with the separation of our spiritual qualities from our overall being – the spiritual being neither the religious nor the state; it is the personal. It's only when we confuse the spiritual with the religious that these quintessential human qualities get buried in the war between church and state. Catastrophically, as our everyday lives become devoid of a spiritual dimension, these very human qualities disappear.

And so, the spiritual revolution through the perspective of the Dalai Lama is a reorientation away from our constant obsession with ourselves. We need to look outward and recognize the impact that our actions have on others, and learn to conduct ourselves with an eye to being more loving and forgiving and patient and compassionate.

Spiritual practice, in short, means acting out of concern for the well being of others, transforming our perspective so that we are truly concerned about the welfare of others. As he says, *To speak of spiritual practice in any terms other than these is meaningless.*" (Italics added)

How much plainer can this I-win we-all-win configuration be stated, a call to turn our attention to the broader community of humankind, to recognize their interests as being as valid and important as our own? Their happiness is our happiness. When society suffers, when the world suffers, we all suffer. And when we are filled with hate and ill will we have no choice but to become miserable. As he says, we can reject everything — religion, ideology, our favorite rituals and wise sayings. But we can never escape the necessity of love and compassion.

It's the only glue that can bind us together.

"This, then, is my true religion, my simple faith. In this sense, there is no need for temple or church, for mosque or synagogue, no need for complicated philosophy, doctrine, or dogma. Our own heart, our own mind, is the temple. The doctrine is compassion."

5

EGO SYSTEMS VS ECO SYSTEMS

As a culture, unfortunately, we have become progressively narcissistic, and it's difficult to see how Narcissus can be compassionate. Instead of expanding our horizons to include a greater number of people in our day-to-day concerns, we have steadily drifted towards an inward-searching focus on the number one preoccupation of the 'me' generation — how *I* am progressing in my life, my spiritual development, my growth as a person. All this effort we expend to find inner peace and wisdom, while somehow ignoring the world around us as it fills up with intolerance. Do we actually believe that the two worlds are not intimately intertwined, that we can have peace in one world while its opposite throbs in the other?

The same is true with our persistent illusions about the spiritual path, and our fondness for navel gazing. As Sam Keen reminds us time and again, the spiritual life is not about individuality or individual accomplishments, but about dropping the illusion of being an individual, un-connected to all others, and accepting that we are a part of a whole, a part of this whole planet at the very least.

This blinkered view finds people vigorously pursuing a spiritual life for themselves, separate and apart from their intimate involvement in the world falling apart all around them. That's just not going to work, Moore says. "That will keep their spirituality narcissistic and infantile, and it will keep our world a dangerous place to be in."

We have to be ever so careful of not letting the superficial trappings and practices distract us from the depths below. He equates this with what Freud called the 'primary narcissism' of childhood, wherein as young children we tend to think that the whole world revolves around us, that everyone is there to service our needs. Alas, one day we grow up, and find it isn't so.

So too with our spirituality. Our narcissism focuses on the quality of our spiritual teacher, what's the best course or book to help us get ahead, and what's the next best step on our road to spiritual enlightenment. All very narcissistic.

Of course there are those who may get into a very good rhythm and eventually arrive at a point where they feel they've mastered yoga and meditation and healthy eco-friendly diets, and then wonder aloud, 'what's next?' Moore answers with astonishment, "next is to go into the world."

Connections Within and Without

We can start by graduating from the childish, moving on to a more adult search of reality; make it a way of life where the growth of our neighbor, no matter where on earth that neighbor lives, is as important as our own personal growth. "Look at all the atrocities and the number of people killed and hurt on this earth in the past hundred years, for all the advantages we've had. If our spirituality does not translate into a better life for our children, what does it mean? It means nothing."

Spiritual maturity is without division, either in the individuals within a people, or in the peoples within the world, nor does it separate itself from the secular.

Which is not to say that maturity means we would all practice the same religion or wear the same clothes or promote the same cultural values; these differences are as important and vital to a healthy world as are the members of a large family who contribute to the clan with their unique personalities, interests, occupations, and eccentricities. As *GAIA II, Song of the Vanishing Tribe* so eloquently states it, "Cultural diversity is vital to the survival of the human race, the human spirit, in the same way that bio-diversity is vital to the survival of the Planet. All life on earth is interdependent, each species part of complex chain reactions."

What it does mean is that ideally we in the modern world would no longer leave our spiritual values at home — as though compassion and love and forgiveness and patience had no worth in the workplace, in the marketplace. These values should inform and affect every single thing we do, especially our secular life because this is where they are most sorely needed, in our relationship to the world.

As we change so changes the world. We cannot change in a void. If the world we live in is neurotic, then we will share in that neurosis. And maybe we are depressed not because of some inner trauma, but because the building we work in is depressing, or the sight of people sleeping in the streets is depressing.

Paraphrasing psychologist Robert Sardello, Moore asks, "Is the cancer that afflicts our human bodies essentially the same as the cancer we see corroding our cities?" Are we and the world also connected in our mental and physical health? Immunity deficiency, cancerous growth, arterial clogging, unbearable pressure, road rage — which is the city, and which me?

As we abuse the things of nature and fill the world with poisons and ugliness, so we redesign and refashion ourselves both inward and out. Yet for the most part we ignore this obvious correlation, tolerating much more ugliness and neglect than we should, even when the pain in the world is reflected in the pain of our individual diseases.

Solitude and the Ability to Enjoy It

Or to look at it from another perspective, if we truly believed that we are what we eat, then what kind of creatures are we that choose our food on the basis of cholesterol level, fat content, vitamins, freshness of the greens, organically grown, recommended for slimming, best for avoidance of cancerous growths, containing all 5 major food groups? Like some chemistry experiment in personal growth.

Of course we're composed of chemicals, but the soul of a house is not the bricks and mortar and roof shingles; it's the life and experiences of those who live within. Then why not more concern about the flair and panache that goes into the preparation of our daily meals, the choice of vegetables based on tang and taste and brilliant color, the ambience and folklore and music connected with this particular ethnic dish, its presentation and table setting, and how it makes our spirit leap with joy and appreciation?

We have become tolerant and complacent about the very things that tear the soul out of us and out of our cities. High-tech billboards and signs of sponsorship have completely taken over, not only on the highways and office towers but in the school cafeterias and on the sides of buses, on playing fields and sidelines, yet somehow, as though in a hypnotic trance, most of us don't even seem to have noticed.

The names of public buildings that used to be named after some local or national hero from the past (thus conveying some sense of history and of who we are as a people), are now, for an appropriate fee, replaced by corporate logos. On sporting broadcasts a 'pitching change' is brought to you by ___, or a 'time out' is sponsored by ____, ad nauseam. The world we present to our children is one where every surface, space, and information byte is up for sale for a buck or two, prostituted to the highest bidder solely for its commercial potential, a value long associated with the vulgar, the uninspired, the crass, and mundane — the complete antithesis of beauty and art and culture and soul.

And then we dare to complain that young people today don't have any values!

"We are destroying both solitude and the ability to *enjoy* solitude," Erica Jong says of the frenetic pace of modern life, and the lack of options it presents to our children. "Try to find a place without mixed media, traffic sounds, deafening music, distracting advertisements. You have to be a billionaire to escape the noisy over-stimulation of selling that is ubiquitous in our cities, suburbs, airplanes, airports, and trains." A constant wall of noise suffocating the sounds of silence that we need to feed our inner calm and strength.

Exactly what I discovered a few years back in an overcrowded elevator in a state-of-the-art hotel, when I complained aloud about the TV monitor, which was bolted to the ceiling, as it smothered its captive audience in non-stop pitches. For my trouble I got a handful of nasty glares, while the rest of the eyes remained glued to our hypnotic pixilated friend.

But then that in the end is the optimum intent of a consumerist society; it's not due to some conspiracy, but the loud cacophony is there simply because it works. Quiet solitude is not the way of the sheep, but the mark of freedom. As Albert Einstein wrote in a letter more than half a century ago to Queen Elizabeth of Belgium, "The individual who has experienced solitude will not easily become a victim of mass suggestion."

Victims, maybe, but we already know the tremendous power of silence, of sitting quietly alone, of stilling the dialogue both without and within. We know the value of 'soul food,' of how beauty and art and music can so transpose us, and deliver us to scintillating heights. So what's keeping us from translating this knowledge into positive change in the world around us? What if these two simple daily indulgences — getting in touch with the eternal moment by feeding our soul, and quieting the incessant babble by meditating or breathing quietly — were practiced as readily as we order fast food or drop in an easy-chair in front of the TV? How cancer-ridden would our cities be then?

A Renaissance Diet

The theme of this chapter, obviously, is compassion, but we can't practice compassion if we don't get involved in the world, and we can't expect to uncover the reality of our world, its truths ephemeral and profound, without improving the reliability of our interactions with those around us. As we grow, the world around us must grow — or we haven't grown at all. We grow our environment as inextricably as our environment in turn provides the lushness for our growth.

"The beauty of Renaissance art is inseparable from the soul-affirming philosophy that tutored it," Moore says of this time well known in history for its exquisite accomplishments in all disciplines of the arts. Indeed some individuals became known as 'Renaissance men,' having cultivated personal mastery in many. This was no accident. The philosophy they lived by was an all-encompassing one in which the soul and its nourishment were the primary concerns of their everyday existence.

As a matter of course, they recommended exposure to only certain types of food and art and music and cultural influences of the finest quality. Which seems to indicate that in savoring that which added to the richness of the soul, they were a special breed of Epicureans.

That is, for those participating in the Italian Renaissance, in particular, life was soul-centered. The architecture, the public squares, the fountains, the sculptures, the paintings that even five hundred years later we still find so appealing and entrancing, are the end product of feeding the soul.

Can we just imagine what we could do today, with all our wealth and technology, if we were to live such an enriched life! "Our schools would change overnight." Moore assures. As would the practice of medicine and healthcare go in a totally different direction. Psychology as a discipline would simply disappear. And people would no longer just surrender themselves to the whims of faceless (soulless?) corporations.

At the very least our schools would again start teaching those deeply human qualities which resulted in those astounding displays of imagination and ingenuity during the Renaissance — qualities such as taking responsibility for who we are and what we do. That alone as a curriculum requisite would raise our culture out of its languishing self-pity and victimhood. Not to mention additional courses in thinking for ourselves, respect, compassion, and listening to our creative urges.

In the ego vs. the eco, the one that best suits my deepest needs is not the world of Narcissus, after all, but the overall environment in which I grow

6

LAUGHING AT OURSELVES

*He wrote his girlfriend a letter every day for two years ...
and she married the mailman.*
— Steve Allen's Private Joke File

I suppose this joke is telling us something profound about who we choose for our messengers, though I think the real point is simply to make us laugh, a point we often overlook in our analyzing of every tick and sound in our lives. It's not difficult to laugh, really; just stop taking ourselves so seriously. Or relish the naiveté hidden in the everyday, as in the following:

WILLIE: Dad, teacher says we're here to help others.
DAD: Of course we are.
WILLIE: Well, what are the others here for?
— Ibid.

But merely laughing at someone else's jokes or naiveté gets us just a momentary chuckle. Far better to see the humor in what comes out of our own mouth, our own blunders, our own naive beliefs. If we were to take all that time we invest in defending our positions and blunders and inane blatherings, and spend it instead on laughing at these silly imperfections, we would not only be a lot healthier in mind and body, but our wisdom would grow hand over hand. Sort of like laughing our way onto the path of wisdom.

In the opening chapter we heard Sam Keen advising us to construct a 'spiritual bullshit detector' to help us through a carnival of so-called up-lifting schemes. At the time it sounded like a harsh critique of our cultural obsessions, but now it's starting to seem that the harsher we then took it to be, the more naive we were at the time, thus giving us yet one more thing to laugh at.

"No one in the Age of Aquarius seemed concerned to offer reasons for what they believed," he further wrote about this 'uncorseted' spirituality, "much less to gather evidence to support their conclusions. The New-age was credulity gone wild — belief in healing crystals, channeling of entities, out-of-body experiences, pyramid power, sorcery, and prosperity for all."

Of course by now we've likely convinced ourselves that such childish ideas worked only on the less tutored; there's no way they could ever ensnare those of us who are wise to the ways of the world. Or could they? The trouble with these types of ideas is that there is no end of them in sight. Our only safeguard is the wit and wisdom to question, question, question, to keep repeating to ourselves that just because something is said in public, or a book written about it, or a seminar given on it, doesn't mean it has the slightest bit of truth or reality to it. It's just that we tend to be so damn trusting; we want to believe, we want to give the benefit of the doubt.

So here we are, the sophisticated, educated West, the most schooled and privileged generation in human history, and here's a sampling of what so many chased after, down the yellow brick road. "EST offered enlightenment in two weekends," Keen recalls of his days in the midst of this whirlwind. "Swamis, enlightened masters, and neo shamans spoke knowingly of the being of the One and *the* Truth. Channelers in trance gave voice to Seth, Ramtha, or other four-thousand-year-old entities."

Can we honestly acknowledge that these were once considered spiritual enlightenment by so many! "Light therapists cleaned your aura, realigned your chakras, and purged you of negative energy. Mystic Traders advertised that 'you will enter into Nirvana with one endless step if you wear the Zen Enso T-shirt ($18.95) and you can tune your Body, Mind and Spirit to the Universe with the fabulous Cosmic Om Tuning Fork ($34.95 + S&H)'."

A Level of Sensitivity

I had an encounter once with this guy who 'talks to dead people.' He packed the largest lecture hall at this spirituality conference, and proceeded to first *open* us up to a high level of sensitivity, then proceeded to get in contact with the deceased relative of someone in the audience. I remember seeing this in a movie once — it's an old vaudeville routine from back in the 20s — but no one in attendance seemed to be aware of this. They waved their hands in fervent hopes that they would be picked, that it was their loved one calling. In a trance-like stance the host called out things like, 'I see a small dog,' 'there is a garage with a workbench,' 'something to do with a bad heart or clogged arteries,' eventually whittling down the crowd to a mere dozen or so who might fill the bill.

The obvious question is, if this medium is genuinely relaying a message from some dead person, why doesn't the dead person just say his name, or, conversely, the name of his relative in the audience? (Hello, this is Sam Grady from beyond. I see my niece Patricia in attendance) Surely if he could reveal all these personal details of a person's life, a name shouldn't be too difficult; would save a lot of time and ultimate disappointment in other members of the audience. In the end, as is usual, the all-important message turns out to be something innocuous like 'Don't worry, I'm fine' or 'everything will be all right with this trouble you're going through.'

As I was heading down the aisle before the show was over, he called out to me through the loudspeakers that I couldn't just leave in my *open* condition, that seeing the streets of New York in hyper-sensitivity could easily land me in a padded cell, or worse. I increased my pace as he continued calling me back with a sense of urgency, and as virtually every eye in the auditorium was focused on me. The strange thing is, though, as they all filed out later on, neither our charming host nor anyone else in the audience so much as gave a second look at the supposedly deranged and incapacitated me – waiting at the hall exit. Or perhaps I always look this way.

So it's not so easy to laugh at ourselves after all, at least not when we're so deadly serious about our image, but the wisdom gained is well worth the effort. For whatever it's worth, we're not the first to be assaulted by such dubious claims; Socrates warned against them two thousand four hundred years ago. The problem seems to be with our innate trust of, and obedience to, authority figures; if someone so much as 'sounds' authoritative, we perk up and pay attention. (Perhaps a remnant of our unconditional obedience to the bicameral mind?)

"A bad thought delivered authoritatively, though without evidence of how it was put together," Alain de Botton, a University of London philosophy professor, explains in *The Consolations of Philosophy,* "can for a time carry all the weight of a sound one. But we acquire a misplaced respect for others when we concentrate solely on their conclusions — which is why Socrates urged us to dwell on the logic they used to reach them."

Teresa of Avila and Intelligence

Or as John O'Donohue said, so many people who pass through the doors of spiritual inquiry today leave their intellects at the door. Even Teresa of Avila, known for her great mystical and spiritual insight, said if you have a choice between a spiritual advisor who is very spiritual but not too intelligent, and one who is intelligent but not too spiritual, always choose the intelligent one. "I think there's great wisdom in that," O'Donohue says of this necessity of protecting the sensitivities of our inner being, as anything less can be very dangerous.

As it can be disconcerting to turn to the spiritual for the wrong reasons. "People turn to spirituality as a means of self improvement," Moore says in amazement of this spreading phenomenon. The idea that you can take classes in spirituality at fitness centers, "as if the two were the same thing." And that about sums up the wrongheaded notion that self-improvement and spirituality are about the same business. How in the world did we so misconstrue it?

Misconstrued it perhaps as a race, as an athletic competition to see who is the most fit, who gets to the finish line first. Keeping in mind what comedienne Lily Tomlin said, "The trouble with the rat race is that even if you win you're still a rat."

Many get lost in the parts and forget the whole, as the Western world did in severing the spirit from the body. In *The Conscious I: Clarity and Direction Through Meditation,* Tai Chi instructor Andy James writes, "In reality, body, mind and energy do not exist separately. They are part of an integrated, inseparable and continually changing whole. It's only our intellect that perceives them as separate and distinct."

Our intellect likes to separate and categorize simply because this makes things easier to study and comprehend. But these separate concepts on their own give a false impression — the whole being not only greater but considerably more complex than the sum of the individual parts. "Ironically, we continue trying to find wholeness through the very process that causes us to feel unwhole and fragmented."

In like fashion, we strive to develop the 'whole' person while ignoring all but his material side, or rail at others for not being compassionate, while fortifying our own barriers between 'us and them'. It would be comical, if only we could learn to laugh at our absurd expectations.

And so one final insight from the comic subtleties of a wise observer of our human condition, Steve Allen:

The warden saw a new arrival was taking his situation rather hard, and asked what the matter was.

"It's that sentence the judge gave me," the new arrival said. "I just can't do all that time."

"How much are you doing?" inquired the warden.

"Life!"

"Well," said the warden, helpfully, "just do what you can of it."

7

OF WHISPERED WORDS

We can be knowledgeable with other men's knowledge
but we can't be wise with other men's wisdom.
— Michel Eyquem de Montaigne

What we really want to know, in the final analysis, is will the Fisher King arise from his sick bed in our time?

From the opening salvos about the humbug of our times, to our attempts to reinvigorate and redefine the nature of our wasteland, the singular drive behind this quest has been to uncover the ever-changing truths of our day-to-day reality, and to perhaps glimpse here and there the deeper honesties, intuitions, and creative inspirations that call to us from some hidden part of who we are.

We are struggling in our culture and in the greater world to define how we should live our lives, how to shape our public will to best incorporate the needs of the many, the needs of the 'all'; and how to tear ourselves away from the comforting lies with which we have deluded ourselves for oh so long.

In 2004, with an eagerness rarely seen in our times, people rushed to movie theatres to experience Michael Moore's *Fahrenheit 9/11*, to be jolted awake to a different take on reality, this alternate perception of what's really going on in America and in the world. Revelations abounded. Heated discussions, public and private, agitated and excited, mushroomed uncontrollably at the office, in family gatherings, with old friends. All this, over a documentary?

The irony is that the true revelations weren't so much about the goings on in the Bush administration, whether you agreed with the film's slant or not, but about these alternate perceptions of reality, none of which our trusted TV networks even hinted may exist. What kind of freedom of speech, freedom of questioning, freedom of access are they offering us? Real debate — what a seemingly novel idea!

The first Age of Enlightenment in the eighteenth century witnessed the birth of a vast array of new ideas, inventions, and

290

revolutionary movements which set the world on a path of discovery and freedoms the likes of which had never been seen before. Dare we try again?

To rid ourselves and the world of lockstep thinking is, after all, what the great wars of the last century were all about. The military battles are long over and won, but the fight for our personal liberation is far subtler, unlikely to generate banner headlines in newspapers. Yet they are the only victories that can free us from our wasteland.

We're living in a time of provocative change and far-reaching promise. It is a time of intensifying voices on left and right, conservative and liberal, Republican and Democrat, world-conscious and isolationist, old school and new thinking – just as it should be in any truly vibrant and creative free society.

In the Gospel of John – that most mystical and enigmatic of New Testament writings – we hear Jesus proclaim forthrightly, "The truth will set you free." This profoundly insightful saying, in its overuse, has lost its power to inflame and incite our imaginations, yet we would do well to ponder its ideal, that only in coming to know the truth can we hope to find true freedom.

And so we come to the truth of our search for truth – that it is in fact our search for freedom. We all long to be free. With this freedom we are awarded a chance to step back and see ourselves for who we really are – surprisingly, compassionate beings of enormous potential for good.

Like The Fisher King, eager to rise from his sick bed, to dance and laugh, to again thrill to the joys of unbound living, our times await the true expression of our deepest humanity, our deepest longing to embrace our lives as free, thinking, and multifaceted creators.

Acknowledgements

This work would not have been possible if it were not for the Quest series on PBS and the research that I was required to do to help prepare for the many in-depth interviews. As such my first acknowledgement and heartfelt thank you goes to Lili for creating the idea behind this imaginative series and all the wizardry that brought it to fruition. Her dedication as director and producer pointed the way to uncovering truths as the raison d'etre for creating.

A special gratitude goes to the many gifted minds who are quoted throughout this book, in particular to Sam Keen for allowing me to use significant portions of his own work in my attempts at clarification, and to Thomas Moore for his support, encouragement and generosity of spirit in providing permission for extensive quotations. I also warmly thank both of them for their enthusiastic endorsements of the book, as I likewise thank Archbishop Desmond Tutu, with whom we danced and sang in Bali a few years back, and Marci Shimoff who was one of our most delightful and happily contagious interviews. And a more personal special thank you to Patricia and André.

I thank Steve Allen and publisher Three Rivers Press for the gift of the jokes in the final chapter. I would like to acknowledge the contribution of my proofreader Kelly Mendoca who worked diligently on short notice. And a very special nod of appreciation to Gokhan Danacioglu who is the man behind *G-Man Creative* and the outstanding job done on the cover of this book.

In the end it is constructive criticism, rewrites, and constant editing that transforms roughly hewn ideas and a fog of thoughts into something approaching a readable book. In this I am privileged to have three champions who have stayed with me from beginning to end. Nick Stephens, editor and dearest friend who suggested, argued, applauded and encouraged the best possible work out of the talent at hand. Mona Bolton for her depth of understanding and compassion along with subtle suggestions when things just weren't going right. And last, though always first, Lili Fournier, wife, mentor, combative instructor, critic and motive force nudging me to take my lamp out from under the table.

CHAPTER NOTES
(Books, unless otherwise noted)

Introduction: Whispers Along the Path
The Dragons of Eden, Carl Sagan

Chapter 1: The Whole Truth and Lots of Lies
Would You Believ, Tom Harpur
On Bullshit, Harry Frankfurt
How Mumb-Jumbo Conquered the World, Francis Wheen
Hyperspace, Michio Kaku
Hymns to an Unknown God, Sam Keen
De Profundis, Oscar Wilde
Eternal Echoes, John O'Donohue
How to Win Friends & Influence People, Dale Carnegie
Sophie's World, Jostein Gaarder
The Hero with a Thousand Faces, Joseph Campbell
Consilience, Edward O. Wilson
The Heart Aroused, David Whyte

Chapter 2: From the Garden of Eden to Reality Bites
Sex in History, Reay Tannahill
Sex and Power in History, Amaury de Riencourt
The Origin of Consciousness in the Breakdown of the Bicameral Mind, Julian Jaynes
Shadows of Forgotten Ancestors, Carl Sagan & Ann Druyan
Jane Goodall Interview, Zolar Entertainment
Blink: The Power of Thinking Without Thinking, Malcolm Gladwell
The Split Brain Revisited, Michael Gazzaniga
The Philosopher's Magazine (Spring, 2003), Anthony Campbell
More Info on Brain's Data Bases, Toronto Star (April 27, 1997), Jay Ingram
The Sizesaurus: Making measures fit for human consumption, Stephen Strauss

Chapter 3: The Mythology of Myths
Testament, John Romer
Before Philosophy, Henri Frankfort
The Encyclopedia of Mythology: Gods, Heroes, and Legends of the Greeks and Romans, Timothy Roberts
The Alchemist: A Fable About Following Your Dream, Paulo Coelho
Martial Arts: The Real Story, Joseph Svinth

Chapter 4: Sophia and the Goddess Within
The Story of Civilization, Will Durant
Bonobo: The Forgotten Ape, Frans de Waal
In the Shadow of Man, Jane Goodall
Sanctuaries of the Goddess, Peg Streep
Goddesses in Every Woman: A New Psychology of Women, Jean Shinoda Bolen
Naomi Wolf Interview, Zolar Entertainment
The Language of the Goddess, Marija Gimbutas
Revolution from Within, Gloria Steinem
Gods and Goddesses of Old Europe, Marija Gimbutas
The Myth of Matriarchy: Why An Invented Past Won't Give Women A Future, Cynthia Eller
States of Grace, Charlene Spretnak
Longing For Darkness: Tara And The Black Madonna, China Galland
What Do Women Want?, Erica Jong
The Witch Hunt in Early Modern Europe, Brian Levack
Witchcraze, Ann Llewellyn Barstow
Counting the Witch Hunt, Ronald Hutton
Witch-hunting and Maternal Power in Early Modern England, Deborah Willis
The Holocaust in Historical Context, Steven Katz
The Gnostic Gospels, Elaine Pagels
The Flowering of the Soul: A Book of Prayers by Women, Lucinda Vardey
Conversations with the Goddesses: Revealing the Divine Power within You, Agapi Stassinopoulos

Chapter 5: Consciousness, Soul and Sensuality
Scientific American Mind, (September 2006), Cameron Smith

Care of the Soul, Thomas Moore
Hymns to an Unknown God, Sam Keen
The Soul's Religion, Thomas Moore
A Mind of its Own: How Your Brain Distorts and Deceives, Cordelia Fine

Chapter 6: Destiny, Character & An Acorn
The Ethical Brain, Michael Gazzaniga
The Soul's Code, James Hillman
Judith Orloff Interview, Zolar Entertainment
On Equilibrium, John Ralston Saul
Zen and the Art of Making a Living, Laurence Boldt
David Whyte Interview, Zolar Entertainment
Something Ignited in my Soul, Pablo Neruda

Chapter 7: Creativity, Perception & Other Mind Tools
Drawing on the Right Side of the Brain, Betty Edwards
Lateral Specialization of Cerebral Function in the Surgically Separated Hemispheres, Roger Sperry
The Doors of Perception, Aldous Huxley
The Role of Language in Intelligence from *What is Intelligence?*, Daniel C. Dennett, The Darwin College Lectures, ed. Jean Khalfa, Cambridge, Cambridge Univ. Press. 1994
The Triune Brain in Evolution: Role in Paleocerebral Functions, Paul MacLean
Anam Cara: A Book of Celtic Wisdom, John O'Donohue
The Power of Myth, Joseph Campbell
Man's Search for Meaning, Viktor E. Frankl
The Re-Enchantment of Everyday Life, Thomas Moore
Grace and Grit, Ken Wilber
Zen and the Art of Making a Living, Laurence Boldt

Chapter 8: The Aging Fountain of Youth
Ageless Body, Timeless Mind, Deepak Chopra
Sam Keen Interview, Zolar Entertainment
Thomas Moore Interview, Zolar Entertainment
Jane Goodall Interview, Zolar Entertainment
Stephen Covey Interview, Zolar Entertainment

Erica Jong Interview, Zolar Entertainment
The Silent Passage, Gail Sheehy
Joan Borysenko Interview, Zolar Entertainment
Healing Words: The Power of Prayer and the Practice of Medicine, Larry Dossey
Ondrea Levine & Steven Levine Interview, Zolar Entertainment
Scientific American: The Quest To Beat Aging, (Summer 2000), Robin Marantz Henig
Anita Roddick Interview, Zolar Entertainment
Bernie Siegel Interview, Zolar Entertainment

Chapter 9: Living in Eternity, Living in Time

A Brief History of Time, Stephen Hawking
In Search of Schrodinger's Cat, John Gribbin
God and the New Physics, Paul Davies
The Time Machine, HG Wells
Timeshifting, Stephan Rechtschaffen
The Mind's Sky: Human Intelligence in a Cosmic Context, Timothy Ferris
Testament, John Romer
Care of the Soul, Thomas Moore

Chapter 10: The Age of Enlightenment II

The Power of Myth, Joseph Campbell
Longing for Darkness, China Galland
Hyperspace: A Scientific Odyssey Through Parallel Universes, Time Warps, and the 10th Dimension, Michio Kaku
The Future of life, Edward O. Wilson
The Story of Civilization, Will Durant
Shadows of Forgotten Ancestors, Carl Sagan & Ann Druyan
Ethics for the New Millennium, The Dalai Lama
The Re-Enchantment of Everyday Life, Thomas Moore
Inventing Memory, Erica Jong
Steve Allen's Private Joke File, Steve Allen
Hymns To An Unknown God: Awakening The Spirit In Everyday Life, Sam Keen
The Consolations of Philosophy, Alain de Botton
The Conscious I: Clarity and Direction Through Meditation, Andy James.

INDEX

Joys   32, 81, 131, 204, 231, 250,
    266, 281, 291
Jung, Carl   52, 60, 75, 98, 105,
    117

K

Kaku, Michio   5, 269-71, 295, 298
Karate   89
Keats, John   207
Keen, Sam   7, 20, 24, 26, 91, 132,
    206-8, 219, 279, 285, 293,
    295, 297, 299
Kerry, John   145
Kieckhefer, Richard   112
King Arthur   66, 77
Kismet   151
Klee, Paul   194
Knights   iii, 49, 66-7, 77, 238, 260-
    1
Knowledge   iii, 6, 19, 22, 51, 55,
    76, 128, 148, 242, 269-70
Konzak, Burt   89
Kung Fu   65, 87-9
Kwai Chang Caine   87, 89

L

Lancelot   66-7
Landscape, inner   119, 123, 125-
    6, 197
Language   25, 48-9, 52, 103, 128,
    179-81, 256, 296-7
Laugh   259, 266, 268, 285, 287,
    291
Laws   42-3, 52, 149, 151, 190
Learning   6, 7, 65, 89, 115, 140,
    144, 149, 177, 181-2, 237,
    259
Legends   37, 66-7, 74, 260, 296
Lennon, John   233
Levack, Brian   112, 296
Levine, Stephen & Ondrea   298
Libidos   174-5
Life expectancy   201
Lifetime   6, 60, 206, 210, 219, 221
Lightsabers   77-8
Lili   15, 46-7, 59, 157-8, 265, 293
Logic   44, 103, 119, 126, 150, 215,
    223
Longevity   199, 201
Longing   10, 24, 71, 76, 91, 114,
    119, 132, 134, 265-6, 296,
    298
Love   51, 84-5, 96, 103, 117-8,
    128, 139, 170, 187, 213,

221, 263-4, 267-8, 277-8,
    280
Lover   72, 81, 137, 151, 166, 221
Luck   42, 156

M

MacLean, Paul   184, 297
Magic   20, 31-3, 51, 67, 87, 111,
    140, 175, 194, 196, 213, 257
  bullet   3, 14, 221
  elixir   232-3
Magical   32-3, 247
Mann, Thomas   196
Martial arts   87-9, 296
Masculine   52, 100, 103, 107, 172,
    175
Materialists   133-4, 162, 165
Matriarchy   57, 93, 98, 105, 117,
    296
McCartney, Paul   233
Medical profession   214, 218, 225
Meditation   124, 139, 203, 215,
    217, 231, 246-7, 254, 280,
    288, 299
Meister Eckhart   25, 188, 242, 246
Mentor   77, 88, 131, 134, 293
Merlin   65-7, 88
Metaphor   25, 48, 50, 67, 98, 180,
    191, 231
Michelet, Jules   112
Mid-wives   112-3
Military   83-4, 88
Millennia   iii, 55, 94, 201, 269-70
Mind-body connection   199, 214,
    218, 220
MIND TOOLS   167, 169-70, 179,
    181, 197, 297
Miracles   190-1, 228
Monroe, Marilyn   227
Montaigne, Michel Eyquem de
    290
Montana, Joe   247
Moore, Thomas   69, 127-8, 134,
    136-7, 139-40, 204, 206-7,
    210-1, 246, 256, 279-80,
    293, 297-8
Mother Earth   31-2, 34, 42, 45
Moyers, Bill   25
Music   85, 127, 137, 139, 143,
    188, 196, 252-3, 256, 265,
    281, 283
Mysterious   25, 32, 61, 82, 86,
    123, 125, 141, 156, 213

Mystical   87, 89, 192, 195, 288,
    291
Mystics   116, 197-8, 217, 250
Myth of Er   155
Mythology   19, 44, 64, 66, 69, 70,
    74-5, 78, 82, 87, 91, 99, 101,
    127, 296
Mythos   83, 85-6
Myths   24, 35, 37, 44, 46, 51, 64-
    5, 68-9, 71, 74-5, 86, 91,
    134, 155, 206, 296-8

N
Neruda, Pablo   167, 297
Neurons   62
Newberg, Andrew   217
Newton, Isaac   19, 149
Norwich, Julian of   116

O
O'Donohue, John   25, 80-1, 133,
    174, 186-8, 219, 239, 242,
    246, 250, 288, 295, 297
Origin of Consciousness   37, 295
Orloff, Judith   161
Oz   72

P
Pagels, Elaine   115, 296
Pamplona   84-5
Particles   148, 152-3
Passion   138, 161, 195, 198, 207,
    211, 230, 233
Passionate   33, 119, 161, 195
Path   i, 19, 65, 72, 78, 81, 89-92,
    136, 154, 156, 163, 166-7,
    171, 275, 285, 291
Patriarchy   31, 39, 98-9, 270
Perceptions, doors of   7, 18, 20,
    35, 45-6, 57, 86, 135, 161,
    176-7, 179-87, 195, 197-8,
    273, 290, 297
Perceval   260-2
Perspective   86, 203, 207, 232,
    277-8, 281
Phallic symbols   85-6
Philosophy   44, 69, 81, 89, 181,
    296, 299
Physics   149, 152, 298
Pineal gland   141
Plato   22, 42, 134, 155, 174, 201,
    239
Poetry   51, 64, 128, 140
Poon, Leonard   211

Potions   10, 225-6, 232
Power   ii, v, 3, 4, 7, 17, 33, 35, 39,
    42, 60, 72, 87, 94, 189-90,
    192, 269
Power of Myth   297-8
Practice
  religious   127, 277
  spiritual   107, 278
Prayers   90, 116, 132, 217-8, 241,
    277, 296, 298
Priests   88-9, 130-2
Programs, spiritual   25
Proofs   105, 107, 223

Q
Qualities   iii, 4, 5, 44, 47, 52, 56,
    93, 107, 117, 164, 184, 221,
    224, 277, 279, 283

R
Reason   18, 20, 32, 47, 55, 92,
    131, 134, 162-3, 171-2, 194,
    257, 270-1
Rechtschaffen, Stephan   247, 249,
    253, 257, 298
Redelmeier, Don   230
Relativity theory   70, 182, 239
Religion   ii, 24, 31, 36, 44, 81, 87,
    90-1, 106-8, 111, 124, 134,
    241, 257, 275, 277-8
Responsibility   14, 38, 46, 149,
    165, 210, 277, 283
Revelations   ii, 112, 213, 290
Revolution   8, 42, 296
Riencourt, Amaury de   33, 39, 40,
    44, 295
Right hemisphere   56-8, 169-70,
    179
Roberts, Timothy   74, 296
Roddick, Anita   225, 227, 298
Romer, John   254, 296, 298
Roots   v, 1, 32, 113, 131, 155,
    214, 224
Round Table   49, 66, 260

S
Sagan, Carl   iv, 36, 268, 295
Saul, John Ralston   160, 297
Scheffer, Louis   62
Schizophrenics   38, 43, 57
Schopenhauer, Arthur   186, 195,
    197
Schweitzer, Albert   79

W

Waal, Frans de   296
War   iii, 4, 7, 96, 99, 118, 277, 291
Wasteland   261-2, 264, 290-1
Whispers   20, 195, 295
Whyte, David   26, 166, 295
Wigan, Arthur   54
Wilber, Ken   133, 195, 220, 297
Wilde, Oscar   i, 9, 295
Williams, Robin   261
Williamson, Marianne   191
Willis, Deborah   112, 296
Wilson, Edward O.   20, 141, 149,
        152, 270-1, 295, 298
Wisdom   i, ii, iv, 15, 18, 20, 22-3,
        26, 37, 65, 69, 89, 115-7,
        119, 224-5, 259, 285-7
Witch trials   111-2
Witches   72, 110-2, 124, 189
Wizard of Oz   72
Wolf, Naomi   296
Women   10, 16, 32-4, 39, 51-2,
        81, 96-100, 102-4, 107-8,
        110-3, 116, 174-5, 201-2,
        210-1, 225-6, 296
Woodstock   84-5

Y

Yamanaka, Ron   89
Youth   199, 205, 211, 221, 223,
        231-2, 249, 298
    eternal   200, 224
    fountain of   218, 221-2, 224,
        228, 230, 232-3

Z

Zen   161, 297

About the Author

Gerard Fournier is the writer and executive producer of the award-winning *Quest* TV series on PBS, most recently *Quest for Success*, which have been renowned for blending eye-opening insights and words of wisdom from some of the world's most influential thinkers and authors. He has worked as a journalist and travel columnist, traveling to over 80 countries in the process.

QUEST
for Success
Powerful Secrets to Wealth,
Happiness and a Deeply Meaningful Life.
A LILI FOURNIER SPECIAL
Today's leading luminaries help you discover your path to achieving success with significance
Sir Richard Branson, Russell Simmons, Stephen Covey, Jack Canfield, John Assaraf, Harv Eker, Marci Shimoff, Byron Katie, Wayne Muller, Archbishop Desmond Tutu and His Holiness The Dalai Lama.
Executive Producer: GERARD FOURNIER
A LILI FOURNIER SPECIAL
ZOLAR
ENTERTAINMENT
www.questthejourney.com
zolar@questthejourney.com

Made in the USA
Monee, IL
08 July 2026